"In this balanced and biblical book, John Phelan de-escalates controversies surrounding Christian eschatology (heaven, hell, divine judgment, the millennium, Israel, the book of Revelation). For Phelan, Christian hope is to be found in God's promised future, in which all things will be set right. Here, he argues, is our motivation for Christian engagement. An accessible and important read."

Robert K. Johnston, professor of theology and culture, Fuller Theological Seminary

"Few areas of Christian belief have garnered more controversy than that of eschatology, the 'doctrine of last things.' It is difficult not to consider it a negative issue that is better ignored. John Phelan's *Essential Eschatology* proves that attitude wrong. He rightly recognizes the positive and important nature of the 'hope' embraced in this doctrine and presents a thoroughly engaging work that is both biblically and theologically satisfying. Of course, not everyone will agree with the answers (e.g., hell as a place of judgment but metaphorical at the core, or the millennium as an actual reign of the Messiah on earth), but all will find it worthwhile and important."

Grant Osborne, Trinity Evangelical Divinity School

"Eschatology is essential to the Christian faith, and Phelan provides a sane, sound, accessible and very helpful treatment of the primary issues, one that steers people away from the silliness that often accompanies the topic. His work can be trusted, and engagement with it will lead to maturity of thought and faith."

Klyne Snodgrass, Paul W. Brandel Professor of New Testament Studies, North Park University

"Jay Phelan shows his readers that eschatology (the doctrine of the 'last things') is not speculative but practical, and not only about the future but also—in fact, especially—about the present. His plea for the church to put kingdom values into practice now, as we await God's new heavens and new earth, is both provocative and persuasive, at once orthodox and radical."

Michael J. Gorman, Raymond E. Brown Professor of Biblical Studies and Theology, St. Mary's Seminary & University, Baltimore

"If eschatology is a casualty of scholarly and popular culture, *Essential Eschatology* artfully resurrects its place in the Christian faith. Phelan weaves together theology, church history and biblical studies, producing a remarkably interdisciplinary treatment of the doctrine of eschatology. I put Phelan's book on my shelf next to N. T. Wright and Scot McKnight who also write accessible biblical theology for the whole church!"

Michelle A. Clifton-Soderstrom, associate professor of theology and ethics, North Park Theological Seminary

"Where does a pastor or teacher turn when those they serve get their eschatology from popular authors who delight in the demise of those who do not share their theology or those authors who joyfully predict the destruction of the planet? Here is the book for which we have been waiting. Dr. Phelan takes seriously biblical authority. This book neither dismisses nor overly literalizes the apocalyptic portions of the Bible. The message is one of hope grounded in the Bible. He discusses the implications for discipleship, for the church and even for contemporary politics."

Glenn R. Palmberg, president emeritus, The Evangelical Covenant Church

Essential Eschatology

OUR PRESENT AND FUTURE HOPE

JOHN E. PHELAN JR.

IVP Academic

An imprint of InterVarsity Press
Downers Grove, Illinois

InterVarsity Press
P.O. Box 1400, Downers Grove, IL 60515-1426
World Wide Web: www.ivpress.com
E-mail: email@ivpress.com

InterVarsity Press® is the book-publishing division of InterVarsity Christian Fellowship/USA®, a movement of students and faculty active on campus at hundreds of universities, colleges and schools of nursing in the United States of America, and a member movement of the International Fellowship of Evangelical Students. For information about local and regional activities, write Public Relations Dept., InterVarsity Christian Fellowship/ USA, 6400 Schroeder Rd., P.O. Box 7895, Madison, WI 53707-7895, or visit the IVCF website at <www. intervarsity.org>.

Scripture quotations, unless otherwise noted, are from the New Revised Standard Version of the Bible, copyright 1989 by the Division of Christian Education of the National Council of the Churches of Christ in the USA. Used by permission. All rights reserved.

Cover design: Cindy Kiple
Interior design: Beth Hagenberg
Images: ladder and cloud © Dmitriy Shpilko/iStockphoto
       wooden ladder © pialhovik/iStockphoto

ISBN 978-0-8308-4025-0 (print)
ISBN 978-0-8308-6465-2 (digital)

Printed in the United States of America ∞

Library of Congress Cataloging-in-Publication Data
A catalog record for this book is available from the Library of Congress.

| P | 24 | 23 | 22 | 21 | 20 | 19 | 18 | 17 | 16 | 15 | 14 | 13 | 12 | 11 | 10 | 9 | 8 | 7 | 6 | 5 | 4 | 3 | 2 | 1 |
| Y | 34 | 33 | 32 | 31 | 30 | 29 | 28 | 27 | 26 | 25 | 24 | 23 | 22 | 21 | 20 | 19 | 18 | 17 | 16 | 15 | 14 | 13 |

To my granddaughter Brenna Kinsale Nelson-Phelan

with a prayer that her generation will see the church

genuinely living in light of the new creation

Contents

Acknowledgments

EVERY AUTHOR IS PART OF A COMMUNITY of the living and the dead. Teachers, colleagues, students, parishioners, friends and family have all made their contributions to this book. Some of them will be pleased with the outcome. Others surely will not! I want first to thank Scott Bolinder who encouraged me to write this book. I am especially thankful to my colleagues in the biblical field at North Park Theological Seminary, particularly Dr. Klyne Snodgrass who read the manuscript and made a number of helpful suggestions and corrections. Klyne has been a conversation partner for decades, and I am deeply thankful for his friendship and encouragement. I am also thankful for the support of Dean of Faculty Stephen Chester and Dean of the Seminary David Kersten. I want to thank the board of North Park University and President David Parkyn for supporting a sabbatical leave. A good deal of the research for this book was done during those blessed months.

I want to thank the ministerium of the Central Conference of the Evangelical Covenant Church and its superintendent, Rev. Jerome Nelson, for the opportunity to share some of the content of this book at its fall retreat. Similar thanks goes out to the North Pacific Conference and its then superintendent Rev. Mark Novak. I would also like to thank Rev. Donn Engebretson for the invitation to present material from the book at the Evangelical Covenant Church's midwinter pastors' conference. The questions and observations at these events and at the many churches where I have shared my ideas have been extremely helpful. Special thanks are due to my friend and supporter of longstanding Rev. Glenn Palmberg, former president of the Evangelical Covenant Church. Glenn has consistently encouraged my writing and leadership at North Park. His friendship is a treasure.

I have been particularly blessed by my ongoing conversations with Rabbi Yehiel Poupko of the Jewish Federation of Chicago. His enduring friendship and fearless questions have been of immense benefit. Although he will clearly not agree with many of my conclusions, I trust this is a better book because I have listened to him. As a result of my friendship with Rabbi Poupko I have over the last few years participated in a Jewish-evangelical dialogue. The friendships formed there and the conversations that have ensued have enriched my life and this book. I wish to thank David Neff for the invitation to participate and Dr. A. J. Levine and Rabbi David Fox Sandmel for being good conversation partners on the biblical text and Jewish-Christian relations.

I wish to thank my editor with InterVarsity Press, Drew Blankman, for his encouragement, support and advice on this project. I thank the entire team at InterVarsity for their work to make this a better book.

Finally, I wish to thank my family: my wife, Dawn, my sons, Bryan and Andrew, and their spouses, Katrina and Dana. Thanks to Dawn especially for putting up with the piles of books. I fear they will not soon disappear.

John E. Phelan Jr.

Introduction

ESCHATOLOGY, OR THE STUDY OF "LAST THINGS," is often considered the periphery of the Christian faith. Some consider it the esoteric purview of fanatics or, more charitably, scholars. Others, of course, are utterly fascinated by the interpretive puzzles of Daniel's prophecy and John's Revelation. By rearranging the pieces they hope to discover a coherent road map to the future—in spite of the fact that history is littered with discarded and discredited maps. Few seem discouraged by this. However, neither indifference nor obsession do justice to the importance of eschatology in Christian faith and life. Far from being at the periphery of the faith, it is no exaggeration to say that eschatology is the *heart* of Christianity.

The Bible is a narrative that begins in creation and ends in new creation. Israel's prophets anticipated a time when their God would rule over all the earth. Jesus came proclaiming the presence of the kingdom of God and called his followers to live out of the values of that kingdom. Paul insisted that the resurrection of Jesus was the initiation of the great and final resurrection, and that through Jesus' death and resurrection the enslaving "powers" had been defeated. John called on the churches of Asia Minor to remain faithful in the face of cultural pressures and outright persecution, confident that God's final purposes would be accomplished. Every part of the Bible is written with the end in view that, as Paul would put it, God would be all in all (1 Cor 15:28).

Eschatology is no more peripheral to Christianity than an engine is peripheral to a car. Without eschatology Christian faith goes nowhere. Without an engine a car may look good. It may be comfortable. But lacking an engine it is at best an interesting museum piece and at worst a rusting piece of junk. Eschatology gives Christianity the power to be more than wistful nostalgia or weekly entertainment. The ethics of the kingdom give Christians and the Christian community character and identity. Biblical warnings of God's judgment provide Christians with a moral vision. The promise of resurrection and new creation provides Christians with hope. Without eschatology Christianity has no mission and the church has no purpose.

Eschatology is more than what will happen in the "last days." It is more than when Jesus will come or whether there will be a "millennium." While these issues are important, eschatology touches on matters that are much closer to home for many of us. Who am I? What does it mean for me to exist? Does my body *have* a soul or is my body *ensouled*—that is, can my soul exist apart from my body? What does it mean to die? What happens to our loved ones when they die? Are they with God in heaven? Do they "sleep" and await the resurrection of the dead? What is heaven anyway? What about those who are not Christians? Will they go to hell forever, or will God give them another chance? What is hell anyway? What is the resurrection of the dead? What will it entail, and when will it occur? What is the final destiny of God's people? Will they "go to heaven when they die" or live on the "new earth"? Will God's people go to heaven, or will heaven come to them? These and other very profound and personal questions are *eschatological* questions.

Eschatology raises corporate questions as well as individual ones. What is the role of the church in the light of God's promised kingdom? Should the church work to realize or even bring in the kingdom of God? Or is the church rather a lifeboat collecting desperate swimmers swept away from the wreckage of a shattered and sinking world? How does the church live the values of the coming kingdom when they seem so antithetical to the values of our various cultures and even to common sense? Is it practical to "love our enemies," "turn the other cheek" or "not worry about your life"? If "Jesus is Lord" both now and in the coming kingdom, how does the church live faithfully when its people are accountable to other "lords"? When are we being "all things to all people," and when are we accommodating to powers antithetical to the rule of God? These are also eschatological questions.

Christianity is about more than my personal salvation. Jesus was not simply calling individuals; he was forming a community of disciples who would live out of the new values of the coming kingdom of God. He was forming an *eschatological community*, a community of the last and ultimate days. This community is not called to map out the future using clues God dropped in the prophets of Israel or the letters of Paul. Nor is it called to sit around and wait for the end. It is called to be a colony of the kingdom of God amid the kingdoms of this world. God calls us not simply to reconcile us to himself, as Paul puts it in 2 Corinthians 5, but to become a part of the advance party of the last days. As part of the colony of the kingdom of God we are "God's ambassadors" sharing our reconciliation and our community with everyone. The church provides an alternative to the kingdoms of this world not simply for the future but in the present.

This book is written to encourage individual Christians and churches to take Christian eschatology seriously. In it I argue that far from being an esoteric fringe doctrine, eschatology is a most *practical* and pastorally significant doctrine. Everything done in the church is, or should be, done in light of the presence of the kingdom of God in Jesus' ministry, message, death and resurrection. The church's message, ministry and communal life are all given shape by the promise of resurrection and judgment, and the coming of the new heavens and new earth. Christians are a people of hope. And our hope is not merely personal but corporate and universal. Christians are also people of *mission*, and that mission is motivated by God's love and longing for the renewal and reconciliation of his creation to himself. The church lives in light of that coming renewal and in hope of the reconciliation of all things to God. By its worship and witness it anticipates that renewal and participates in that reconciliation.

1

Hope and Promise

An Overview and Invitation

DOES THE WORLD HAVE A PURPOSE? Does my life have a purpose? Most of us have asked questions like these at one time or another in our lives. They arise for many reasons. Perhaps the violence and chaos plaguing the planet bring such despair in their wake that we wonder if history has a guiding hand. Or perhaps personal failure and gnawing disappointment with the course of our lives bring us to the very edge of disillusionment. We wonder if the world is really under the control of a good and compassionate God or if it is governed by indifferent and impersonal forces acting without regard for virtue, vice or vision. We wonder if there is a bright and hopeful future before us or only darkness and disappointment.

A bewildering variety of sages, religions and sects offers an equally bewildering variety of religious answers to these and other significant questions. Another group of advisers offers us more secular advice regarding life struggles. They call on us to join a particular political party or social movement. Meaning will be found, they say, in fighting for social justice or an equitable tax policy or protection of the environment. Still others despair of finding answers at all and advise us to bravely accept the reality of the world's meaninglessness and try to make the best of it.

The sages, mystics and prophets have offered two principal answers to the question of life's direction and purpose. Some have argued life is an unending cycle of birth, death and rebirth. Just as spring turns to summer and summer to fall and then winter, so our lives ascend, descend and then ascend again. Many ancient societies, in fact, saw the seasons as an important picture of human life itself. A human life is rather like the agricultural cycle. We move through life like a plant, sprouting like a seedling, growing to fruitful maturity and then sinking back into the earth to nurture the next generation. The cycle is repeated over and over again. In some traditions the cycle is a spiral that takes human beings from a lower to higher state—or vice versa! But in others the world is a closed cycle of birth, death and rebirth with no destination, no purpose but its own perpetuation.

Jews and Christians look at the purpose and direction of life very differently from these sages, mystics and prophets. For them the metaphor is not the endless cycle of death and rebirth, but the journey, the pilgrimage. Life is depicted not as a circle or a spiral but as an arrow. Jews and Christians are not wandering in the wilderness but heading purposefully for the Promised Land. There are certainly birth, death and rebirth, but there is completion to the cycle. The journey finally comes to an end. God's mysterious purposes are finally fulfilled. The force that acts upon the world is not indifferent, impersonal and purposeless, but personal, loving and *full* of purpose. Life is not, as Macbeth declared, "a tale told by an idiot, full of sound and fury, signifying nothing."[1] Rather,

> The steadfast love of the LORD never ceases,
>   his mercies never come to an end;
> they are new every morning;
>   great is your faithfulness. (Lam 3:22-23)

Judaism and Christianity, in other words, are *eschatological*. They believe God intends to bring his great work of creation to completion.

Among other things, this means the study of eschatology, or "last things," is not important because it gives insider information about the end of the world. The prophecy charts and end-time scenarios more often than not obscure the significance of prophetic texts. The attempts to identify the antichrist or predict the time of Jesus' return have done little more than provide occasions for mockery and embarrassment. Consider the following:

---

[1]William Shakespeare, *Macbeth,* act 5, scene 5, lines 27-28.

- Followers of Joachim of Fiore believed that the year 1260 "was the pre-determined date that marked the final early age."

- The Taborite sect predicted Christ would return in 1420.

- John Napier of Scotland predicted the world would end in 1688.

- Heinrich Alsted of Germany thought the judgment would begin in 1694.

- Others predicted the end would come in 1697, 1714, 1798, 1830, 1847, 1866 and so on.[2]

Jewish mystics were no less enthusiastic in predicting the date of the arrival of the Messiah.[3] And such predictions have not ceased. When I arrived at my office on the first day of my pastoral ministry in Salina, Kansas, a booklet titled *88 Reasons Why the Rapture Will Be in 1988* was on my desk. Many Christians have been taken in by such rash predictions. Unfortunately, neither the failure of the predictions nor the words of Jesus seem to dampen the enthusiasm of some folk (see Mk 13:32). For others the bizarre fantasies of such "prophets" and mystics lead to cynicism. They avoid books like Daniel and Revelation, claiming to be "panmillennialists"—believing it will all "pan out" in the end. But neither obsession nor indifference does justice to the eschatological teachings of the Bible.

There is much more to Christian eschatology than mere prediction. Eschatology is not about the end only, but also about the beginning and middle of faith and life as well. Christianity, as suggested, is eschatological to its core. This means, as suggested, that Christians believe the world has a purpose—it is headed somewhere. The Christian faith is about hope. The Christian message is good news. The world is not locked in an endless cycle of death and rebirth or trapped in a death spiral leading to annihilation. God's promise is "new heavens and a new earth" (Is 65:17; Rev 21:1-4). But this does not mean God's future is a remote reality we passively await. For Christians the future spills into the present. Jesus would assert that in a profound sense the kingdom of God was already here. The apostle Paul would insist that we are already raised with Christ (Rom 6) and already "seated . . . with him in the heavenly places" (Eph 2:6). The rulers and authorities have already been

---

[2]Robert G. Clouse, Robert N. Hosack and Richard V. Pierard, *The New Millennium Manual* (Grand Rapids: Baker, 1999), pp. 108-9.

[3]Ibid., pp. 109-12.

disarmed and defeated (Col 2). Christians are called to live in light of a victory already secured. They are called, in the words of poet Wendell Berry, to "practice resurrection."[4]

JESUS AND THE HOPE OF ISRAEL

The Gospel of Mark tells us that after his baptism by John the Baptist and a time of testing in the wilderness, Jesus returned to Galilee to begin his public ministry. Mark says Jesus was "proclaiming the good news of God, and saying, 'The time is fulfilled, and the kingdom of God has come near; repent, and believe in the good news'" (Mk 1:14-15). Almost immediately he began teaching in the synagogues, calling disciples, casting out demons and healing the sick. What did Jesus mean by all this? How would his Jewish audience have understood it? How was all this good news for them? To answer these questions we need to explore the situation of the Jewish people in the first century.

Six hundred years before the ministry of Jesus began, the Babylonians had destroyed the city of Jerusalem, leveled Solomon's temple and carried away the people into exile (see 2 Kings 25:1-17). Although the Persian king Cyrus eventually permitted Jews to return to their homeland and rebuild their temple, they were still under the control of a mighty empire (see Ezra 1). The Greeks of Alexander the Great followed the Persians. And following a brief period of relative freedom under their own kings, precipitated by the successful Maccabean revolt against their Greek rulers, the Jews found themselves once more at the mercy of an empire: Rome. Although Cyrus permitted the Jews to return to Jerusalem and rebuild the temple, it must have seemed to many in Israel that the exile had never really ended.[5]

This was particularly galling because of the high expectations generated by their prophets. Isaiah 35 had predicted that at the end of the exile God's people would experience the flowering of the desert preceding the arrival of God himself. Exiles from distant pagan lands would joyfully journey to Jerusalem. The "eyes of the blind" would be opened. The "ears of the deaf" would be unstopped. The lame and broken would join the return journey to

---

[4]Wendell Berry, "Manifesto: The Mad Farmer Liberation Front," *New Collected Poems* (Berkeley, CA: Counterpoint, 2012), pp. 173-74.
[5]N. T. Wright, *Jesus and the Victory of God*, vol. 2 of *Christian Origins and the Question of God* (Minneapolis: Fortress, 1996), pp. 202-9.

the land whole and free. The brutal wasteland would flow with water and flourish with lush grasses. God's exiled people would return to the land

> and come to Zion with singing;
> everlasting joy shall be upon their heads;
>   they shall obtain joy and gladness,
>   and sorrowing and sighing shall flee away. (Is 35:10)

The reality of the return from the exile was something else entirely.

The prophet Haggai bluntly confronts the disappointments of the returnees in his brief and poignant prophecy. "Consider how you have fared," he declares. "You have sown much, and harvested little; you eat, but you never have enough; you drink, but you never have your fill; you clothe yourselves, but no one is warm; and you that earn wages earn wages to put them into a bag with holes" (Hag 1:5-6). Although the people had returned to the land, the temple was still in ruins, the walls of the city were rubble and they were barely surviving in a hostile environment (see Neh 1–2). Only a small percentage of the exiles had returned to the city, and the ones there were disheartened and frustrated. This was hardly what Isaiah had led them to expect! Over the years the situation of God's people did not greatly improve.

By the time of Jesus the disappointment was painfully obvious. Some still lived in hope of God's intervention, perhaps through his "anointed one," his Messiah. Others formed communities of protest in the desert to escape the compromises of their rulers as well as the hated Romans. Still others called for opposition to the Romans and anyone who sympathized with them, bloodying their knives to foment rebellion. Some sought solace in the community, the Scriptures and the traditions of the elders. Others simply gave up on God and the "hope of Israel" (Jer 14:8; Acts 28:20). Perhaps we hear their voices in the words of the "scoffers": "Where is the promise of his coming? For ever since our ancestors died, all things continue as they were from the beginning of creation" (2 Pet 3:3-4). Palestine at the time of Jesus was a swamp of hostility, depression, indifference and hope as Jesus began to proclaim the good news.

According to the Gospel of Luke, Jesus began his synagogue teaching in his hometown of Nazareth. He appears to have laid out his program in Luke 4:16-30. He began by quoting from Isaiah 61:

The Spirit of the Lord is upon me;
    because he has anointed me
        to bring good news to the poor.
He has sent me to proclaim release to the captives
    and recovery of sight to the blind,
        to let the oppressed go free,
to proclaim the year of the Lord's favor. (Lk 4:18-19)

So far as Jesus was concerned, Isaiah's hopes were not dead. However deep their disappointment at their continuing oppression, Jesus insisted there was good news. Not only that, he insisted, "Today this scripture has been fulfilled in your hearing" (Lk 4:21). The promises of Isaiah, so long delayed and frustrated, were coming to fruition. The sermon did not end well for Jesus. Enraged at his presumptuousness, they drove him out of town. It was hardly an auspicious beginning!

Nevertheless, in Nazareth Jesus had launched his program. To a great extent it was Isaiah's program. I believe Jesus took his cues from the book of Isaiah and framed his ministry around the book's hopes and expectations. Even his death reflects that of the Suffering Servant of Isaiah 53. Why was Isaiah so important to Jesus? I would suggest that Isaiah's importance was found in that, while he certainly prophesied national renewal, he seemed to go far beyond the requirements of rebuilt temple, restored walls and renewed institutions. He looked not only to the fulfillment of Israel's future but to the fulfillment of God's intention for the whole of creation. Isaiah's message contains a strikingly transcendent element. Two passages are key: Isaiah 65:17-25 and 25:6-9. Did these striking prophecies refer only to a national revival for Israel, or does the prophet have something more in mind? And what do these ancient words have to do with hopes of first-century Jews or, for that matter, with people living in the twenty-first century?

ISAIAH AND THE RESTORATION OF ALL THINGS

Imagine you are one of those discouraged postexilic Jews eking out a living in a devastated city or desolate countryside. You live in rubble. Your neighbors are hostile. You fret over the future of your children and perhaps doubt the very survival of your community. You are part of a tiny and defeated people, living at the edge of a vast, powerful and violent empire. You have heard tales of what your God did in the past to call a people to himself out of slavery and humiliation. Will he do so again, you wonder, or was your God defeated by the gods of Babylon and now humbled before the gods of Persia? How would you hear these words?

> I am about to create new heavens
>   and a new earth;
> the former things shall not be remembered
>   or come to mind.
> But be glad and rejoice forever
>   in what I am creating;
> for I am about to create Jerusalem as a joy,
>   and its people as a delight.
> I will rejoice in Jerusalem,
>   and delight in my people. (Is 65:17-19)

There is no question you would hear this as good news. Perhaps your heart would beat a little faster and your dormant hopes would stir. You see before you a restored city, fruitful fields and happy children playing in prosperous villages. You see peace, prosperity and security—what every human being, every human family, longs for.

But then Isaiah says something startling:

> No more shall there be in it
>   an infant that lives but a few days,
>   or an old person who does not live out a lifetime. (Is 65:20)

This could just be a fancy way of speaking of the security and health of the community. But it raises your eyebrows a bit. And then the prophet makes another startling proclamation:

> The wolf and the lamb shall feed together,
>   the lion shall eat straw like the ox;
>   but the serpent—its food shall be dust!
> They shall not hurt or destroy
>   on all my holy mountain,
>   says the LORD. (Is 65:25)

For wolves and lambs to feed together and lions to eat straw like an ox, something dramatic would need to happen. Predators and prey do not normally get along, to say the least. Once again you could take this as rather high-flung prophet talk—exaggeration for the sake of effect. But perhaps you would wonder just what it could mean.

If Isaiah 65 raised your eyebrows, Isaiah 25 would cause your jaw to drop. The passage promises victory for Israel over her enemies. In the victory's aftermath there will be a great celebration:

> On this mountain the LORD of hosts will make for all peoples
>> a feast of rich food, a feast of well-aged wines,
>> of rich food filled with marrow, of well-aged wines strained clear.
>>> (Is 25:6)

So far, so good, but then, once again, Isaiah says something quite unpredictable and startling:

> And he will destroy on this mountain
>> the shroud that is cast over all peoples,
>> the sheet that is spread over all nations;
>> he will swallow up death forever. (Is 25:7)

This would have been something quite new to the returning exiles. As we will see later in this book, for much of Israel's history there was no expectation of resurrection from the dead. The dead, small and great, sinners and saints, went to Sheol, the abode of the dead where, at best, they lived a shadowy existence.[6] This passage does not yet speak of resurrection, but it does seem to predict an end to death. What could this mean?

There was something else startling about these words. The prophet speaks of "the sheet that is spread over *all nations.*" Does this mean that the Gentiles were somehow to be included in this blessing? When the prophet said this would be a feast for "all peoples," did he mean to include the Gentiles? Another prophet would look forward to a time when "the LORD will become king over all the earth" (Zech 14:9). The defeated Gentiles would make the pilgrimage to Jerusalem "to worship the King, the LORD of hosts, and to keep the festival of booths" (Zech 14:16). Israel's God would not simply be a tribal deity, the local God of a weak and defeated people. Rather he would show himself to be God of heaven and earth, of Jew and Gentile alike. At

---

[6]Alan F. Segal, *Life After Death: A History of the Afterlife in the Religions of the West* (New York: Doubleday, 2004), pp. 120-40.

some point in the future this would become clear to everyone!

Isaiah combines the normal hopes of normal people for prosperity, peace and security with more transcendent hopes: the swallowing up of death, the end of predatory behavior and the renewal of the entire creation. People would live in their own land and worship their own God without fearing their more powerful enemies. In fact, those enemies would be converted and come to Israel to worship their God alongside them at their great festivals. All of this suggests fundamental changes not only in the nature of wolves and lions but in the nature of human predators as well. In fact, Isaiah had predicted that too:

> They shall beat their swords into plowshares,
>   and their spears into pruning hooks;
> nation shall not life up sword against nation,
>   neither shall they learn war any more. (Is 2:4)

This is no ordinary peace. This is not the temporary and wary cessation of violence that so often marks human relationships, be they personal or national. This is not the enduring tension of mutually assured destruction (MAD). This is the peace of God: "He shall judge between the nations, and shall arbitrate for many peoples" (Is 2:4). This peace is not produced by human cleverness on the basis of human military or diplomatic skill. This is an act of God. Isaiah suggests God works through an heir of great David who will reestablish David's kingdom "and uphold it with justice and with righteousness from this time onward and forevermore" (Is 9:7). This "shoot . . . from the stump of Jesse" (Is 11:1) will possess the very Spirit of God and produce the righteousness and peace the Israelites so longed for (see Is 11:2-9).

Return to Nazareth. Take a seat in the synagogue to hear a word from Joseph and Mary's boy. Hear again those stirring words of Isaiah—words that never grow stale no matter how often they are read. And yet, you think, hundreds of years have passed and the peace, prosperity and security you and so many others have so long anticipated seems nowhere in sight. The people of Israel had been battered by the Greeks, by the Romans and by their own internal dissension. Could they cling to hope much longer? Were God's promises empty? And then hear this young man insist that "today this scripture has been fulfilled in your hearing" (Lk 4:21). Who did he think he was? What did he think he was doing? But he was not done. This fulfillment, he declares, would not be just for Israel. It would, as Isaiah had suggested, include the Gentiles as well—even Sidonians and Syrians (Lk 4:25-27). "All in the synagogue," Luke writes, "were filled with rage" (Lk 4:28).

The good news the Jews of Jesus' day were awaiting was the end of the long exile. They were looking for peace, prosperity and security in their own land and the opportunity to be ruled by their own king and worship their own God. They were anticipating the humiliation and defeat of their enemies, the Gentiles—especially the Romans. Some, with the prophet Daniel, were expecting more than military victory. They were anticipating the resurrection of the dead: "Many of those," Daniel had written, "who sleep in the dust of the earth shall awake, some to everlasting life, and some to shame and everlasting contempt. Those who are wise shall shine like the brightness of the sky, and those who lead many to righteousness, like the stars forever and ever" (Dan 12:2-3). Others were anticipating a more prosaic victory over their enemies—nothing so transcendent or eternal. Into this ferment of disappointment and expectation steps Jesus with his message of hope, his announcement of the kingdom of God. What did he mean by the kingdom of God?

JESUS AND THE MESSAGE OF THE KINGDOM

I will have more to say about the kingdom of God and the ministry of Jesus later in the book. Here I want simply to explore how Jesus represented the kingdom of God in his teaching and ministry and what that could have meant to his hearers. Remember Isaiah 35:5-6 and the predictions of "the eyes of the blind" being opened, "the ears of the deaf" being unstopped, the lame "leap[ing] like a deer" and "the tongue of the speechless" singing for joy? Jesus' ministry is characterized by just such acts of healing and liberation. These are not simply impressive mighty acts; they are signs of the presence of God's kingdom. In the ministry of Jesus in some profound sense the kingdom is already here. When Jesus healed the sick and cast out demons "by the finger of God," then "the kingdom of God has come to you" (Lk 11:20). Jesus healed the sick and cast out demons in anticipation of a new heaven and a new earth where, as Isaiah proclaimed, death is defeated and creation is healed. In this ministry of Jesus, the kingdom is now but not yet. God's rule of justice and peace was coming in its fullness, but, Jesus seemed to be saying, in his ministry it was present now.

Jesus' healings and exorcisms are not the only part of his ministry to anticipate and represent the presence of the kingdom. In his teachings he identifies a way to live and love that looks forward to the time when swords would become plowshares and spears pruning hooks. This is seen in his most famous teaching—the Sermon on the Mount in Matthew 5–7. In the "poor in spirit" he sees a people who can become "the salt of the earth" and "the light of the world" (Mt 5:3, 13-14). They go beyond the dictates of the ancient law. They refuse to engage evil by using its own tools. They pull the sting out of enmity by loving their enemies. They live with simplicity, humility and trust. They leave judgment to God and live in obedience to the teaching of Jesus. Their lives are unusual—contrary to the frantic and acquisitive ways of their neighbors. They are, in fact, living kingdom lives *before* the kingdom arrives in its fullness (see Mt 5–7). They are "the salt of the earth," "the light of the world," "a city built on a hill" (Mt 5:13-14). They are, for the world around them, the presence of the kingdom.

In the life and ministry of Jesus there is a profound sense that the present and the future come together. In the life, death and resurrection of Jesus, the kingdom was inaugurated, the new age begun. For the apostle Paul, for example, Jesus' resurrection was not simply Jesus' restoration to life. Jesus' resurrection was the "first fruits" of the great and final resurrection (1 Cor 15:20). Paul argues that when we entrust ourselves to God's love in Christ, we die and rise with him (Rom 6). For Paul this means we have already experienced Jesus' resurrection in a profoundly real sense. As individuals and as a Christian community this means we are called, as I suggested earlier, to practice resurrection. All that is anticipated in a new heaven and a new earth is to be lived out in the Christian community—a community that has already died and been raised with Christ.

AS IT WAS IN THE BEGINNING: JOHN'S FINAL VISION

The life and ministry of Jesus is not the only place in the New Testament where the prophecy of Isaiah figures prominently. Isaiah promised a new heaven and a new earth where righteousness would dwell. War, famine, disaster and premature death would be a thing of the past. God's people would live securely under the direct, righteous rule of God. Jesus had declared that in his life and ministry the kingdom had begun and a new community was being called to live out of kingdom realities. Empowered by God's Spirit and energized by the resurrection of Jesus, this community would announce this good news and model kingdom life as its members called people to repentance and invited them to participate in the resurrection life of Jesus. Together, members of the new community would bear witness to Jesus and await the consummation—a new heaven and a new earth.

More than sixty years after the death and resurrection of Jesus, a prophet named John had a series of visions on the remote Greek island of Patmos. He sent these powerful and disturbing visions to seven churches in Asia Minor—present-day Turkey. He addressed each church with a letter. The letters commended faithfulness in the midst of persecution and warned of compromise. The infant church, like the people of Israel before it, was now suffering from the oppression of Rome. While the threat of violence and even bloodshed was ever present, perhaps the greatest danger, so far as John was concerned, was for Christians to conform to the expectations of the empire. Some folk in the churches of Asia Minor seemed to think that there was no inconsistency in following Jesus while also fulfilling one's civic obligations by making an offering to Caesar as a god. Others seemed to think it was not all that bad to go to a banquet in honor of a local deity only, of course, for the express purpose of making business contacts. Perhaps others wondered if people would respond more readily to the good news if Christians made an effort to fit in a bit better? John had no tolerance for this kind of thinking. Such people, he insisted, bear not the marks of Jesus but the mark of the beast.

John's final vision loops back around to Isaiah: "Then I saw a new heaven and a new earth; for the first heaven and the first earth had passed away, and the sea was no more. And I saw the holy city, the new Jerusalem, coming down out of heaven from God, prepared as a bride adorned for her husband" (Rev 21:1-2). As Isaiah had predicted, God would dwell with his people:

> See, the home of God is among mortals.
> He will dwell with them as their God;
> they will be his peoples. (Rev 21:3)

John continues, using words very similar to Isaiah 25:

He will wipe every tear from their eyes.
Death will be no more;
mourning and crying and pain will be no more,
for the first things have passed away. (Rev 21:4)

As in Isaiah, there is even a great banquet, "the marriage supper of the Lamb" (Rev 19:9). And everyone will be invited to worship God in the heavenly city come down to earth: "The nations will walk by its light, and the kings of the earth will bring their glory into it" (Rev 21:24).

In the end, John makes clear, we don't go to heaven; heaven comes to us. According to Isaiah and John, our destiny is an earthly destiny. I will say more about this later, but the popular notion of our ultimate fate as going to heaven when you die disregards the true, and much more exciting, expectation of the Bible.[7] In John's vision God returns to the garden from which Adam and Eve were once banished. The garden is now in the midst of a great city. There "the water of life, bright as crystal, [is] flowing from the throne of God and of the Lamb." There "on either side of the river is the tree of life with its twelve kinds of fruit, producing its fruit each month; and the leaves of the tree are for the healing of the nations" (Rev 22:1-2). God's people will rule in peace and righteousness alongside God himself, "for the Lord God will be their light, and they will reign forever and ever" (Rev 22:5). In the end God does not abandon his creation or his people but sets both the world and his people right. This is our hope and the world's destiny.

IMPLICATIONS AND EXPECTATIONS

We are not given all this information merely to satisfy our curiosity. Isaiah, Jesus, Paul and John offer both hope and warning. They are not simply concerned with the church's future or even its current endurance; they are concerned with its mission. Eschatology is not just about the future return of Jesus, the last judgment, and a new heaven and a new earth. It is about how we live into that hope in the present. It is about how the church is the

---

[7]N. T. Wright, *Surprised by Hope: Rethinking Heaven, the Resurrection, and the Mission of the Church* (New York: HarperOne, 2008), pp. 3-30.

"presence of the future"[8] and the sacrament of the kingdom. The values of the future kingdom are to be our values now. We do not bring in the kingdom, but *we make the kingdom present in our lives and ministries.* The Jews who heard Isaiah speak of the glories of the coming intervention of God did not experience the fullness of their expectations. But they did experience the providential care of God in the midst of their suffering and struggle. And they lived in hope, clinging to the promise. Followers of Jesus have not yet experienced the fullness of our expectations. Are we still living with the same hope?

But, some people may think, all that was a long time ago. Those messages were given to a people very different from us. Is such a hope even possible for us today? Can modern people really look forward to a new heaven and a new earth? Can we really anticipate the coming of Jesus, the establishment of God's kingdom of peace, the healing of all wounds and the stilling of all fears? Isn't that all rather primitive? Aren't we beyond that now? Books like Ezekiel, Daniel and Revelation may seem too strange, even distasteful, to many of us today. And yet there are portions of these great, strange books that could have been written yesterday, that seem to warn of very contemporary dangers. Read Revelation 8 with its warnings of environmental devastation or Revelation 12–13 with its warnings of political domination and see if this is not so. Many in our contemporary world see these dangers but have no real answers to them; at most they offer despair or resignation. In the next chapter I will suggest that we have been betrayed by the modern era and that as a people, particularly in the West, we need the Christian hope more than ever.

Ultimately this is what it means to be a Christian, a follower of Jesus. We are people of hope. Such hope is not wishful thinking or a vague desire for things to work out—somehow. Because we have entrusted ourselves to Jesus, Paul writes, "we have peace with God through our Lord Jesus Christ, through whom we have obtained access to this grace in which we stand; and we boast in our *hope* of sharing the glory of God" (Rom 5:1-2). To share the glory of God is to be in the presence of God. This hope does not make us smug. It does not make us passive. It provides us with our mission, our direction, our

---

[8]George Eldon Ladd, *The Presence of the Future* (Grand Rapids: Eerdmans, 1996).

goal in life—both individual and communal. In another letter Paul will declare us "ambassadors for Christ" entrusted with a "ministry of reconciliation." Our mission is from God because "God was in Christ reconciling the world to himself, not counting their trespasses against them" (2 Cor 5:18-20). Our ministry, our mission is about the reconciliation of the world—all God's people and the entire created order! No one and nothing are left out of God's love and God's peace. But the church of the West faces the same dangers of compromise as those ancient churches of Asia Minor. This book is written in part to confront us with our compromise, our passivity, our indifference—even our disbelief. We all need hope as never before.

2

Hope and Accommodation

Why do we need to reclaim a vibrant Christian eschatology, an eschatology that is not merely abstract speculation or smirking complacency? Isn't Christian eschatology a discredited doctrine valued only by scholars and fanatics? What does such strange and esoteric biblical material have to offer a world facing myriad challenges: crippling natural disasters, economic collapse, threats of violence, grinding poverty and crushing despair? To begin answering these questions I will turn to the Christian past. There was a time when the Christian church lived in a world very much like this—a world of imperial violence, economic collapse, urban poverty and deadly plagues. While the primitive Christian church should not be romanticized, this relatively powerless group of Jesus followers living under a cloud of suspicion and facing frequent outbreaks of violent persecution was able to move from being a small sect of Judaism to a dominant religious force in the Roman Empire in less than three hundred years. How did they do it, and why does it matter to us today?

ESCHATOLOGY AND THE EARLY CHURCH

In his famous and controversial book *The Rise of Christianity,* Rodney Stark argues that the early Christians were able to accomplish all this because, in short, they showed the violent, troubled and divided Roman Empire a better way to live.[1] They were able to do this because they were practicing resurrection. Not only were they convinced that Jesus had been raised from the dead, but they believed in their own resurrections. This conviction enabled them to face persecution and even martyrdom with calmness and confidence. It also enabled them, as we will see, to face plagues without fear and to serve the suffering and dying in the fetid Greco-Roman cities. They formed small communities of hope that provided a new family and new vision for life—a life not controlled by fate, the capriciousness of gods, or the all-powerful economic and political life of Imperial Rome. These communities of hope offered family and freedom in the present and the new heaven and new earth in the age to come. And these communities of hope brought that future into the present in their worship and service.

Stark, noting that early Christianity was an urban movement, argues that the early Christians were effective in dealing with the problems of the city. Greco-Roman cities were every bit as troubled as our own. They were as densely populated as the great contemporary Indian cities of Calcutta or Mumbai.[2] These ancient cities were filthy beyond our imagining. The poor, in particular, lacked the most basic of services—sewage removal and clean water among the most prominent! The result was, of course, dirt, squalor and frequent outbreaks of infectious disease and even plagues. The cities were also diverse, filled with people from all over the empire. They had different customs, different gods and different political loyalties. The result was frequent ethnic and cultural strife leading to frequent violence, rebellion and bloodshed. Cities in the region were also subject to natural disasters, earthquakes being the most deadly.

The cities were controlled by powerful political and economic aristocracies. Many if not most citizens were obligated to an important political family headed by a powerful patron. These patrons insisted on loyalty and were not above using mob violence to protect their interests. Guilds also wielded significant influence in many cities, requiring their members to conform to their expectations. Above all these powers was the absolute

---

[1]Rodney Stark, *The Rise of Christianity: How the Obscure, Marginal Jesus Movement Became the Dominant Religious Force in the Western World in a Few Centuries* (San Francisco: HarperSanFrancisco, 1997), pp. 161-62.
[2]Ibid., p. 153.

power of Rome and her deadly legions. The patrons and the guilds competed to show their loyalty and servility before Roman power. Rome, of course, did not hesitate to send in the legionnaires with their deadly short swords if it sensed any threat. The individual butcher, baker or tentmaker in a Greco-Roman city would feel powerless and even hopeless in the face of such might.

Many millions lived at the bottom of Greco-Roman society. The economy was kept healthy by millions of slaves. Some slaves lived in great households and served as domestics, managers and even teachers of the young. But others lived brief and brutish lives in mines, fields or galleys, Roman fighting ships. A few could win their freedom, but most were doomed to live out their lives in servitude. Women were also relatively powerless in Greco-Roman society. Considered first as possessions of their fathers and second as possessions of their husbands, they had few rights or opportunities. Upon the death of her husband, a woman could find herself under the control of her son. A girl had little or no say regarding whom and when she would marry. It was the rare Greco-Roman woman that exercised cultural, economic or political power in that patriarchal society.[3]

According to Stark, these were all factors in the early success of the church. Since they were living in hope of resurrection, Christians did not fear when plague and disease swept these great cities. In fact, they were known for remaining in the cities and caring for the sick and suffering. The Roman emperor Julian complained that the pagan priests fled the cities when plagues struck while the hated Christians cared for Christian and pagan alike.[4] Many of the early martyrs were not killed by animals or beheaded by Roman officials but died caring for the sick in plague-stricken cities. As many as a quarter to a third of a city's population could die during a plague.[5] Since Christians stayed and served, they not only gained credibility with the populace, but they formed a new family for those who had lost everyone during the plague. They served not only out of compassion but in full expectation of the resurrection of the dead. They were also convinced that the

---

[3]Ibid., pp. 106, 120-21.
[4]Ibid., p. 84.
[5]Rodney Stark, *The Triumph of Christianity: How the Jesus Movement Became the World's Largest Religion* (San Francisco: HarperOne, 2011), pp. 114-19.

healing power of the new age was present in them as it had been in Jesus.

Stark also argues that a major element of the early church's success was its appeal to women. The apostle Paul had insisted that "there is no longer Jew or Greek, there is no longer slave or free, there is no longer male or female; for all of you are one in Christ Jesus" (Gal 3:28). Since in a profound sense the new age had already arrived, the old divisions and subjugations were no longer in place. This gave women a role, a place and a dignity in the early church that they lacked in the wider culture. Two other factors were significant in the church's appeal to women. First, early Christians followed Jews in their opposition to abortion and the exposure of unwanted children to the elements. This meant that Christian women did not die as frequently from the deadly methods of abortion often required by a husband or father. It also meant a growing number of females in the Christian movement since girl babies were the ones most frequently exposed by the pagans. Second, Christian women frequently married later than their pagan contemporaries and had more choice in mates.[6] All of this obviously would appeal to Greco-Roman women and perhaps enrage Greco-Roman authorities. And, it should be said, many of the factors that appealed to women would also appeal to slaves. They too received a new status in Christ that transcended their servitude.

Christians offered the Greco-Roman world a new community ethic. All were brothers and sisters in Christ, not aliens and strangers. This ethic offered a community relationship that transcended their statuses as slaves or free, patrons or powerless, women or men. In Christ they were all one regardless of their status, wealth, power or gender. Christians also offered a new ethic of compassion. All the sick and suffering were offered the healing power of Christ, regardless of their economic status, ethnic identity or religious commitment. The early Christians did this because they were convinced of the resurrection of the dead and the very presence of the kingdom of God. They were practicing resurrection.

As I said earlier, we should not romanticize the early church. It was not perfect. It had its failings and departures from the simplicity of the message of Jesus. As time went on, it was attracted to the same hierarchy and power

---

[6]Ibid., pp. 121-36.

dominant in the empire. It was given to embarrassing theological squabbles and charges of heresy that would even lead to violence between the partisans of various theological positions. We, in short, cannot and should not aspire to return to an earlier era as if that would solve our problems. Nevertheless, I am convinced we can learn something about living out of the resurrection from those early Christians. They faced a hostile and divided world as we do. They spread the message of Jesus through living faithfully and freely in the face of threats of violence, deadly plagues and social suspicions. The question we should ask is not how can we be like them, but how can we, in a very different world, live out of the same resurrection life that emboldened them?

THE ACCOMMODATION OF CONSTANTINE

As time went on, the immediate kingdom expectations that fired the primitive church virtually disappeared. Perhaps it is simplistic and unfair to blame everything that subsequently went wrong with the church on the Roman emperor Constantine. But something did change in the early fourth century when Constantine embraced Christianity. He credited a vision of the cross for a military victory that brought him to power. From this rather ambiguous beginning, Christianity gained greater and greater influence within the Roman world until it overshadowed paganism. Its leaders became officers of the state and would eventually use state power to enforce their will. The state would even step in to solve forcibly the theological squabbling mentioned earlier. Human beings were as clever then as they are now. Many in the Roman Empire could see which way the wind was blowing. Pretty soon the church had more converts than it knew what to do with. Some celebrated this newfound recognition as a sign of God's favor and power. Others fretted about the diminishment of purity of doctrine and commitment of life. Roman recognition meant the diminishment and eventual elimination of persecution of Christians. It meant governmental patronage and support of the church. But many will argue that this support came with a heavy price.

Scholars of history continue to argue about the significance and results of the conversion of Constantine. But it cannot be doubted that Roman patronage set the church on a road that led to it imitating the imperial state.

Eventually church officials would wield as much power in their own realm as Roman political and military officials wielded in theirs. Eventually church officials would be as gloriously attired and comfortably housed as the Roman aristocracy. They would be as committed to preserving their power, personal comfort and status as any secular official. For many within the political and religious aristocracy, the preservation of the status quo became the most critical factor in their decisions. Few people who acquire wealth, status and comfort willingly relinquish them, even for the common good.

Many believe this linking of the power of the state with the power of the church resulted in the sapping of the spiritual power of the latter. Throughout the subsequent history of the church, many protest movements have criticized these compromises and recalled the church to its earlier commitments. In the very earliest period, monks fled the cities for the desert and formed communities of protest and resistance. The monks saw only compromise and corruption in the official church and called its officials to live by the gospel, not by the Roman rules of power and influence. Eventually monasticism was included within the church and throughout its history acted as a brake and a critique upon the imperial aspirations of many church leaders. It is no surprise that the Protestant Reformation was begun by an Augustinian monk, Martin Luther.[7]

The Protestant Reformation was certainly, in part, a protest against the imperial accommodation of the Roman Catholic Church. Protestants insisted that the Bible was to be the guiding force for faith and life—not church hierarchies, church traditions or accredited theologians. In that all believers were considered priests, the ordained priest was not at the top of the heap. Nevertheless, Protestants, no less than Roman Catholics, were seduced by state power. Throughout northern Europe great state churches arose in which all or most the citizens of a given country or region were baptized as Lutherans or Anglicans or Reformed. Kings and princes claimed power over the regional or national church and appointed or deposed leaders at will. Opposition was often crushed by sword and flame.

The result was a powerful, but flaccid church. Certainly there were many faithful, committed and passionate Christians who sought to follow Jesus in

---

[7]On this section, see Rodney Stark, *For the Glory of God* (Princeton, NJ: Princeton University Press, 2003), pp. 33-46.

all these state churches. But there were also millions of nominal Christians who inherited their faith as a part of their national identity. Stark suggests this meant that many of these European countries were only lightly evangelized and not fully converted.[8] When the so-called Enlightenment arrived and gained ground, such nominal Christianity was largely swept away. The state of the current church in Western Europe bears witness to the weakness of these state churches. Depending on the power of the state to enforce the rights and beliefs of the church has normally been deadly to the church. That is as true in the United States as in Europe.

It is not an accident that one of the first casualties of the rise of the national and state church was a healthy eschatology. When the goals of the state and the goals of the church coalesce, eschatological critiques of the state are obviously muted. In the protest movements of monks and reformers, eschatology would occasionally make an appearance as a tool of protest. But for many throughout the history of the church, the institution itself was bringing in the kingdom in cooperation with the various powers. To resist the church or resist the powers was to resist the very work of God to produce the kingdom. Since eschatology was often seen as a tool of resistance, its role was diminished, explained away or pushed into the distant future. Complacent in the support of the state, the church ceased practicing resurrection or expecting the kingdom of God.

LIVING BETWEEN ROMANS 13 AND REVELATION 13

If this is what the state does to the church, how should the Christian church live in relation to the state? Jesus famously told a group of Pharisees and Herodians trying to get him in trouble that they should "give to the emperor the things that are the emperor's, and to God the things that are God's" (Mk 12:17). This is often interpreted to mean that there are two spheres of Christian existence—the sphere of the state and the sphere of the church. I believe this is wrong. Jesus' response is cleverer than that. Is there any sphere of life that does not belong to God? Clearly not. We owe everything to God as far as Jesus is concerned. In some ways this is a trick response. In the long run what belongs to the emperor? Nothing. What belongs to God? Every-

---

[8]Ibid., pp. 255-72.

thing. For Jesus, following God, doing the will of God, always and at all times took precedence over human authority. This does not mean Christians are in a constant state of revolt against the authorities; rather, the values and commitments of Christian discipleship trump the values and commitments of national citizenship. Sometimes these values come into direct conflict.

Christians live between Romans 13 and Revelation 13. In Paul's great letter the believers in the capital city are told: "Let every person be subject to the governing authorities; for there is no authority except from God. . . . Therefore whoever resists authority resists what God has appointed" (Rom 13:1-2). These very same Roman authorities would in a few short years execute Paul and Peter and slaughter many ordinary Christians in the wake of the great fire of Rome. Emperor Nero would become infamous for his cruelty and brutality toward a despised minority. And yet, the words of Paul remind Christians of an obligation of respect for human government and human leadership.

John, as you might expect, offers a different perspective. In Revelation 13 he sees "a beast rising out of the sea" (Rev 13:1). This beast "was allowed to make war on the saints and to conquer them" (Rev 13:7). A second beast "rose out of the earth" and made "the earth and its inhabitants worship the first beast" (Rev 13:11-12). Many scholars believe this is a reference to a Nero-like figure and to the pagan priesthood that supported the worship of the emperor. It is for us a sober reminder that all human government has the capacity to become beastly. The beastliness could denote efforts to force a compromise of our commitments, or it could refer to outright persecution. Some scholars believe the churches John addressed in the book of Revelation were facing painful choices of fidelity to Jesus or compromise for the sake of survival. John commands resistance even to the point of death.

This is what it means to live between Romans 13 and Revelation 13. We respect the state and its authority as a gift from God. But we are wary of the state and its authority because of the pressure of compromise. The rulers are "servant[s] of God" (Rom 13:4). But sometimes the rulers are "beasts" (Rev 13). Christians live between these realities seeking to be faithful to God's call on their lives. The soft power of the state can lull us into complacency perhaps even more than the hard power of outright persecution. We resist both soft and hard power by seeking first God's kingdom (Mt 6:33). This means we develop an eschatological consciousness—that is, we live with the end in view. We are respectfully wary of what Paul calls the "rulers and authorities," knowing they have their sphere of influence and responsibility. But we know that those powers are frequently hostile to Jesus and have been finally and completed defeated by him through his death and resurrection (Col 2:15).

Having said all this, I would offer a warning. I have observed that when their own party is in office, some Christians will frequently quote Romans 13. But when the other party is in office, they darkly cite Revelation 13. Their candidates are servants of God while the other party's candidates are beasts. Such an approach is dangerous and simplistic and a misuse of Scripture. All leaders can be servants of God, and all leaders can be beastly, regardless of their political affiliation. We should not be taken in by the powers through such demands for loyalty. We should remember that all our loyalty is due first to God and only secondarily and warily to Caesar.

BABYLON THE GREAT

John has much more to say about the beastly character of human government and its seductive power. In Revelation 17, he savagely depicts the Roman Empire as "Babylon the great, mother of whores and of earth's abominations" (Rev 17:5). To symbolize the current imperial power, John reaches back into Jewish history to ancient Babylon—the empire that had destroyed the city of Jerusalem, razed Solomon's temple and carried the people into exile. The woman is seated on "a scarlet beast" and is dressed in purple and scarlet (Rev 17:3-4). She is said to be "drunk with the blood of the saints" (Rev 17:6). She is a picture of violence, wealth and power. John says that "the kings of the earth have committed fornication" with her and "the inhabitants of the earth" have become drunk on the "wine" of their fornication (Rev 17:2).

These graphic and disturbing images speak to the seductive power of empires and governments throughout history. Not only do they possess the very real threat of policing powers and persecution; they possess the more subtle powers of the economy. They can threaten with the sword and seduce with wealth. Some scholars think the woman on the beast is a symbol of Rome's wealth and economic power. She is seated on a powerful beast symbolic of Rome's military power. Rome's military power made her wealth possible. It protected trade routes, opened new opportunities to exploit new markets and brought in millions of slaves as prisoners of war. This interpretation of Revelation 17 is supported by the weeping of kings, merchants and sailors over the fall of Babylon in Revelation 18. Rome's fall would mean they were no longer able to make money.[9]

Revelation, of course, does not simply speak of ancient Rome. As I have already suggested, it speaks of any cultural and political power throughout human history that would seek to compromise and seduce the people of God. Any culture, any society, any government can become demonic. In the letters to the seven churches that began his prophecy, John, as we have seen, worried as much about cultural, social and economic compromise as he did about outright persecution. As Paul would warn, the world around us is always trying to squeeze us into its mold (see Rom 12:2). An eschatological worldview will keep us wary and alert to such compromises. It will take account of the seductions of the church throughout history and be more accountable to the words of Jesus than to the expectations of the larger society. This is a particular challenge for us in that we live in a society capable of marshaling astonishingly powerful resources through marketing, technology and propaganda to convince us that the nature of the world is other than we think. This requires careful attention to the message of Jesus lest it be drowned out by other messages that may seem more attractive. Jesus offers his disciples and his community a way to resist the powerful influences of the culture and the state.

THE COUNTERCULTURAL MESSAGE OF JESUS

So what does it mean for us to seek first God's kingdom? What is an eschatological consciousness? The Sermon on the Mount in Matthew 5–7 is perhaps the most famous and least regarded piece of teaching in human history. It has been admiringly explained away for centuries by people purporting to be followers of Jesus. Some interpreters might as well say, "This is quite wonderful, very moving, but he surely didn't really mean it." For many centuries only the religious, monks and nuns, aspired to live by the dictates of the sermon. For others the teachings of Jesus might offer prin-

---

[9]Michael J. Gorman, *Reading Revelation Responsibly: Uncivil Worship and Witness; Following the Lamb into the New Creation* (Eugene, OR: Cascade, 2011), pp. 123-30, 145-50.

ciples or ideals but were regarded as impossible requirements for the real world. In later church history only oddballs or extremists sought to live by the words of Jesus in the sermon, even though he warned at the end of the sermon, "Everyone who hears these words of mine and does not act on them will be like a foolish man who built his house on sand" (Mt 7:26).

I think Jesus meant for us to take the sermon seriously. This does not mean it does not bristle with difficult questions of interpretation and application—for surely it does. But I will argue that the Sermon on the Mount points us in the direction of fidelity to God and away from accommodation with "the rulers and authorities" (Col 2:15). It calls God's people to a specifically Christian way of life that always settles uncomfortably within the "kingdom of this world" (Rev 11:15). It is amazing how this call to love, generosity and simplicity has aroused such hostility and scorn. If you don't believe me, suggest in a public forum that we should love our enemies (Mt 5:44) and "not resist an evildoer" (Mt 5:39) and you will see what I mean.

Jesus thought the kingdom had in a profound way "come upon" us (Lk 11:20). His followers were already breathing kingdom air and living by kingdom rules. There was a blessedness to all this even for the poor, the mourners and the meek (Mt 5:3-5). Jesus, in fact, turned the values of the Greco-Roman world on their heads. Greco-Roman culture valued wealth, power, possession, influence and honor—rather as we do. If you had walked the streets of, say, Ephesus, at the time of Jesus, you would have seen statues, plaques, buildings and inscriptions honoring the benefactors of the city. Well-to-do Romans vied for honors and the best seats at the table and sought to avoid anything that would bring shame on them or their families. This was no less true in Galilee, as Jesus' parables make clear. Then as now the wealthy benefactors wanted their names on the important buildings. As one of my friends once told me, at a college no one wants his or her name on the maintenance shed. There is little honor in that.

As we saw in the last chapter, Jesus said his people are the "salt of the earth," "the light of the world" and "a city built on a hill" (Mt 5:13-14). But all this does not bring them honor. They do not carve their names in stone. Rather, when their contemporaries "see your good works," they "give glory to your Father in heaven" (Mt 5:16). The attention is directed away from them toward God. "When you give alms," Jesus told them, "do not let your left hand know what your right hand is doing" (Mt 6:3). "And whenever you pray," he insisted, "do not be like the hypocrites; for they love to stand and pray in the synagogues and at the street corners, so that they may be seen by others" (Mt 6:5). For a follower of Jesus, neither ostentatious generosity nor ostentatious spirituality is appropriate. We do not give or pray or serve to get our names on the building, to gain honor. Giving or withholding honor, Jesus seemed to suggest, is our culture's way of trying to control us and conform us to its expectations and values. Living obscurely and refusing to seek honor are ways of avoiding such temptation.

Perhaps we are not as much an honor-and-shame culture as they were. But in little and large ways we want to make sure we receive proper credit. We want such credit because it appeals to our egos. Our generosity, piety and compassion frequently seem to require validation for them to continue. Over the years I have been amused by the number of letters to advice columnists complaining about the failure of family and friends to send thank-you notes in response to gifts. Sometimes it appears that the only reason the gift is given is to receive a thank-you note in reply. The offended gift givers often complain bitterly at the failure of a child, grandchild or friend to acknowledge their generosity. They wonder if this failure justifies their no longer giving gifts until the thoughtless recipient responds appropriately. Now I am all in favor of thank-you notes. But is a gift really a gift if it requires proper acknowledgment (and not merely an email message or verbal thank you—but a handwritten note, addressed, stamped and sent through the mail)?

This is a small and trivial example of how credit, or honor, can control us. When our gift giving, our piety or our service makes us miserable because we are not properly acknowledged, Jesus would suggest we have ingested the values of the world. These values would control us through recognition and credit, a bigger salary or a corner office. But our audience, Jesus insists, is not our society but God himself. You don't let your "left hand know what your right hand is doing, so that your alms may be done in secret; and your Father who sees in secret will reward you" (Mt 6:3-4). If Jesus' followers live this way, the culture has lost a powerful tool of control, compromise and accommodation. The voices that insist we call attention to ourselves by the way in which we live will fall on deaf ears. The voices that insist we live like

everyone else and don't buck the trends will be ignored. The whore of
Babylon will have not power over us.

Worry and trust. Then as now, people sought credit and honor. And
people have always sought to secure their future by storing up "treasures on
earth" (Mt 6:19). Throughout much of human history people have seemed
to worry about little more than what they will eat, drink and wear and where
they will live. So it is counterintuitive that Jesus would tell us "do not worry
about your life, what you will eat or what you will drink, or about your body,
what you will wear. Is not life," he insists, "more than food, and the body
more than clothing?" (Mt 6:25). Someone once suggested to me this was
either the wisest or the craziest thing Jesus ever said. Jesus' words here are
certainly about trusting God: "If God so clothes the grass of the field . . . will
he not much more clothe you—you of little faith?" (Mt 6:30). But there is
more than this going on.

Our cultures and our economies seduce and compromise us through fear
and intimidation. Politicians panic us by warning of the weakness of the
economy. We will put up with just about any nonsense from our leaders if
the economy is strong. We will meekly do what powerful business and political bosses want if we think we can save our paychecks, our homes, our
careers. For the sake of the economy we will "strain at gnats" and "swallow
camels." For contemporary Americans this is the most powerful force of
compromise and seduction. I once heard of a pastor in a contentious de-
nomination who said, "When the big split comes, I am going with the
pension fund." Every politician knows that in the United States, Social Security is the third rail of a political career. Step on it, and your services will
no longer be required by the electorate! Some Christians seem to have no
difficulty in trusting God for their eternal salvation but balk at trusting him
for their next meal.

But Jesus wants us to really trust God and not the economic policies of
the Republicans or the Democrats. He wants us to value the kingdom of
God over capitalism or socialism. Those who trust God, really trust God,
for their daily bread will not be seduced by fear or manipulated by threats.
As difficult as it is for those of us who worry about little else, Jesus wants us
not to "worry about tomorrow, for tomorrow will bring worries of its own"
(Mt 6:34). To have an eschatological consciousness is to trust in God and

look to God's kingdom and not to the kingdoms of this world. We do not need the gold and silver and purple of the "great whore" or the violent power of the "scarlet beast" (Rev 17). We have the power of the slaughtered Lamb (Rev 5)! This liberates us from fear and anguish and enables us to rest in the certainty of God's final redeeming work, in the promise of a new heaven and a new earth.

The other. A final countercultural teaching of the Sermon on the Mount is directed to our relationship with others. We are seduced by culture and society when we give another person power over us. The grumpy gift-givers I mentioned earlier are miserable because they have given someone else the power to make them happy or miserable. Anger and alienation from a brother or sister gives that person power over you. Forgiveness and reconciliation eliminate an obligating debt (Mt 5:22-26). Seeking revenge, trying to even the score, is another way of giving power to the other. Refusing to get even, refusing to continue the cycle of violence by returning one blow for another, completely changes the power relationships (Mt 5:38-40). Loving enemies and persecutors, rather than hating and despising them, gives you freedom (Mt 5:43-48).

These are among the most controversial teachings of Jesus. But they contain an irrefutable logic. It is difficult to continue a conflict in which the other party refuses to participate. But there is a larger picture here. The renowned Christian thinker René Girard has argued that human culture is based on what he calls a principle of "scapegoating."[10] Ancient people discovered that they could find unity and create peace and order if they identified some "other" as their common enemy. Throughout history, nothing has rallied a divided people like a common enemy, a scapegoat who is deemed the source of all their problems. Political leaders have always known this. Blame your problems on someone else—the Jews, the communists, the terrorists or the American "crusaders"—and you will find a previously elusive unanimity, albeit a unanimity of hatred.

Girard argues that entire cultures were founded upon some form of violence against an enemy. Even today we are often held together only by the people we hate. Girard insists that Jesus in his teachings and his death ex-

---

[10]See René Girard, *The Scapegoat*, trans. Yvonne Freccero (Baltimore: Johns Hopkins University Press, 1989).

posed this deadly way of forming culture. By calling us to love our enemies and forgive them, he shows us how we have used and persecuted others to gain power and find unity. Scapegoating the other is the way our culture controls us and seduces us into accepting its values and standards. Loving our enemies frees us from this control and enables us to live out of the values of the kingdom of God rather than the values of the "kingdom of this world" (Rev 11:15). Is this easy? Clearly not. As I suggested before, it bristles with difficulties and questions. But the difficulties and questions are no reason to ignore the countercultural teachings of Jesus. When we resort to violence and scapegoating, whether our enemies are terrorists in the Middle East or political opponents in our city or country or even in our church, we have abandoned the gospel. We have left off practicing resurrection.

The church accommodated itself when it failed to live out of the kingdom of God and the values of the gospel in the teachings of Jesus. It will reclaim its identity and purpose when it reclaims the teachings of its Lord and frees itself from the rulers and authorities he died to defeat. When as a community and as individuals we seek first God's kingdom (Mt 6:33) and live out of kingdom values, we will offer a genuine alternative to the violence, bloodshed and hatred that characterize our world. We will not be seduced by the economic power of the whore of Babylon or the military might of the great scarlet beast. We will hunger for righteousness and commit ourselves to mercy, purity and peace even if we are scorned and persecuted (Mt 5:6-10). When the followers of Jesus and his community, the church, do all this, it will once again have something to offer a modern world now cast adrift by the failure of the "modern project."[11]

THE FAILURE OF THE MODERN PROJECT

The church clearly needs to reclaim a powerful eschatology for the sake of its own mission and identity. But it also needs to renew its commitment to God's promises because society as a whole needs the message of hope in Jesus Christ. The modern project has failed, and our society is in the grip of what some would call a postmodern despair. Secular hope is evaporating, and confidence in progress has become a sick joke. Boosters of what came

---

[11]Martin Heidegger uses the phrase "modern project" in *Being and Time*, trans. John Macquarrie and Edward Robinson (London: SCM Press, 1962).

to be called the Enlightenment convinced us that human wisdom, human intelligence, human science and human technology would eventually solve all our human problems. We had no need of God. Eschatology, the vision of a new heaven and a new earth, was a primitive pipe dream we should give up—and the sooner the better. God was pushed to the margins. Religion was acceptable only as a part of our private world and was not to be brought into the public square, where the real problems were addressed. It was perhaps a nice extra in one's life, but not strictly necessary.

Whole disciplines were developed to take advantage of this new enthusiasm for human control. Nature would be controlled for human benefit by science. Human nature would be explored and corrected through psychology. The human community would be analyzed and directed through sociology. Human power relationships would be explored and eventually regulated through political science. Human exchange of goods and services would be understood and managed through economics. The high priests of this new religion of humanity would be the scholars, experts and technocrats who gazed upon the mysteries of the world in laboratories, libraries, think tanks and corporate offices. Let me hasten to say that these are valuable disciplines, but better, in my opinion, at describing human problems than at solving them.

Individualism and community. The Enlightenment made the individual king or queen of his or her own realm. Human beings were liberated from aristocrats, priests and even their own families. They were "free" to pursue their pleasures without restrictions imposed from above. The shackles of cultural and religious restraint were thrown off. Individuals could rise as dramatically or fall as disastrously as their ability would take them. While there was much in this liberation to be applauded, much of it was an illusion. Many then and now exchanged one kind of servitude for another. Cutting oneself loose from the restrictions of church, community and family frequently brought loneliness and confusion.

The Enlightenment brought humanity many advantages. It resulted in a dramatic increase, at least in the West, in material wealth and personal freedom. People who once had no hope of receiving an education were enrolled in school. Imaginative and creative people in every field were able to put their creativity to work to benefit both themselves and society. There were also dramatic advances in technology in medicine, communications, transport, building and construction, and the like. People lived longer, ate better and were more comfortably housed than even their recent forebears. They were also better educated, with higher rates of literacy and greater technical skills—at least in the West. But all these things came at a cost.

The West suffered a loss of faith and community ties. People shook off their old habits of faith and morality. They moved frequently and established few ties with neighbors or coworkers. Many of them lived by a Darwinian creed, turning in on themselves and putting aside compassion for others or society as a whole. The other was not to be loved as much as used to benefit one's own survival and as a source for one's own pleasure. Even marriage, children and friendship were seen as utilitarian commodities to be dropped when they no longer served one's ego needs. While it is itself profoundly individualistic, the current so-called postmodern culture recognizes the emptiness and destructiveness of such extreme individualism. Postmodern people long for community but have no idea how to form and sustain it. They long for genuine relationships but fear accountability to and responsibility for another. They want to have the cake of freedom and eat it too. Like the academic disciplines mentioned above, postmodern people frequently are better at diagnosis than finding a cure.

Blessings and curses of technology. The aforementioned technical progress has brought nearly as many curses and blessings. We have developed amazing capacities to heal but equally terrifying capacities to kill and destroy. We rightly fear weapons of mass destruction with their capacity to eliminate whole continents and wipe out whole peoples. We can communicate more quickly, easily and frequently than any generation in human history. But the same technology that has made such rapid communication possible has made it possible for governments and businesses to spy on us, monitor our behavior and manipulate our desires. Our technology can also isolate us. Some of us are more comfortable in front of a screen than in front of a real person.[12] Our technologies also raise serious and complex questions of justice. We in the West expect and demand the kind of medical care that most ordinary Africans can only imagine. This should, at least, make us uncom-

---

[12]See Sherry Turkle, *Alone Together: Why We Expect More from Technology and Less from Each Other* (New York: Basic Books, 2011).

fortable—unless we have bought into the Darwinian worldview mentioned earlier and consider it simply their bad luck to be born outside of the West.

Ecological disaster. Finally, the way we use our various technologies has brought us to the edge of ecological disaster. Our topsoil is eroding at an alarming rate. The soil that remains is often poisoned and infertile. Our great freshwater aquifers are quickly disappearing, making it increasingly difficult and expensive to raise food in once-fertile fields. Our groundwater is often polluted and undrinkable, and our air not breathable. In more poverty-stricken regions of the world the ecological problems are even direr. Millions are suffering and dying today because of our waste, exploitation and ignorance. And yet, in the West many argue this is not a moral issue but an economic one. Nothing must be done, they insist, to limit profit or the freedom to exploit current opportunities no matter how serious our future challenges.

In Revelation 8 John sees a number of angels blowing trumpets of judgment. After the first trumpet, "a third of the earth was burned up, and a third of the trees were burned up, and all green grass was burned up" (Rev 8:7). In the wake of the second trumpet, "a third of the sea became blood, a third of the living creatures in the sea died, and a third of the ships were destroyed" (Rev 8:9). The third trumpet sees "a third of the waters become wormwood, and many died from the water, because it was made bitter" (Rev 8:11). Wars and plagues and other disasters follow. And in spite of all this "humankind . . . did not repent of the works of their hands or give up worshiping demons and idols of gold and silver and bronze and stone and wood" (Rev 9:20). John sees that when we worship the "works of [our] own hands" and value our "idols of gold and silver," we, in the end, bring disaster on our world. By staying the course of greed and abuse and refusing to repent, we are bringing these disasters upon ourselves.

Some readers are perhaps uncomfortable with this analysis. I want to suggest as gently as possible that perhaps Christians in the West have sometimes let the marketplace, rather than the word of God, form our morality. We have let our individual good take precedence over human flourishing. I hasten to say that I add myself to the number of those valuing my own comfort over the larger human good. This is as persistent a challenge for me as it is for anyone else. But if we want to practice resurrection and bring the realities of the kingdom of God into the present, we will need to let the words of the Jewish prophets and the teachings of Jesus of Nazareth reframe our thinking. If we want to have an impact as the church of Jesus Christ in the midst of postmodern despair, we will need to point out a different path.

It is not hard today to find evidence of postmodern despair. While our politicians confidently boast that they can give us all we want, lower our taxes and protect us from all we fear, we know better. We recognize that our world is headed toward a crisis. War, economic collapse, growing poverty and ecological degradation have brought with them growing social and political divisions. Fearful of the angry voices from within our own country and crude threats from without, some despair and withdraw into protective enclaves. These enclaves could be economic, religious, ethnic or strictly personal. Some build gated communities or military compounds; some become mystics and withdraw into a private religious world; some become Trekkies or collect baseball cards or Roman glassware; some follow a famous band around the country or sink in the swamp of the Internet. When there is no community or corporate meaning, all that is left is personal escapism. When there is no hope, we close our eyes and look the other way. Tragically, many Christians and even churches have done something very like this.

Followers of Jesus and members of his community, the church, have something to say about all this. They represent a countercultural solution to the problems of the world because *Christians are people of hope!* We do not give up on the world because we know that God created it and Christ died to redeem it and will make all things new. We do not give up on the world because we know God loves everything and everyone he made. Some perhaps view the coming end of the world with gloom and hopelessness. Others may view it with gleeful expectation. Christians accept neither extreme. We see both as self-indulgent and escapist. To the despairing and hopeless we offer a new community of love, faith and joy. To the greedy and indifferent we offer a serious warning of judgment—a judgment they are bringing on themselves. To the poor, hungry and desperate we offer the bread of this world and the bread of the world to come. To all we offer the hope of resurrection and a new heaven and a new earth where righteousness and peace will dwell. Ironically, Christian eschatology is a critical source of hope, not just in the future but in the present as well. In the next chapter we explore the resurrection hope that forms the backbone of Christian life and action in the world.

3

Hope for Resurrection

IN MANY CHRISTIAN CHURCHES THE CONGREGATION affirms each Sunday, in the words of the Apostles' Creed, "I believe in . . . the resurrection of the body." This is a statement of profound hope. This hope is not for a disembodied existence in some ethereal realm but for a full-blooded human experience in a transformed but very real human body on a renewed earth. This was the hope of the earliest Christians, though it was not without its skeptics. Paul challenged a group in Corinth who said "there is no resurrection of the dead" (1 Cor 15:12). For many Gentiles the thought of resurrection was distasteful. They were hoping to escape their bodies, not be trapped in them. They perhaps believed in the immortality of the soul and looked forward to a sort of disembodied union with God. But this was not the Christian and Jewish hope. The resurrection of both Jesus and the believer is the cornerstone of Christian eschatology. In fact, without resurrection there is no Christian eschatology.

Perhaps the most enduring of all human questions is, what happens after we die? For a large and perhaps increasing number the answer is, nothing. With our death we pass forever out of existence. No heaven or hell, no judgment or blessing awaits us. If we live on at all, it is in the memories of those we love. We are perhaps known through journals, letters and fading photographs, but we no longer exist and will never be recalled to life. The Christian church, of course, has a very different answer to this foundational question. Unfortunately, many Christians, even those who declare their belief in the resurrection of the body, are rather vague about their expectations. Their ideas of heaven, hell and judgment may be drawn more from popular culture than from the Bible and Christian tradition. And they may not know what to make of the promise of the resurrection of the body. They may be more comfortable with the idea of the immortality of the soul and an eternal existence in heaven.

N. T. Wright has cogently argued that Christians have misread their own tradition by focusing on going to heaven when they die. He insists that the ultimate hope for Christians is not heaven, but a new heaven and a new earth.[1] As indicated in chapter one of this book, the book of Revelation insists that at the end we do not go to heaven; rather *heaven comes to us*. The seer writes:

> Then I saw a new heaven and a new earth; for the first heaven and the first earth had passed away, and the sea was no more. And I saw the holy city, the new Jerusalem, coming down out of heaven from God. . . . And I heard a loud voice from the throne saying,
>
> "See, the home of God is among mortals." (Rev 21:1-3)

Our eternal destiny is not in heaven but on a renewed earth in a renewed, resurrection body. This is the Christian hope—a robust, vigorous hope that affirms the goodness of creation and the human body.

In subsequent chapters I will explore heaven, hell and judgment, but in this chapter I will consider the resurrection of the body. I will examine the development of the notion of resurrection in ancient Israel and Judaism, the firmly grounded hope for resurrection within early Christianity and the meaning of the doctrine today. I will also show how Greek notions of the immortality of the soul have plagued both Judaism and Christianity and continue to distort our understandings of the resurrection hope to this very day. I trust that in the process the reader will be encouraged to reclaim the full vigor of the resurrection hope. If there is no resurrection of the body, Paul insists, "we are of all people most to be pitied. But in fact Christ has been raised from the dead, the first fruits of those who have died" (1 Cor 15:19-20). One day we will be able to cry with Paul, "Where, O death, is your victory? Where, O death, is your sting?" (1 Cor 15:54-55).

---

[1]N. T. Wright, *Surprised by Hope: Rethinking Heaven, the Resurrection, and the Mission of the Church* (New York: HarperOne, 2008), pp. 13-20.

LIFE AFTER DEATH IN THE ANCIENT MIDDLE EAST

According to the Old Testament, ancient Israel lived and formed itself within the orbits of two ancient cultures: Egypt and Mesopotamia. The Israelites' views of life after death were developed in response to and often in conflict with the views of their influential neighbors. The principal, indeed crucial difference between the Israelites and their neighbors was their view of God. For the Israelites there was one God, not many. This God was responsible for the whole of creation, not a small part of it. Responsibility for the various aspects of human existence was not parceled out among a host of divine beings, but the enduring task of one. And this God was *for* his people. He even *loved* them. To be sure, God's people were responsible to him for keeping his covenant with them. But the responsibilities between God and people were mutual. As time went on, this mutuality was to be critical. The Israelites' God was committed to them, and his commitment was enduring.

Egypt. One of the most important and enduring myths of the ancient world originated in ancient Egypt.[2] It is a complex myth developed over hundreds of years and exists in many varieties, but the gist of it is as follows: Isis and Osiris were brother and sister and lovers. After Osiris was killed and dismembered by his evil brother Seth, Isis sought out his body parts and reassembled and restored him. Osiris became lord of the underworld and, perhaps ironically, lord of fertility. Some interpret this myth as a nature myth. Osiris was restored to life as the land of Egypt was restored to life through the floods of the Nile. But the myth also addressed life after death. At least during part of their history, Egyptians believed that to gain immortality they needed to be embalmed by the priests of Osiris. What were the Egyptian expectations of the afterlife?

The Egyptian dead were required to go on a journey in the afterlife. Hieroglyphics in tombs provided spells to help the dead make their way through the perils of the underworld to reach Egyptian "heaven." One could either die forever or be resurrected into a realm of pleasure and peace. Tomb paintings from certain periods of Egypt's history show a human heart being weighed on a scale. The good deeds of the deceased needed to outweigh the complaints against them for them to continue on their journey. The dead

---

[2]Alan F. Segal, *Life After Death: A History of the Afterlife in the Religions of the West* (New York: Doubleday, 2004), pp. 27-69.

asserted their innocence in words like these from the so-called Egyptian Book of the Dead:

> I have not done that which the gods abominate.
>
> I have not defamed a slave to his superior.
>
> I have not made (anyone) sick.
>
> I have not killed.
>
> I have given no order to a killer.
>
> I have not caused anyone suffering.[3]

Not only were there spells and prayers to assist the dead in their perilous journey, but the living were required to offer prayers for the dead. A so-called mortuary cult developed first for the pharaoh and eventually for all Egyptians who could afford it. The dead could help the living by making the proper offerings and saying the proper prayers. None of this, obviously, speaks to the security of the dead. The journey after death could only be viewed with anxiety. No one was guaranteed a place in the next world. Furthermore, human beings were responsible for their own fate. Both the living and the dead were bound in an uncertain task with an uncertain outcome. Their fates were in their own hands.

Mesopotamia. The view of the ancient Mesopotamians was, if anything, a great deal more pessimistic than that of the Egyptians.[4] Abraham journeyed from a land that had little, if any, hope for the dead. The dead lived in an underground kingdom estranged and separated from both the gods and living humans. None of these societies had a beatific vision, a heaven to hope for. An example of this is the famous Epic of Gilgamesh. This epic poem is one of the oldest surviving works of literature. It tells the tale of Gilgamesh, a semidivine but rather unruly being. The gods send him a companion named Enkidu to civilize him. When his friend Enkidu dies, Gilgamesh is distraught and sets out to find a way to revive him. When he seeks Enkidu in the house of death, he learns that only the gods live forever; death is the lot of human beings. In light of this, Gilgamesh receives the following advice in words very similar to Ecclesiastes 9:7-10:

---

[3] J. B. Pritchard, ed., *Ancient Near Eastern Texts Relating to the Old Testament,* 3rd ed. (Princeton, NJ: Princeton University Press, 1969), p. 34, quoted in Segal, *Life After Death,* p. 59.

[4] Segal, *Life After Death,* pp. 70-119.

As for you, Gilgamesh, let your belly be full,
Make merry day and night.
Of each day make a feast rejoicing,
Day and night dance and play!
Let your garments be sparkling fresh
Your head be washed; bathe in water.
Pay heed to the little one that holds on to your hand.
Let a spouse delight in your bosom,
For that is the task of a [woman].[5]

In other words, make the best of life now. There is nothing better awaiting you—only existence as a shade in the realm of the dead. There is no returning to this life, and there is no expectation of a meaningful life to come. There is only the shadowy realm of the dead.

First Temple Judaism. By the phrase First Temple Judaism scholars mean the religious tradition of the Jews during the existence of Solomon's great temple in Jerusalem. This era came to an end with the destruction of Jerusalem and its temple by the Babylonians in the sixth century B.C. The Jews who rebuilt the city, the temple and the communal life of Israel after the exile had been tempered and changed by their experiences of exile and loss. Their prophets had reframed their understanding of God and his expectations and promises. There was, of course, profound continuity with the earlier era but significant developments as well. God would still be the God of promise. God would still speak in the present as he did in the past. God would continue to reveal more about himself as the Israelites read, prayed, obeyed and questioned. But all of that was in the future.

During the First Temple era, Jews' views of death were quite sober and not unlike those of the Canaanites they had displaced. They had no concrete narrative of the afterlife. There was no elaborate mythology of gods and goddesses. There were no prayers for the dead and no cult of the dead. These things, in fact, were opposed. There was no mythologizing of nature. There was only one God who was responsible for everything. There were no gods of the underworld and no perilous journey to the realm of the gods. The Old Testament, in fact, says almost nothing about the realm of the dead. Life and

---

[5]John Gardner, ed., *Gilgamesh*, trans. John Maier (New York: Vintage, 1984), p. 214, quoted in Segal, *Life After Death*, p. 87.

death were in the hands of the one God, and the focus was on how life was lived before that God *now*.

There was no heaven or hell in our sense in First Temple Judaism. There was, of course, the realm of God. But this was not heaven as it is now popularly conceived. And there was no hell, only *Sheol*—the Hebrew word used for the realm of the dead. Sometimes *Sheol* referred to the residence of the dead. At other times the word simply referred to the "pit" or the grave. It was not a place of punishment. Both good and evil ended up there. Furthermore, according to Job 10:21-22 the dead go there "never to return." It is a "land of gloom and deep darkness, the land of gloom and chaos, where light is like darkness." "The dead do not praise the LORD," says the psalmist, "nor do any that go down into silence" (Ps 115:17). On this even the prophets agree:

> Sheol cannot thank you,
> > death cannot praise you;
> those who go down to the Pit cannot hope
> > for your faithfulness. (Is 38:18)

Such sentiments are repeated over and over again, especially in the Psalms. The "preacher" warns "there is no work or thought or knowledge or wisdom in Sheol, to which you are going" (Eccles 9:10). Clearly the idea of a resurrected and restored life had not yet developed in Israel. The Jews hope was for a good death at a ripe old age surrounded by sons and daughters who would carry on their name (see Gen 25:7-22; 49:33; Job 5:26).[6]

But there were minority voices. Consider the story of the so-called witch of Endor in 1 Samuel 28:6-14. Contrary to Israelite law, a desperate Saul asks this witch to recall Samuel from the realm of the dead. Samuel is annoyed at being disturbed and comes with really bad news for the hapless king. This story hints at the existence of a larger view that had not yet been spelled out. Consider also the stories of Enoch and Elijah. The first "walked with God" and is taken, perhaps, to the very realm of God (Gen 5:18-24). The second is carried away to God's realm in God's own chariot (2 Kings 2:9-14). These are perhaps the exceptions that

---

[6]Kevin J. Madigan and Jon D. Levenson, *Resurrection: The Power of God for Christians and Jews* (New Haven, CT: Yale University Press, 2008), pp. 69-80.

prove the rule. But the stories suggest that the ancient Israelites contemplated the possibility of a human being gaining admittance into God's presence after death.

Why were the Israelites so cautious? Why were they so reluctant to develop a more robust view of the afterlife? They were perhaps wary of the influence of their neighbors with their elaborate ceremonies and multiple deities. They were also focused on obeying God's covenant in the present and demonstrating the love and hope of God, not only for Israel but for the entire creation. And they wanted people to understand that there was a clear difference between God and God's creation. God was the Lord of life and death. There was no question that God could both "kill" and "make alive" (Deut 32:39). God could certainly elevate someone to his own realm if he wanted, but God could not be manipulated by rites or magic. Although God remained sovereign over life and death, he appeared to be most concerned about how Israel lived before him in this life.

Second Temple Judaism: exile and return. After the exile, Jews came to believe in the resurrection of the body and look for the "new heavens and a new earth" (Is 65:17). How did this happen? Scholars have long debated this, and there is not yet a consensus. Some scholars think the question of divine justice provided impetus for new thinking about the world to come. Some Jews may have wondered, in light of the suffering of the exile, If there is no beatific vision, no promise of paradise, how is one to justify the suffering and death of the righteous? What is one to make of the injustice of the world? Does this mean the God of Israel is uncaring and unjust? Psalms like 37 and 73 struggle with this conundrum. How is it that the wicked seem to flourish and the righteous suffer? The entire prophecy of Habakkuk is also addressed to this agonizing question: "Why do you look on the treacherous, and are silent when the wicked swallow those more righteous than they?" (Hab 1:13). Would God do nothing about the suffering of his people?

The entire book of Job addresses the question of the justice of righteous suffering. Job, although a righteous man, has suffered a series of appalling disasters. Far from patient, he rails against the unfairness of it all. Neither God nor his friends seem to appreciate the depth of his sufferings. Job wonders if the record will ever be set straight. Job wants to get God into court. He wants him on the witness stand faced by a competent, no-nonsense defense attorney who will demand an account of his shabby treatment of Job. Job cries:

O that my words were written down!
    O that they were inscribed in a book!
O that with an iron pen and with lead
    they were engraved on a rock forever! (Job 19:23-24)

And then Job says something astounding:

For I know that my Redeemer lives,
    and that at the last he will stand upon the earth;
and after my skin has been thus destroyed,
    then in my flesh I shall see God. (Job 19:25-26)

These verses are fraught with controversy. The word *redeemer* can be translated "vindicator" and can perhaps refer to a defense attorney of sorts who will plead Job's case. More controversial is the question of whether Job was expecting an after-death tribunal where he could plead his case. Generations of Christian interpreters have seen in Job's words an allusion to Jesus the redeemer/vindicator who would plead the believers' case with God. When Job finally does get his longed-for encounter with God, he rather wishes he had kept his mouth shut. God asks him a series of rhetorical questions that silence his complaints but in the end do not answer his, or our, questions (Job 38–42). Job's health, family and wealth are restored, but the questions of justice and the world to come are left unanswered.

It is Israel's prophets who begin to open up the possibility of resurrection, both for the nation and the individual.[7] The prophet Ezekiel is taken "by the spirit of the LORD" to a valley full of bones (Ezek 37:1). God asks the prophet, "Can these bones live?" (Ezek 37:3). He then instructs his prophet to "prophesy to these bones, and say to them: O dry bones, hear the word of the LORD. Thus says the Lord GOD to these bones: I will cause breath to enter you, and you shall live. I will lay sinews on you, and will cause flesh to come upon you, and cover you with skin, and put breath in you, and you shall live" (Ezek 37:4-6). As Ezekiel prophesies, the bones clatter together, skin covers them,

---

[7]Ibid., pp. 132-55.

breath enters them "and they lived, and stood on their feet, a vast multitude" (Ezek 37:10).

God goes on to tell Ezekiel "these bones are the whole house of Israel" (Ezek 37:11). They complain that they are beyond hope, lost forever in exile and dry as a bone. But God insists, "I am going to open your graves, and bring you up from your graves" (Ezek 37:12). They will return to the land of Israel, their "own soil." Furthermore, "I will put my spirit within you, and you shall live" (Ezek 37:14). Does this passage refer only to the rebirth, the resurrection, of the nation? Or could it also refer to the resurrection of individuals? On the surface it certainly refers to the rebirth of national hopes, to the return to the land and the renewal of God's covenant with his people. Both Jews and Christians have seen in this passage allusions to a larger hope for resurrection of the dead. But this resurrection is not simply my hope as an individual; it is a hope for the restoration of God's people and God's world. As Madigan and Levenson put it, "The question [Jewish expectations] is not the familiar, self-interested one, 'Will I have life after death?' but rather a more profound and encompassing one, 'Will God honor his promises to his people?' Ezekiel's answer to the latter question is a resounding, 'Yes!'"[8] They are not simply raised as individuals but as a people. The resurrection of the individual is accomplished in the context of the resurrection of God's purposes for his people.

This is also beautifully illustrated in Isaiah 25 and 26. The prophet anticipates "a feast of rich food," a banquet "for all peoples." He promises God will destroy death, "the shroud that is cast over all peoples." He continues, "Then the Lord GOD will wipe away the tears from all faces, and the disgrace of his people he will take away from all the earth" (Is 25:6-8). In the next chapter the prophet, in response to the anguish of his people, has God promise,

> Your dead shall live, their corpses shall rise.
> O dwellers in the dust, awake and sing for joy!
> For your dew is a radiant dew,
> and the earth will give birth to those long dead. (Is 26:19)

Once again, scholars have wondered if this referred to the rebirth of the

---

[8]Ibid., p. 155.

people rather than the rebirth of individuals, but there seems no reason it cannot in the end be both. All of this paves the way for the promise of a new heaven and a new earth that God makes later in Isaiah. This is a God who makes all things new! (See Is 65:17-25.)

The most explicit, and some say only, reference to the resurrection of the individual in the Old Testament is found in Daniel 12:2. After a time of suffering and anguish, Daniel is promised, "many of those who sleep in the dust of the earth shall awake, some to everlasting life, and some to shame and everlasting contempt." This is what will later come to be known as the general resurrection and judgment of the dead. Once again the key is God's justice. The martyrs who suffered at the hands of God's enemies and kept the faith, as did Daniel and his three companions, will be resurrected to everlasting life. The rebellious and violent will be raised to shame and contempt. But this is no resurrection to a heavenly realm. As in Isaiah, what is anticipated here is God's rule over all the earth through his people. Earlier in Daniel the prophet was promised:

> The kingship and dominion
>> and the greatness of the kingdoms under the whole heaven
>> shall be given to the people of the holy ones of the Most High;
> their kingdom shall be an everlasting kingdom,
>> and all dominions shall serve and obey them. (Dan 7:27)

This is the kingdom of God that Jesus came to proclaim.

Resurrection and the life to come at the time of Jesus. At the time of Jesus, there was a variety of views of the fate of the dead among the Jews. The Sadducees did not believe in the resurrection (see Acts 4:1-2; 23:8). They clung to the old ways. Their views are typified by the apocryphal book Sirach. "At death the person abides in Sheol, a place of unending sleep (Sir. 30:17; 46:19) and silence (Sir. 17:27-28); and immortality is restricted to the nation and the person's good name (Sir. 37:26; 39:9; 44:8-14)."[9] Some Jews were influenced by the philosophy of Greece and spoke of the "immortality of the soul" rather than the resurrection of the body.[10] The Pharisees, however, strongly supported belief in the resurrection of the dead. In spite of his conflict with

---

[9]Joel B. Green, Scot McKnight and I. Howard Marshall, eds., *Dictionary of Jesus and the Gospels* (Downers Grove, IL: InterVarsity Press, 1992), s.v. "Resurrection," by G. R. Osborne.
[10]Ibid.

them, Jesus and the early church were as firmly committed to resurrection as the Pharisees were. Paul even used the division between the Sadducees and the Pharisees to his advantage (Acts 23:6-10)!

After the fall of Jerusalem in A.D. 70, belief in the resurrection of the dead became more the standard among the Jews. The apocalyptic book *4 Ezra* famously speaks of the resurrection of both the righteous and the wicked for the purpose of judgment and blessing (see *4 Ezra* 7:26-44). The Mishnah, the earliest written account of traditional rabbinic interpretations and applications of the Torah, promised that all Jews would have a part in the world to come—except the heretics and apostates. It does not go into the sort of detail one finds in books like *4 Ezra*. The resurrection of the dead and the world to come are more promised than described. Nevertheless, Orthodox Jews to this day expect the resurrection of the dead in the last day.

THE RESURRECTION OF JESUS AND THE FINAL RESURRECTION

Jesus clearly anticipated the resurrection of the dead. His controversy with the Sadducees makes this abundantly clear. In Mark 12:18-27 they try to trap him with a ridiculous story of a woman who had suffered through marriage to seven brothers without producing an heir. Seeking to discredit the whole notion of resurrection, they ask, "In the resurrection whose wife will she be?" (Mk 12:23). Jesus rather bluntly tells them, "Is not this the reason you are wrong, that you know neither the scriptures nor the power of God?" (Mk 12:24). It is clear that the dead are raised, Jesus insists, because God says, "I am the God of Abraham, the God of Isaac, and the God of Jacob." And this God "is God not the of the dead, but of the living" (Mk 12:26-27). Additionally, Jesus also expected and predicted his own resurrection (e.g., Mk 10:32-34). His resurrection became the cornerstone of Christian conviction and mission. For the apostle Paul it was the beginning of a whole new world.

Paul and the new creation. "If anyone is in Christ," Paul wrote, "there is a new creation: everything old has passed away; see, everything has become new!" (2 Cor 5:17). In Jesus, according to Paul, the new creation had already begun, a new heaven and a new earth had in some sense already arrived. In the teaching of Jesus, the kingdom of God was inaugurated, the new age was beginning, but the fullness of new creation and kingdom was still to come. There was an overlap between this world and the world to come. This was illustrated and demonstrated, for Paul, by the resurrection of Jesus from the dead. Paul's eschatology, his understanding of the last days and the world to come, flowed from his understanding of the resurrection of Jesus. Pauline scholar J. Christiaan Beker argues that Paul used four basic categories to interpret the resurrection of Jesus in light of God's intentions for the renewal of his creation: vindication, universalism, dualism and imminence.[11]

Vindication. Most importantly, Jesus' resurrection was a *vindication* of Jesus and of Paul his messenger. In 1 Corinthians 15 Paul insists the message and hope of Jesus are invalidated if he was not raised by God. "If there is no resurrection of the dead, then Christ has not been raised; and if Christ has not been raised, then our proclamation has been in vain and your faith has been in vain. We are even found to be misrepresenting God, because we testified of God that he raised Christ—whom he did not raise if it is true that the dead are not raised" (1 Cor 15:13-15). If Jesus was raised, Paul argues, we too have hope for resurrection. Jesus was, in fact, the "first fruits" (1 Cor 15:20) of the great final resurrection of the dead. His resurrection was not unique but anticipated the resurrection "at his coming [for] those who belong to Christ" (1 Cor 15:23). Jesus' resurrection vindicated himself, his messengers the apostles, and all those who believe in him and await a new heaven and a new earth.

This vindication required the defeat of the forces opposed to God and to God's kingdom. Paul tells the Colossian Christians that God had rescued them "from the power of darkness" and "transferred" them "into the kingdom of his beloved Son" (Col 1:13). Once again, in some sense the kingdom had already been inaugurated. God had reconciled them when they were "hostile in mind, doing evil deeds" (Col 1:21). All this had been done through Jesus and his cross. In fact, "he disarmed the rulers and authorities and made a public example of them, triumphing over them in it" (i.e., the cross; Col 2:15). The Colossians gain all this because "when you were buried with him in baptism, you were also raised with him through faith in the power of God, who raised him from the dead" (Col 2:12). Participating in the death and resurrection of Jesus enabled the Colossians to be victorious over the forces of evil ranged against them. In 2 Corinthians 2, Paul

---

[11]J. Christiaan Beker, *Paul's Apocalyptic Gospel: The Coming Triumph of God* (Minneapolis: Fortress, 1982), pp. 29-59.

compares the believers' vindication by Christ to a Roman triumphal procession. Followers of Jesus are like victorious soldiers following their triumphant general through a cheering throng with their captives chained in the rear, expecting the worst (2 Cor 2:14-16).

Finally, Jesus' resurrection is a vindication for those who had already died in Christ. In 1 Thessalonians 4, Paul encourages his grieving converts who evidently were concerned that those who had died would somehow miss the kingdom of God when it came in its fullness. Paul insists that "since we believe that Jesus died and rose again, even so, through Jesus, God will bring with him those who have died" (1 Thess 4:14). Those who died before the arrival of the great final day will not miss out. Jesus' resurrection is a guarantee of their resurrection. Notice that Paul says God will bring them with him. I will come back to this important passage, but suffice it to say that this passage does *not* anticipate "raptured" Christians going up to heaven; rather, it describes God bringing the resurrected saints with him to the earth.

Universalism. As far as Paul was concerned, Jesus' resurrection had to do with everything and everybody. Through the resurrection of Jesus, God was about setting all things right. When the rulers, authorities and powers opposed to God have been finally and thoroughly defeated, God will destroy "the last enemy"—"death" (1 Cor 15:26). All things will be put "in subjection under his feet" (1 Cor 15:27). Paul concluded this powerful section with a startling pronouncement: "When all things are subjected to him, then the Son himself will also be subjected to the one who put all things in subjection under him, so that God may be all in all" (1 Cor 15:28). God's victory is a universal victory, and God's salvation is a universal salvation.

This will involve great acts of reconciliation: human beings are reconciled to God and to each other (see 2 Cor 5:18-21; Col 1:19-23); Jews and Gentiles are reconciled in Christ (Eph 2:13-21; see also Rom 11:25-27). Creation itself will be redeemed and restored, "set free from its bondage to decay" (see Rom 8:18-23). God's work in Jesus is not just for a little corner of the world but for everybody and everything. "Therefore," he wrote to the Romans, "just as one man's trespass led to condemnation for all, so one man's act of righteousness leads to justification and life for all" (Rom 5:18). This does not mean that Paul believed that everyone will be saved, whether they want to be or not. Rather, it means that Jesus' work has a universal scope and cannot be limited by racial, theological or cultural differences. God's creation will return to God. God, as Paul put it, will be all in all.

Dualism. I have argued that Paul saw this age and the age to come as overlapping. He anticipated the defeat of the powers and authorities ranged against God. This victory had already been won in the death and resurrection of Jesus. But this did not mean that Paul thought believers would face no struggle or opposition in following Jesus—quite the contrary. It is the burden of Paul's letters to make it clear that the battle continues. "Our struggle," he told the Ephesians, "is not against enemies of blood and flesh, but against the rulers, against the authorities, against the cosmic powers of this present darkness, against the spiritual forces of evil in the heavenly places" (Eph 6:12). This battle is not just cosmic but profoundly personal. Each of us is to take up the armor of God to face this threat. Key in this battle is "the sword of the Spirit, which is the word of God" (Eph 6:17).

In Galatians Paul spoke of these cosmic forces in a different way. He commanded his converts to "live by the Spirit . . . and do not gratify the desires of the flesh" (Gal 5:16). By flesh, Paul did not mean to suggest our physical bodies per se. Rather, he was referring to the danger of living in the world as if God did not exist. The person who lives according to the flesh lives in rebellion against God. For Paul, the Spirit is the power of God present through the resurrection of Jesus: "If the Spirit of him who raised Jesus from the dead dwells in you, he who raised Christ from the dead will give life to your mortal bodies also through his Spirit that dwells in you" (Rom 8:11). The resurrection power of God, present in us through the Spirit, enables us to resist the evil that attacks us from within, that is, from our inclinations to sin and rebellion.

But there are more than internal forces ranged against us. The forces of "the flesh" are not the only ones arrayed against us. We are also threatened by forces of lawlessness and rebellion entirely external to us. Second Thessalonians 2:1-12 is a difficult and obscure passage, but it offers a sober warning to followers of Jesus. In spite of Jesus' victory on the cross over the powers of evil, "the mystery of lawlessness is already at work" (2 Thess 2:7). What did Paul think this was? Did he anticipate that the military and economic power of Rome would eventually be used against Christians? Certainly it was eventually used against him! By the time of John's great vision in Revelation, Rome was well on its way to becoming a "beast." First John 2:18 and 4:13 warn of the spirit of antichrist already present in the world and insist there have already been many antichrists. Followers of Jesus are faced with powerful economic, political and cultural forces that work against their faithfulness. Some of the forces of antichrist are clearly recognizable. Others come to us as angels of light (see 2 Cor 11:14). These are present as well as future dangers.

Imminence. New Testament scholars have long pondered the problem of the delay of the parousia. Jesus and his followers seemed to expect him to return to establish his kingdom rather more quickly than has happened. Some have suggested that Paul expected Jesus' return within his lifetime. Paul evidently believed that when Jesus returned with the risen saints and made his progress toward the earth, Paul would be among those who would go to meet Jesus: "*We* who are alive, who are left, will be caught up in the clouds together with them to meet the Lord in the air" (1 Thess 4:17). But Paul, like Jesus before him, insisted in the end that no one really knows: "You yourselves know very well that the day of the Lord will come like a thief in the night" (1 Thess 5:2). Rather than attempting to calculate the time of Christ's coming, believers are to live soberly and alertly in the face of opposition and threat.

We do not know God's intentions but are called to live in the overlap of this age and the next. We are called to live as those who have already died and been raised with Christ (Rom 6). Our communities are already communities of the coming kingdom, of the world to come, present in *this* kingdom, *this* world. For Paul, Jesus' resurrection was the beginning of the age to come. It was the beginning of the great process of reconciliation of everything to God so that God may be all in all. We have been entrusted, Paul said, with a "ministry of reconciliation" (2 Cor 5:18). By seeking to reconcile people to God, we are carrying out God's work of new creation in anticipation of the completion of his work. We are doing *eschatological* work, kingdom work, even resurrection work. As we await the resurrection of the dead, we bring resurrection life into the deadness of the world.

THE RESURRECTION BODY

I will have more to say about heaven, hell and judgment, and the return of

Jesus in subsequent chapters. I will also have more to say about the question of what happens to believers between their death and resurrection. But in this last section of this chapter on resurrection I am going to examine what the Bible suggests about the resurrection body. There are two principal sources of information on this: Jesus' resurrection appearances and Paul's teaching on the resurrection body in 1 Corinthians 15.

Jesus' resurrection body. In the most spiritual of the Gospels, John wants to make it abundantly clear that Jesus was not a ghost, vision or hallucination. In John 20, Jesus tells Mary, "Do not hold on to me" (Jn 20:17). He invites the skeptical Thomas to "put your finger here and see my hands. Reach out your hand and put it in my side. Do not doubt but believe" (Jn 20:27). In Luke when the disciples "were startled and terrified, and thought they were seeing a ghost," Jesus asks them, "Why are you frightened, and why do doubts arise in your hearts?" (Lk 24:37-38). He invites them, as with Thomas, to touch him: "Touch me and see; for a ghost does not have flesh and bones as you see that I have" (Lk 24:39). He goes so far as to eat a piece of broiled fish—hallucinations do not eat! Jesus' resurrection body was, furthermore, recognizable by its scars. He could be touched, held and fed. He was recognizable by appearance and bodily peculiarities. This was a human body of "flesh and bones." If Jesus is, as Paul put it, the first fruits of the resurrection, this would suggest that his resurrection body is a model for the believers' resurrection bodies. In fact, Paul would tell the Philippians that Jesus, "by the power that enables him to bring everything under his control, will transform our lowly bodies so that *they will be like his glorious body*" (Phil 3:21 NIV).

Paul and the resurrection body. So how did Paul understand the resurrection body? The same skeptics who questioned the resurrection of the body evidently pressed him to explain how a resurrection body was even possible: "How are the dead raised? With what kind of body do they come?" Paul has little patience with them: "Fool! What you sow does not come to life unless it dies" (1 Cor 15:35-36). Paul goes on to use, for him, a relatively rare metaphor from nature. What you sow in the ground and what emerges from the ground may appear to be utterly different. Nevertheless, there is continuity between seed and plant. They are both different and the same. The body that dies, that is "sown," Paul says "is sown a natural body" and "raised a spiritual body" (1 Cor 15:44 NIV). Paul is not talking about the substance of the body. It is not a body made out of spirit. N. T. Wright explains it well:

> Greek adjectives ending in *-ikos* describe not *the material out of which things are made* but *the power or energy that animates them.* It is the difference between asking on the one hand, "Is this a wooden ship or an iron ship?" (the material from which it is made) and asking, on the other, "Is this a steamship or a sailing ship?" (the energy that powers it). Paul is talking about the present body, which is animated by the normal human *psyche* (the life force we all possess here and now, which gets us through the present life but is ultimately powerless against illness, injury, death, and decay) and the future body, which is animated by God's *pneuma,* God's breath of new life, the energizing power of God's new creation.[12]

The spiritual body, Paul insists, is imperishable, glorious and powerful. But it is a body, not some sort of ghostly ectoplasm. Many questions remain, of course. How will our bodies be recognizable to those we loved? Some knew us as infants; some knew us as teenagers or in our vigorous youth; some knew us as old men or women. How old will we be in our resurrection bodies? Furthermore, Jesus still had his scars. Will we still have our scars and disabilities, or will our bodies be completely renewed? There is a great deal of, largely fruitless, debate about such issues. The church fathers and early theologians, Wright points out, offered a number of answers to these and other questions. The gruff Tertullian brushed them aside suggesting it was God's business as creator and he would undoubtedly sort it out. The medieval theologian Hugh of Saint Victor thought the resurrection body "will be at the height of its powers, free from disease and deformity, and around thirty years old, the age at which Christ began his ministry."[13] Even C. S. Lewis in his book *The Great Divorce* tried his hand at imagining not only heaven and hell but the resurrection body.[14] In the end all we have is speculation and imagination—both helpful and unhelpful.

---

[12]Wright, *Surprised by Hope*, pp. 155-56 (emphasis original).
[13]Ibid., p. 158.
[14]C. S. Lewis, *The Great Divorce, a Dream* (1946; repr., San Francisco: HarperCollins, 2009).

CONCLUSIONS

Why is the resurrection of the body so important? Here creation and consummation come together. God created human beings from the dust of the
earth. If God intends to make all things new, if God intends the lion to lie
down with the lamb and the fruits trees in the holy city to be for the healing
of the nations, then God must also intend to make the human body new. The
early Christians found themselves engaged in a bitter battle with so-called
Gnostics who despised both the physical creation and the human body. Tertullian wrote:

> Their great burden is . . . everywhere an invective against the flesh: against its
> origins, its substance, against the casualties and invariable end which await it;
> unclean from its first formation from the dregs of the ground, uncleaner af-
> terwards from the mire of its own seminal transmission; worthless, weak,
> covered with guilt, laden with misery, full of trouble, and after all this record
> of its degradation dropping into its original earth and the appellation of a
> corpse and destined to dwindle away even from this loathsome name.[15]

But Tertullian knew that the flesh was God's creation and was declared
good. Jesus himself was incarnate, enfleshed. Both creation and incarnation
declared that the world and the flesh, though flawed and battered by sin,
were good. God intended to renew and restore both of them. The resurrection was more than just the reanimation of a corpse; it was the renewal
of the whole person, restored to creation glory, fresh from the hand of God,
to enjoy his new world and sing his praises.

---

[15]Tertullian, *De Resurrectione Carnis* 4, quoted in Madigan and Levenson, *Resurrection*, p. 231.

4

Hope for Judgment

THE TITLE OF THIS CHAPTER MAY SEEM A BIT STRANGE. Most people fear rather than hope for judgment. At the most they may hope that judgment falls on someone else, not them. As a former colleague of mine used to say, "Grace for me. Justice for everyone else." But this betrays a lack of appreciation for the nature of God's judgment. Judgment in the Bible, I will argue, is never merely punishment. Judgment is not about God getting even. Rather, God's judgment is concerned with setting the world right. God's judgment is a form of restorative justice. Evil is overturned in the process of doing good. I hope to show that God's people anticipated, rather than feared, God's judgment because it meant God's broken world would be whole again. Good would replace evil. Justice would replace injustice. Love would replace hate.

Nevertheless, even on the more positive account of judgment there are questions and problems. Anyone who has taught a Sunday school class, participated in a Bible study or pondered a sermon has confronted them. What about the question of final judgment? An earnest junior high student asks, "Would God really condemn people to hell and suffering for all eternity? What about the people who never heard of Jesus? What about babies, young children or mentally challenged people? Isn't a god who would send people to eternal torment a monster?" On the other hand, after serial killer Ted Bundy repented on the eve of his execution, a fellow pastor wondered where the justice was. It didn't seem right, he said, for Bundy to go to heaven after all the monstrous things he had done. What would we make of a deathbed confession of a Hitler, a Stalin, a bin Laden? Could history's monsters avoid judgment that easily? For some people, God's judgment seems too harsh. But for others it may appear to be too lenient.

Some people, of course, seem to relish the idea of judgment. They are untroubled by the cruel suffering of the wicked. They are not haunted by the notion of hell and the possibility of eternal suffering. Perhaps they have not sufficiently contemplated the horror they so blithely invoke. Other folks, living a comfortable middle-class suburban life, are perhaps far too squeamish about the possibility of God's judgment. But those who suffer oppression, whose sons have been "disappeared," whose daughters have been raped, or who bear the lash of racial prejudice and injustice are more likely to cry out for God's judgment—and rightly so. Like the saints under the altar, they shout, "How long, O Lord?" (see Rev 6:9-11). With Mary, they wonder, How long before the powerful will be brought down from their thrones? How long before the lowly are lifted up? How long before the hungry are filled with good things and the rich sent away empty (see Lk 1:46-55)?

In the pages that follow I will examine the nature of God's judgment and explore the final fate of human beings.[1] I will consider especially the last judgment, the nature of hell and the possibility of universal salvation. I will insist that, whatever our views of hell and judgment, the Bible tells us we live in a morally serious universe. The way we live our lives matters. Our decisions matter. God has given us the freedom to follow the way of life or the way of death. He has honored and will honor our decisions. As C. S. Lewis famously insisted, in the end we either say to God "Your will be done," or God says to us, "Your will be done."[2] It is a fearful thing to be free! Nevertheless, God has done everything possible to enable us to escape the implications of our own decisions. We call this the grace of God, and we live with hope for that grace.

---

[1]Parts of this chapter were drawn from my article "God, Judgment and Non-Violence," in *Compassionate Eschatology*, ed. Ted Grimsrud and Michael Hardin (Eugene, OR: Cascade, 2011), pp. 116-33.

[2]C. S. Lewis, *The Great Divorce, a Dream* (1946; repr., San Francisco: HarperCollins, 2009), p. 75.

GOD AS JUDGE IN THE BIBLE

From the beginning to the end, the Bible depicts the God of Israel as a judge. In his dispute with God over the fate of Sodom, Abraham declares, "Shall not the Judge of all the earth do what is just?" (Gen 18:25). Moses uses legal terminology in seeking forgiveness for Israel after the Israelites' rebellion in the wilderness: "Forgive the iniquity of this people according to the greatness of your steadfast love, just as you have *pardoned* this people, from Egypt even until now" (Num 14:19). Abraham and Moses recognize God's right to judge, but appeal to God's grace, love, patience and generosity on behalf of his erring people. And in both cases God is gracious—to a point. Sodom is destroyed in the end, and the disobedient Israelites will not see the land of promise (Num 14:22-23). In both cases God's judgment is not arbitrary or cruel, but a function of the disobedience and stubbornness of the people themselves. Their judgment is the logical outcome of their actions. I will have more to say about this shortly.

In ancient Israel, a judge was not like a contemporary judge at a criminal trial. The judge did not merely hear the case, interpret the law and decide on the punishment of the offender. The task of the judge was to set things right. In this sense these ancient courts and judges were more often like our civil courts. Ancient judges most frequently decided for or against plaintiffs in lawsuits or other civil matters. They decided what was right and acted to set things right. Think of the elders in Ruth 4 deciding on the possession of Elimelech's land and of Ruth the Moabite. Think of Solomon deciding which mother had a claim on a living child (1 Kings 3:16-28). Think of David hearing the cause of the woman whose son was threatened by familial revenge for killing his brother (2 Sam 14:4-11). The king was the supreme court of the land. He could certainly decide on capital punishment. But more often than not the decisions rendered were much more mundane. The judge was to restore justice, peace and wholeness to the land.

One of the charges against Israel by the prophets was that justice was perverted. Through Isaiah the Lord declared,

> Your princes are rebels
> and companions of thieves.
> Everyone loves a bribe
> and runs after gifts.

They do not defend the orphan,
    and the widow's cause does not come before them. (Is 1:23)

A bit later Isaiah records,

The LORD enters into judgment
    with the elders and princes of his people:
It is you who have devoured the vineyard;
    the spoil of the poor is in your houses.
What do you mean by crushing my people,
    by grinding the face of the poor? says the Lord GOD of hosts.
        (Is 3:14-15)

God will be the judge, the one to set things right. God will make sure that
the poor are heard, the orphan and the widow are sustained, and justice is
done. The purpose of God's judgment is not the vindictive punishment of
evildoers, although they will suffer the consequences of their own actions.
The purpose of God's judgment is a society, a world, set right. God declares,

I will restore your judges as at the first,
    and your counselors as at the beginning.
Afterward you shall be called the city of righteousness,
    the faithful city. (Is 1:26)

Jesus anticipated a final assize. In Matthew 12:41 he called it "the judgment."
He warned his contemporaries that repentant Nineveh would condemn
them at the judgment along with the "queen of the South." The citizens of
Nineveh had responded to Jonah and the queen of the South to Solomon,
but Jesus' contemporaries were ignoring someone greater (Mt 12:38-42). In
a series of parables near the end of his Gospel, Matthew depicts Jesus com-
paring the consummation of "the kingdom of heaven" to "wise and foolish
virgins" waiting for the bridegroom (Mt 25:1-13), to servants entrusted with
their master's money (Mt 25:14-30), and to the separation of sheep and goats
(Mt 25:31-46). In the latter scene, the Son of Man sits on a throne and renders
judgment based on the compassion demonstrated by those standing before
him. It was not so much the bad things they did that condemned the goats.
It was rather the good they failed to do: feeding the hungry, clothing the
naked, visiting prisoners. The sheep had served Christ himself even if they
didn't know it.

Paul speaks of "the judgment seat of Christ" where "each may receive recompense [literally "receive back"] for what has been done in the body, whether good or evil" (2 Cor 5:10). In 1 Corinthians he warns those building on the foundation of his work in their city that "the work of each builder will become visible, for the Day will disclose it." Some of the work will endure, but some of it will be destroyed: "If what has been built on the foundation survives, the builder will receive a reward. If the work is burned up, the builder will suffer loss; the builder will be saved, but only as through fire" (1 Cor 3:10-15). Once again, the issue here is not the evil they have done but the good they have aspired, and perhaps failed, to do. Both Paul and Jesus seem more interested in the positive rather than the negative side of judgment. Both are concerned to encourage their followers to love and to do good deeds rather than simply to warn them away from sin.

This does not mean, of course, that evil deeds do not matter. Clearly they do. In Revelation 20:11-15 John describes the "great white throne" judgment. The "dead, great and small," stood before God. The "books were opened" and "all were judged according to what they had done." Both evil deeds and good deeds matter here as does having one's name recorded in "the book of life." I will come back to this passage, but suffice it to say that Jesus, Paul and John agree that how one lives matters. They all agree that this is a morally serious universe. According to Jesus, some of those standing before the throne will be surprised. They did not realize that in serving the poor, clothing the naked and visiting prisoners—or failing to do so—they were serving him: "Lord, when was it that we saw you hungry?" (Mt 25:37).

In Ephesians 2:8-10 Paul insists, "by grace you have been saved through faith, and this is not your own doing; it is the gift of God—not the result of works, so that no one may boast. For we are what he has made us, created in Christ Jesus for good works." God intends to restore the world through a generous act of his grace. He intends to rescue and restore us along with his world. He demonstrated his love and determination to reclaim us in the life, death and resurrection of Jesus. The world's salvation is totally an act of God's grace. But Paul himself would insist to the Philippians that in spite of all this he was not resting on his laurels. After speaking of gaining Christ and "not having a righteousness of my own that comes from the law, but one that comes through faith in Christ," he speaks of his hope of attaining "the resurrection from the dead." Paul had experienced God's grace, but the race was not over: "not that I have already obtained this or have already reached the goal; but I press on to make it my own, because Christ Jesus has made me his own." He concludes, "Let us hold fast to what we have attained" (Phil 3:7-16).

How are the grace of God and the judgment of God held together? A key in all this is the God-given agency of human beings. God created human beings with the freedom to turn away from him. Although God desires to be in a relationship with his creation, he will not compel people into such a relationship. But he does act to call them back to his love. According to Stephen Travis, this is actually the focus of God's judgment:

> A key to understanding the tension between inevitable retribution and God's forgiving mercy is the nature of justice in the Hebrew thought and its relation to God's covenant with Israel. . . . Christian ideas about justice have often owed more to Greco-Roman philosophical and legal concepts than to biblical thought. In the Old Testament judgement (whether exercised by God or by the king as his agent) is not a matter of dispassionately dispensing justice but of establishing or restoring right relationships.[3]

As I suggested earlier, God judges not merely to punish, but to set things right, to restore relationships and creation itself. The Israelites were sent into exile not simply to punish them for their sin but to restore them to God. Consider the prophet Hosea, whose fraught marital life became a metaphor for God's relationship with Israel. Although wounded by Israel's faithlessness, God did not abandon her:

> How can I give you up, Ephraim?
> > How can I hand you over, O Israel?
> How can I make you like Admah?
> > How can I treat you like Zeboiim?
> My heart recoils within me;
> > my compassion grows warm and tender.
> I will not execute my fierce anger;
> > I will not again destroy Ephraim;
> for I am God and no mortal. (Hos 11:8-9)

---

[3]Stephen H. Travis, *Christ and the Judgement of God: The Limits of Divine Retribution in New Testament Thought,* 2nd ed. (Peabody, MA: Hendrickson, 2008), p. 20.

God warns of judgment not simply to threaten Israel but to restore it to intimacy with him. Isaiah depicts God's longed-for world as a world of peace between Israel and the nations, peace between human beings and the animals, and peace between human beings and God (see Is 9:2-7; 11:1-9; 35:1-10; 61:1-11; 65:17-25). Paul alludes to this expectation in Romans 8. He looks forward to the time "that the creation itself will be set free from its bondage to decay and will obtain the freedom of the glory of the children of God" (Rom 8:21). He tells the Corinthians that at the "end" Christ will hand over "the kingdom to God the Father, after he has destroyed every ruler and every authority and power" (1 Cor 15:24). These are spiritual powers ranked against God, and the last of these enemies is death (1 Cor 15:26; see also Is 25:6-9; 26:16-19). After this final victory, "when all things are subjected to him, then the Son himself will also be subjected to the one who put all things in subjection under him, so that God may be all in all" (1 Cor 15:28).

In the end, the whole creation and all people are restored to relationship with God. Through the life, death and resurrection of Jesus from the dead, Paul thought the entire creation would be reclaimed from death and alienation. The enemies of God would be defeated and destroyed, and the peace of God would be established. "Just as one man's trespass," he wrote to the Romans, "led to condemnation for all, so one man's act of righteousness leads to justification and life for all. For just as by the one man's disobedience the many were made sinners, so by the one man's obedience the many will be made righteous" (Rom 5:18-19). Paul shares this universal vision with Isaiah and with the book of Revelation: "I saw a new heaven and a new earth; for the first heaven and the first earth had passed away, and the sea was no more" (Rev 21:1). The holy city, the new Jerusalem comes down from heaven and "the home of God is among mortals. He will dwell with them as their God; they will be his peoples, and God himself with be with them" (Rev 21:3).

The very last verses in the Bible describe the restored relationship between God, his creation and his people. I repeat: God's judgment is directed toward restoration, not punishment. According to Jesus, his Father loves his enemies and "makes his sun rise on the evil and on the good, and sends rain on the righteous and on the unrighteous" (Mt 5:45). The Father of Jesus is the waiting father eager to receive back the prodigal son (Lk 15:11-32). He is a patient God, a forgiving God, a God who "is not slow about his promise, as some think of slowness, but is patient with you, not wanting any to perish, but all to come to repentance" (2 Pet 3:9). Lamech may pay back seventy-seven times (see Gen 4:24-25), but Jesus' disciples, in imitation of God, are to forgive seventy-seven times (Mt 18:22). This is the God of Jesus Christ, who cried out from the cross, "Father, forgive them; for they do not know what they are doing" (Lk 23:34).

How do we hold together God's deep desire and intent to save and restore the whole earth and all people to him, and his warning of judgment? How do we hold together his passionate love and his equally passionate holiness? We hold them together, first, of course, in Jesus. On Jesus' cross God's love and holiness met, and the possibility of human salvation was revealed. "When you were dead in trespasses," Paul wrote, "God made you alive together with him, when he forgave us all our trespasses, erasing the record that stood against us with its legal demands. He set this aside, nailing it to the cross" (Col 2:13-14). We no longer need to fear the judgment of God. We no longer need to fear our bad record. But Paul is well aware that however much God has done for us, we are capable of turning away from him. In this case our judgment is not the fault of God, who made every effort to forgive and restore us, but the result of our own refusal to receive his love and grace. God honors our freedom even to reject his love.

If a man jumps off a cliff, we do not blame the rocks for killing him. If a woman steps in front of a bus, we do not blame the wheels for crushing her. These could be the deliberate actions of human beings or tragic accidents, but their deaths are not the fault of the inanimate objects that destroyed their lives. God is not willing that any should perish. God loves his world and his people with the passion of an estranged father for a wandering son, a wayward daughter. He will make the way clear for them to return, but he will not force them. He will do all he can to love them, but he will not demand that they love him. Some have wondered if God's love is so powerful that it will win over everyone in the end. If God is not willing that any should perish, perhaps no one will. This view of God's ultimate purpose is called universalism, and I will discuss it a bit later in this chapter. Suffice it to say at this point that this seems to violate God's dangerous gift of freedom.

God is a judge. He wants to set the world right and would include everyone and everything in that restoration. Sadly, it seems, some will refuse to be included in the "new heavens and a new earth." What will happen to them? What will be the outcome of their judgment? This brings us to the vexed question of hell and the final fate of humans who refuse God's grace. This is perhaps the most controversial and difficult of the doctrines of the Christian faith. In recent years this troubling doctrine has received a good deal of attention from both proponents and opponents of the traditional view. There is, in fact, a good deal of variety in the way hell has been understood throughout the history of Christian doctrine. I will explore the various views in the pages that follow.

THE DOCTRINE OF HELL

On the surface at least, the most popular views of hell seem to contradict the notion of God's judgment as setting things right rather than as mere punishment. It is hard to see how eternal conscious torment, as many understand hell to be, contributes to the restoration of justice. Pastor Rob Bell, in his book *Love Wins,* created a significant controversy when he not so much denied the existence of hell but raised serious questions about the most popular conceptions of hell among evangelical Christians.[4] Sharon L. Baker of Messiah College set out to "rethink everything you've been taught about God's wrath and judgment" in her book *Razing Hell.*[5] John Walvoord, on the other hand, mounted a vigorous defense of the traditional view of hell in *Four Views on Hell.*[6] Those who object to the traditional view often see it as a monstrous affront to the love and dignity of God. Those who support the traditional view see it as a crucial means of sustaining the justice and sovereignty of God. How are we to proceed with this vexed question?

Ironically many studies have shown that while Americans in large numbers believe in heaven, they for the most part claim not to believe in hell. Years ago David Clayton-Thomas of the rock group Blood, Sweat and Tears sang, with what I hope was conscious irony, "I can swear there ain't no

---

[4]Rob Bell, *Love Wins: A Book About Heaven, Hell, and the Fate of Every Person Who Ever Lived* (New York: HarperOne, 2011).

[5]Sharon L. Baker, *Razing Hell: Rethinking Everything You've Been Taught About God's Wrath and Judgment* (Louisville, KY: Westminster John Knox, 2010).

[6]John F. Walvoord, "The Literal View," in *Four Views on Hell,* ed. William Crockett (Grand Rapids: Zondervan, 1996), pp. 11-28.

heaven but I pray there ain't no hell."[7] With these words he perhaps summed up the anxiety of many. And yet, one still hears the declaration that a particular criminal or other miscreant is "rotting in hell." It seems that when it comes to hell and judgment many of us are like my previously mentioned colleague: we want grace for ourselves but justice for everyone else. Heaven for me; hell for them.

WORDS FOR HELL

In chapter three I noted that the Hebrew word for the dwelling place of the dead is *Sheol.* I suggested Sheol is not actually hell, as many Christians have come to understand it. Both sinners and saints end up there. If the dead can be said to exist at all, they are only fleeting shadows. In many passages *Sheol* should simply be translated as "the grave." We also saw that in the postexilic time Israel's views began to change. In the course of its history Israel suffered bitterly at the hands of its enemies. God would finally set things right via extraordinary acts of power and grace. The prophets, I argued, anticipated a time when the entire creation would be reordered. The armies of the Gentile oppressors would be destroyed and even their people would join Israel in the worship of God. This is, of course, the great vision of Isaiah. Both Isaiah and Ezekiel looked forward to the resurrection of the nation. But it was finally the prophet Daniel who clearly affirmed the resurrection of the dead: "Many of those who sleep in the dust of the earth shall awake, some to everlasting life, and some to shame and everlasting contempt" (Dan 12:2).

The latter phrase perhaps suggests that not only saints will be raised from the dead. Some will awake to face "everlasting contempt." If God were going to set things right, it would require the judgment of the oppressors as well as the resurrection of the saints. But there is, as yet, no reference to hell here. And the reader is not told exactly who is raised. It says many—not all. Are those raised only the best and the worst? Does the writer have in mind the holy martyrs and those who killed them?[8] The prophet says the "wise shall

---

[7]From his song "And When I Die" on the album *Blood, Sweat and Tears,* released by Columbia in 1968, CS9720.

[8]John J. Collins, *The Apocalyptic Imagination: An Introduction to Jewish Apocalyptic Literature,* 2nd ed. (Grand Rapids: Eerdmans, 1998), pp. 112-13.

shine like the brightness of the sky" (Dan 12:3). We are not told the fate of the wicked. Some, at least, of both the righteous and the wicked have escaped from Sheol, but as yet their final fate is unclear.

In the New Testament one finds a different world. In the years between the return from the exile and the birth of Jesus a much richer collection of descriptions and ideas regarding the fate of the dead had been introduced. During the years under their Persian and Greek overlords, the Jews had greatly developed their ideas of divine blessing and divine judgment, but there was not a unified view of the character of the world to come. Pharisees and Sadducees had very different ideas about the resurrection. The Qumran sectarians living in the desert south of Jerusalem differed from both on the nature of the coming kingdom. The surviving writings of the centuries leading up to the birth of Christ offer a bewildering variety of views on the final judgment and the fate of the dead. In such a theological context, great care is needed to understand and interpret how Jesus spoke of the judgment of the wicked.

Two key words are used in the New Testament to speak of the place of the final judgment of the wicked: *Gehenna* and *Hades.* The latter word is borrowed from the Greek world and is often used for *Sheol* in translations from Hebrew to Greek. In Jewish literature outside of the Bible, *Hades* is used in a variety of ways. It can mean the same thing as *Sheol* in the Old Testament: the final resting place of the dead, both good and evil. But it can also be used for a temporary "holding tank" for those awaiting the final judgment. This notion is found, for example, in a Jewish work composed roughly during the time of Jesus and the rise of the church. In *The Apocalypse of Zephaniah,* Hades is depicted not as a place of fire but as a great sea into which those awaiting judgment sink (*Apoc. Zeph.* 10:3-14). In any event, neither here nor elsewhere does Hades appear to be the final place of judgment for the wicked. Hades, in other words, is not our popular conception of hell. It is either the abode of the dead or a temporary place for the wicked to await judgment. In the end, according to the book of Revelation, Hades itself is thrown into the lake of fire (Rev 20:13-14).

The most common word for the place of judgment used by Jesus is *Gehenna.* The reference is to an actual place located southwest of Jerusalem. From ancient times it had an evil reputation:

It gained its infamous notoriety during the reigns of Ahaz and Manassah, both of whom burned sacrifices there to Molech, even to the point of sacrificing their own sons in the fire (cf. 2 Chron 28:3, 33:6; 2 Kings 16:3). This elicited prophetic condemnations on the valley, identifying it as the scene of future carnage and desolation resulting from God's judgment (Jer 7:30-33, 19:1-13, 32:34, 35 . . .).[9]

Gehenna became synonymous with the place of God's final judgment. Jesus frequently warns of the judgment of Gehenna. The real question is the nature of this judgment. Is it really, as some think, eternal, fiery torment? Or does it refer simply to the finality of God's judgment? There are clearly places where Jesus appears to refer to eternal judgment (see Mt 25:46). But Jesus also says, "Do not fear those who kill the body but cannot kill the soul; rather fear him who can *destroy* both soul and body in hell" (Mt 10:28). Here Gehenna is a place of destruction, not a place of eternal conscious torment. Some would see a similar reference to the final destruction of the wicked in Revelation 20:14-15, where Death and Hades are thrown into the "lake of fire." This is called the "second death." It certainly implies a kind of finality.

The view that the wicked are destroyed and not subjected to eternal torment is called annihilationism. According to Sharon Baker:

> The lake of fire imagery suggests a fire that completely consumes whatever is thrown into it rather than eternal torment. We see the same type of imagery in Psalm 37:38, which tells us that the wicked will be utterly destroyed. Malachi 4:1 tells us basically the same thing: "The day is coming, burning like a furnace; and all the arrogant and every evildoer will be chaff; and the day that is coming will set them ablaze, . . . so that it will leave neither root nor branch." The arrogant and evil will be as chaff. God will burn them so that there is nothing left. These verses speak of complete destruction or annihilation.[10]

However appealing or unappealing one finds Gehenna as either eternal torment or complete annihilation of the wicked, both views face exegetical and theological challenges. If the unbelieving dead are subjected to eternal torment, this raises questions about God's love and justice. If the unbelieving

---

[9]Joel B. Green, Scot McKnight and I. Howard Marshall, eds., *Dictionary of Jesus and the Gospels* (Downers Grove, IL: InterVarsity Press, 1992), s.v. "Heaven and Hell," by J. Lunde.
[10]Baker, *Razing Hell,* pp. 142-43.

dead are simply destroyed, this raises questions about God's ability to finally set things right—to be all in all. And this raises, once again, the question of universalism. But before I turn to that question, I want to explore a passage that has profoundly shaped our view of heaven and hell: the parable of the rich man and Lazarus (Lk 16:19-31).

THE RICH MAN AND LAZARUS

In this story Jesus describes an indifferent rich man who daily passes by the suffering poor man Lazarus (Lk 16:19-31). When both die, Lazarus is carried away to "Abraham's bosom," whereas the rich man finds himself in Hades (Lk 16:22 KJV). The rich man is depicted as being "tormented" in the "flames" of Hades (Lk 16:23-24). Lazarus is being comforted in recompense for the evil he suffered during his lifetime (Lk 16:25). The point of the parable is obviously to warn against the kind of callous indifference demonstrated by the rich man. As with the parable of the sheep and the goats in Matthew 25:31-46, Jesus is warning that it is not simply our evil deeds that will condemn us. The rich man is shown not abusing Lazarus but simply ignoring him. It was his cruel indifference to the suffering of the poor that condemned him and, Jesus implies, will condemn us as well.

But what are we to make of this description of Hades? First, I would argue this is *not* the place of the final judgment of the rich man. Hades here is rather, as suggested above, the holding tank for the final judgment. In 2 Peter 2:4 we are told "God did not spare the angels when they sinned, but cast them into hell [literally *tartarus*] and committed them to chains of deepest darkness to be kept until the judgment." In 1 Peter 3:19 we are told Christ "went and made a proclamation to the spirits in prison, who in former times did not obey, when God waited patiently in the days of Noah." These are obscure and difficult passages, but both suggest that the disobedient angels and spirits were temporarily imprisoned until the final disposition of their cases. Whether there was any hope for them in the end is ambiguous. What kind of proclamation was Christ making? What kind of response did he expect? This is not at all clear. But according to Revelation 20 Hades, however we understand it, will be emptied out ahead of the final judgment.

In any case, in Jesus' story, the rich man finds himself suffering in Hades. Perhaps he is simply awaiting the final judgment. But does not the depiction

of torment in flames at least support the traditional view of hell as a place of
torment? Yes and no. It should first be said that Jesus' descriptions here of
heaven and hell are clearly metaphorical. To take the flames literally would
require you also to take "Abraham's bosom" literally. Hades is clearly depicted
as a place of pain and alienation. The rich man is cut off from his brothers by
death and from Abraham and Lazarus by a "great chasm" (Lk 16:26). Flames
are a source of torment here, but in other passages the place of the wicked
dead is described as a place of darkness (2 Pet 2:4), as a prison (1 Pet 3:19) or,
as in the *Apocalypse of Zephaniah,* as an ocean. Such images speak to the pain
of isolation and loss of freedom. Someone imprisoned is cut off from those
they love and forced to exist in cramped and painful quarters. Lazarus, in
contrast, finds himself in a place of intimacy and comfort. Nevertheless, all
these passages use metaphors, images, to describe the place of the dead and
cannot be taken to be literal descriptions of the fate of the dead.

WHAT ABOUT PURGATORY?

The doctrine of purgatory was developed by the Western church well after the
earliest days of the church. The logic of the doctrine is included in the word
itself. To *purge* is to cleanse or purify. It assumed that sins not adequately
confessed or atoned for in this life needed to be addressed in the life to come
before one could come into the presence of God. While the most serious and
unrepentant were sent to hell, ordinary sinners paid off their debts in purgatory. This logic of salvation is rooted in the sort of legal mindset that shaped
the Western church. Debts must be paid. The ledger must be balanced. But
this is not the logic of salvation found in the New Testament. It undercuts the
notion of God's forgiveness, the completeness of the work of Christ and the
fact that, as N. T. Wright puts it, death itself is purification from sin.[11] Furthermore, what has been forgiven does not need to be atoned for. Why would
God forgive our sins through Jesus and then require us to pay for them after
we die? Even Pope Benedict modified the more popular notion of purgatory.
According to Wright, the pope appealed to 1 Corinthians 3 to suggest "that the
Lord himself is the fire of judgment which transforms us as he conforms us to
his glorious resurrected body. This happens not during a long, drawn-out

---

[11]N. T. Wright, *Surprised by Hope: Rethinking Heaven, the Resurection, and the Mission of the Church* (New York: HarperOne, 2008), p. 170.

process, but in the moment of final judgment itself."[12] This obviously detaches the idea of purgatory from any sort of intermediate state.

Perhaps there is another way of looking at this. I would distinguish, for example, between purgation and growth. If we are told very little about the character and nature of hell, we are perhaps told even less about heaven. I have already argued that the Bible foresees not eternal life in heaven but eternal life on the re-created earth—a new heaven and a new earth. The ideas we have about the nature of heaven—golden streets, pearly gates and the like—are drawn entirely from the description of "the holy city Jerusalem coming down out of heaven from God" (Rev 21:10). This city is not located in the clouds but resides on the re-created earth. We are not told what we will do or how we will live in this new reality. But it could be suggested that even here we will continue to grow toward God. In Revelation 22 John sees "on either side of the river . . . the tree of life with its twelve kinds of fruit, producing its fruit each month; *and the leaves of the tree are for the healing of the nations*" (Rev 22:2). Is our life in the new heaven and earth meant to complete our healing, to enable our completion as human beings in the likeness of God? This is not purgation or punishment any more than the growth from childhood to adulthood represents movement from sinfulness to sainthood. In the new heaven and new earth do we become in the end what God intended us to become in the beginning? Is our task in the new heaven and new earth to grow toward God?

THE QUESTION OF UNIVERSALISM

Paul speaks in 1 Corinthians of God becoming "all in all," with everything in creation subjected to him. Some have wondered how God could become all in all if some were still in rebellion, still being punished in hell. Does not God being all in all rather suggest that in the end everyone will be restored to God? Will God make new all people along with the new heaven and earth? There are certainly passages in the New Testament that could be taken to support this view. In Romans 5:18 Paul wrote, "therefore just as one man's trespass led to condemnation for all, so one man's act of righteousness leads to justification and life for all." In the same book he said, "God has imprisoned all in disobedience so that he may be merciful to all" (Rom 11:32).

---

[12]Ibid., p. 167.

He told the Ephesians God's plan was "to gather up all things in him, things in heaven and things on earth" (Eph 1:10; see also Eph 1:23; Col 1:20; 1 Tim 4:10). Peter tells us "the Lord . . . is patient with you, not wanting any to perish, but all to come to repentance" (2 Pet 3:9).

Universalism has had its supporters throughout Christian history. Church fathers like Clement of Alexandria, Origen and Gregory of Nyssa taught a universal restoration to God. And even though the church condemned universalism as a heresy, mystics and theologians throughout history have believed in it. Some years ago I heard Robert Farrar Capon say that universalism wasn't biblical, but it was a thought! Roman Catholic theologian Hans Urs von Balthasar wrote a book titled *Dare We Hope: "That All Men Be Saved"?*[13] Balthasar argued that it was at least a theoretical possibility that God could in the end save everyone. This honors God's freedom. Rob Bell says something similar in *Love Wins*. And of course, this is true. If we believe God is sovereign, we must believe that God can do whatever he likes. But Capon, Balthasar and, as far as I can tell, Bell recognize that the biblical text and human experience militate against this. The warnings of judgment in the Bible must be given their full weight. Human freedom must be honored. It is not God's desire to judge or destroy—quite the contrary. But God's love must be freely chosen to be genuine. And God, perhaps with sorrow, will honor our decision not to love him.

Having said this, we can depend on the judge of the world to do right—as we heard from Abraham. We should not base our ideas of God or of God's judgment on hard cases, either serial killers or people who have never heard of Jesus. The Bible makes it clear that God is not willing that any should perish. He is neither arbitrary nor cruel and has gone to great lengths to save us and his world. In the end he will show mercy on whomever he wishes. We cannot bind God. God is free. Nevertheless, it would be naive to expect that in the end all will be saved—however much we might like it to be true. In a handout to students, my colleague Klyne Snodgrass wrote:

> I do not revel in the thought of judgment, nor do I think any of us can be presumptuous about the outcome of judgment. Yet, we can have confidence

---

[13]Hans Urs von Balthasar, *Dare We Hope: "That All Men Be Saved"?*, trans. David Kipp and Lothar Krauth (San Francisco: Ignatius Press, 1988).

in accord with the themes of 1 John 3:19-22 and the assurances of texts like Romans 8:31-39. Judgment is a positive thing as well as a negative thing. Truth will be demonstrated to be truth. God will be vindicated and so will his people. Evil will be shown to be evil and will be defeated. God will be "all in all" (1 Cor. 15:28), but I do not think this type of "universalism" precludes judgment or assumes the involvement of every creature.[14]

There is considerable wisdom in these words. We can trust in the mercy and love of God for his whole creation, but we cannot presume on that mercy and love.

A VISION OF HEAVEN AND HELL

I have argued that all descriptions of heaven and hell are metaphorical. The descriptions speak of a reality that can only be expressed in analogies and pictures. The place of judgment can be described as a place of darkness, flame or deep water while the heavenly city is depicted as a Middle Eastern walled city with gates of pearl and streets of gold. One of the most powerful attempts to paint a contemporary picture of heaven and hell is found in C. S. Lewis's 1946 book *The Great Divorce*. Hell is depicted as a gray, gloomy city full of quarrelsome and suspicious people. Its suburbs extend great distances, and the farther out you go the more isolated and alone its residents are. The protagonist of the tale joins a group of citizens taking a bus ride to heaven. When they get there, the vast majority of them elect not to stay but return to hell.

Lewis skillfully draws a picture of people who are convinced they are right and God is wrong. One person refuses to stay in heaven if someone else is there. Another refuses to stay unless she can once again take control of her husband. They refuse to shed the prejudices, fears and opinions that kept them out of heaven in the first place. They refuse to grow. The Scottish author George MacDonald acts as a tour guide for Lewis's visitor. The visitor asks, "Is there really a way out of Hell into Heaven?" MacDonald replies,

It depends on the way ye're using the words. If they leave that grey town behind it will not have been Hell. To any that leaves it, it is Purgatory. And perhaps ye had better not call this country Heaven. Not *Deep Heaven,* ye

---

[14]Klyne Snodgrass, in a handout for eschatology class, North Park Theological Seminary, undated.

understand. . . . Ye can call it the Valley of the Shadow of Life. And yet to those who stay here it will have been heaven from the first. And ye can call those sad streets in the town yonder the Valley of the Shadow of Death: but to those who remain there they will have been Hell even from the beginning. . . . Not only this valley but all this earthly past will have been heaven to those who are saved. Not only the twilight in that town, but all their life on earth too will then be seen by the damned to have been Hell.[15]

Lewis is not trying to describe the reality of heaven and hell. *The Great Divorce* is an extended metaphor. Lewis is not saying hell is a gray city or heaven a lovely valley. His book is rather a warning that the patterns and expectations that frame our lives here will follow us into the life to come. If we have not responded to the love of God here, why would we expect we would respond to the love of God there? Those who cling to their own peculiar visions of themselves and of reality will increasingly, as Luther put it, curve in upon themselves. The gospel intends to straighten us out through the love of God and of one another. Otherwise, we grow in narcissism and paranoia until no one or nothing exists except our own fears. As Abraham warned the rich man in Hades regarding his brothers, "If they do not listen to Moses and the prophets, neither will they be convinced even if someone rises from the dead" (Lk 16:31).

At the beginning of this chapter I suggested that the warnings of judgment in the Bible suggest we live in a morally serious universe. The way we live today matters. The decisions we make today matter. Who we are today matters. You can make a case that *hell* in the Bible refers to a place of eternal isolation from God. You can make a case that in the end those who resist God are utterly destroyed. You can even make a case that God in the end will restore all things and people to himself. But God's great gift of freedom suggests that we human beings are perfectly free to choose against our own best interests. We can sink into misery, fear and loss here and, as George MacDonald suggested, have our decisions confirmed in the life to come. We can also rise in love and faith to the one whose love is eternal. We can turn in upon ourselves, or we can open like a flower in the sun of God's love.

---

[15]Lewis, *The Great Divorce*, p. 67 (emphasis original).

5

Hope for the Kingdom of God

THE GOSPEL OF MARK BEGINS WITH VERY FEW PRELIMINARIES. There are no angel visitations, no shepherds, wise men or murderous kings. Mark begins in the middle of the ministry of John the Baptist, who graphically predicts the coming of a powerful individual who will go beyond John's ministry of repentance. "I have baptized you with water," he tells the crowds; "but he will baptize you with the Holy Spirit" (Mk 1:8). John does not explain this startling statement, but the biblically literate among the crowd could not help but think of Joel 2:28-29:

> Then afterward
> I will pour out my spirit on all flesh;
> your sons and your daughters shall prophesy,
> your old men shall dream dreams,
> and your young men shall see visions.
> Even on the male and female slaves,
> in those days, I will pour out my spirit.

John was clearly anticipating the great day of consummation and judgment, when God would set things right.

Jesus appears in the narrative as suddenly as John has. When John baptizes him, the Spirit descends on Jesus "like a dove" (Mk 1:10). A voice from heaven commends him as God's beloved Son. The pouring out of the Spirit has begun with Jesus himself. The same Spirit drives Jesus into the wilderness to be tempted by Satan. When he returns, he begins his own proclamation: "The time is fulfilled, and the kingdom of God has come near; repent, and believe in the good news" (Mk 1:15). At the beginning of his Gospel, Mark is making sure the essential message of Jesus is clear. The time of Israel's deliverance is at hand. God's kingdom is near. All Israel should prepare for God's deliverance by repenting and believing the good news, that is, the gospel. In this very succinct summary, Mark sets the stage for everything Jesus will say and do in the coming chapters.

To understand Jesus you need to understand what he meant by the kingdom of God. For many followers of Jesus the kingdom of God is a rather vague concept. Perhaps it refers to God's rule in their lives now. Perhaps it is something the church works toward in society. Or perhaps it is something God will establish in some future era. For Jesus' first hearers it would suggest that the creator God is coming to rescue his people and rule over the entire earth. "The LORD will become king over all the earth; on that day the LORD will be one and his name one" (Zech 14:9). God would deliver them from the oppression of the Romans, establish them in their own land and give them peace and prosperity.

According to N. T. Wright, the phrase "the kingdom of God" would call to mind a complex story.[1] Saying "the kingdom of God is at hand" is the same as saying "Frodo and Sam have arrived at Mount Doom!" for readers of J. R. R. Tolkien or "Harry Potter has returned to Hogwarts!" for readers of J. K. Rowling. It suggests that the consummation of the story is at hand. The time of crisis has arrived. This is the beginning of the end of the story. The last act of the play, the climactic scene of the movie, is about to begin. The arrival of the kingdom was the last scene of a well-known story in Israel. Wright gives the story as follows:

1. The first temple, built by Solomon, was the place where the LORD chose to dwell. It was a place of prayer, worship and celebration.

2. The true king, like Solomon, is a temple builder and temple keeper.

3. The temple was the center of the earth, indeed, the entire cosmos. It was the spot where heaven and earth met.

4. The sixth-century B.C. destruction of the temple by the Babylonians was a catastrophic abandonment of the temple, king and nation by God (see Ezek 10:18-19; 11:22-24—the glory leaves the temple).

---

[1]For what follows see N. T. Wright, *Jesus and the Victory of God*, vol. 2 of *Christian Origins and the Question of God* (Minneapolis: Fortress, 1996), pp. 202-9.

5. As Jeremiah predicted, the people returned to the land after seventy years—but not fully. There was no defeat of paganism, no true Davidic king and no reestablishment of the true temple. Even though a temple was rebuilt, it was a disappointment. The postexilic period was a "day of small things" (Zech 4:10; see also Hag 1:6; 2:3). The true Davidic king would finally come, rebuild the temple and reestablish the kingship, and God would return to his people forever. But now they were under the dominion of Persia, then Greece and then Rome. "The longing for the *return from exile* thus contained as a major component, the equal longing for *the return of YHWH to Zion* with, as its components, the defeat of evil, . . . the rebuilding of the Temple, and the re-establishment of the true Davidic monarchy."[2]

6. They were, then, not expecting the end of the world but a new heaven and a new earth and the direct rule of God—the kingdom of God. Their expectations were entirely earthly and certainly not about merely going to heaven when they died. Their expectations were in line with Isaiah 65 (see chapter one of this book). They "were *not* expecting the end of the space-time universe" but the coming of God.[3]

JESUS' FULFILLMENT OF ISAIAH'S KINGDOM PROPHECY

This story of the kingdom was deeply rooted in the prophets of Israel. I have often told students that the book of Isaiah was Jesus' "ministry manual." If you want to understand the ministry and teaching of Jesus, you need to understand the prophecy of Isaiah. Jesus framed his version of this great story in terms of Isaiah and used Isaiah to both preach and demonstrate his gospel, his good news. Consider the following examples.

Isaiah 35:5-6 // Matthew 11:4-6. The healings of Jesus were signs of the nearness of the new creation. When Jesus healed, he was not simply doing something impressive to wow the crowds. His mighty works were signs of the presence of the kingdom. His healings anticipated the time when God would heal the entire creation and make all things new. When this occurs,

> The ransomed of the LORD shall return,
>   and come to Zion with singing;

---

[2]Ibid., p. 207 (emphasis original).
[3]Ibid. (emphasis original).

everlasting joy shall be upon their heads;
they shall obtain joy and gladness,
and sorrow and sighing shall flee away. (Is 35:10)

Isaiah 61:1-3 // Luke 4:16-30. Jesus boldly declared that in him was good news to the poor, freedom for prisoners and the oppressed, and recovery of sight for the blind. These were all things Isaiah anticipated in the great day of God's coming and deliverance. These were things the Nazareth crowd was expecting as well. But they were perhaps not expecting that Jesus himself would be the one who brought them about. And they were clearly not expecting that God would widen the net on that great judgment day to include even the Gentile oppressors. Jesus was telling the familiar story, but he was giving it a twist they did not expect. They were outraged enough to try to kill him (Lk 4:28-30).

Isaiah 25:6-10 // Matthew 8:11 // Luke 13:29. Jesus expected there would be a great messianic banquet at the end of the age. But Isaiah spoke rather startlingly of the end of death and perhaps even implied the possibility of resurrection. (For more on this, see chapter three of this book.) During his ministry Jesus spent a good deal of time at symbolic meals, eating with sinners and prostitutes, and he finally provided a meal for his disciples that looked back to his death and forward to the time he would eat with his followers in the kingdom of God (see Mt 26:29). A number of Jesus' parables speak of glorious banquets (e.g., Mt 22:1-14 and parallels), and this image is reprised in the so-called marriage supper of the Lamb in Revelation 19:6-9. A banquet is the ultimate symbol of joy and fellowship with God's children and with God himself.

Isaiah 52–53 // Matthew 8:17. Finally, and perhaps most importantly, Jesus is depicted as the Servant of God who suffers on behalf of the people and for the sake of their restoration. Isaiah 52 begins with a reference to captive Israel and to the promise of God that the Israelites will finally leave their places of exile. This is "good news" brought by heralds who proclaim "Your God reigns!" (Is 52:7). God's Servant will silence kings (Is 52:15), bear the sins of the people (Is 53:4-6) and "make many righteous" (Is 53:11). He will engineer the final great return of God's people. Through his own suffering and oppression, he will lift the suffering and oppression of the people and bring them peace: "The righteous one, my servant, shall make many righteous, and he shall bear their iniquities" (Is 53:11). Perhaps the words of Jesus in Mark 10 are an echo of this great passage: "Whoever wishes to become great among you must be your servant, and whoever wishes to be first among you must be slave of all. For the Son of Man came not to be served but to serve, and to give his life a ransom for many" (Mk 10:43-45).

All of this is implied in those bare words of Mark: "The time is fulfilled, and the kingdom of God has come near; repent, and believe in the good news" (Mk 1:15). In Jesus the kingdom has been inaugurated. The last part of the story has started. The climax is in view. But—and this is important—it would not quite be what they expected. To the foundational story, Jesus added a twist that perplexed and angered many of his listeners. Questions arose from a number of quarters. John the Baptist himself wondered if Jesus was the one (see Lk 7:18-20). Jesus had announced freedom for prisoners, but John was still languishing in Herod's jail and would eventually lose his head there. We have already seen the outrage of the crowd in Nazareth in Luke 4. Jesus' own disciples didn't really understand what he was doing. This is one of the major themes of the Gospel of Mark (see Mk 8:14-21 and throughout the Gospel).

Wright argues that Jesus was telling Israel that the route to the kingdom was not through eschatological violence and armed rebellion against Rome. That, in fact, was a route to disaster. They would not win their freedom and restore their kingdom through forming an army to fight the Romans. The kingdom's arrival would be an act of God, not an act of communal violence.[4] In fact, the route of revolutionary violence was the route to utter disaster. It would lead to the destruction of the temple, the people and all they valued. Jesus' predictions of apocalyptic disaster in Mark 13 and parallels must be seen in this context. The Jewish rebellion against Rome is not world-ending disaster but a very earthly tragedy brought about by Israel's leaders' poor decisions.

Wright does not believe that Jesus' so-called eschatological discourse has a future reference. I do not entirely agree with him and will discuss the discourse more fully in a subsequent chapter. Nevertheless, his point remains. Jesus was not advocating eschatological violence. He was not anticipating the dissolution of the "space-time universe." He was expecting a new heaven and

---

[4]Ibid., pp. 323-33.

a new earth. He was anticipating that God himself would establish his kingdom. To the surprise of many in Israel, Jesus insisted that even Gentiles and sinners would receive the benefits of the kingdom (see Mk 2:15-17; 7:24-29). Some parts of the Jewish law would even be transcended to make this possible (Mk 7:17-22). The old barriers between Jews and Gentiles would be broken down. "Many will come from east and west and will eat with Abraham and Isaac and Jacob in the kingdom of heaven" (Mt 8:11).

According to S. S. Bartchy, the inclusive banquet is a major image in Jesus' teaching. He eats with Zacchaeus, a tax collector and sinner (Lk 19:1-10). He joins a banquet at Levi's home (Lk 5:27-32) with a large crowd of such sinners. And in Luke's version of the parable of the great banquet, "the poor, the crippled, the blind, and the lame" are included (Lk 14:15-24). The most unexpected people are to be participants in the great eschatological banquet of Isaiah 25. "From the perspective of Luke and Acts together," Bartchy writes, "God intends his new community to offer reconciliation and solidarity among Jews and Gentiles, men and women, rich and poor."[5] For Jesus does not mean to simply proclaim the kingdom of God's coming. He intends to form a community of the kingdom. To this we now turn.

THE COMMUNITY OF THE KINGDOM

Jesus began his ministry by calling disciples. In Mark 3:13-19 he appoints twelve—obviously a highly symbolic number since ancient Israel was formed by twelve tribes bearing the names of Jacob's (and Joseph's) sons. The community around Jesus and his disciples could be seen as the reconstitution of Israel. Clearly Jesus did not think he was starting over. The new Israel was in continuity with the old. Nevertheless, the coming of the kingdom of God required new commitments and new directions for God's people. Mark says Jesus chose the twelve "to be with him, and to be sent out to proclaim the message, and to have authority to cast out demons" (Mk 3:14-15). In other words, they were to be extensions of his ministry. The disciples were also to proclaim repentance and the coming of God's kingdom. But the disciples were not the only ones in this new community.

Mark often juxtaposes texts so that one story throws light on another. In

---

[5]Joel B. Green, Scot McKnight and I. Howard Marshall, eds., *Dictionary of Jesus and the Gospels* (Downers Grove, IL: InterVarsity Press, 1992), s.v. "Table Fellowship," by S. S. Bartchy.

Mark 3, the calling of the twelve disciples is followed by the story of Jesus in conflict with both his family and "the scribes who came down from Jerusalem." His family thinks he is crazy, and the scribes, less charitably, think he is possessed by Beelzebul (Mk 3:21-23). In addition to Jesus' disciples, his family and his Jerusalem opponents, there is a fourth group: "a crowd . . . sitting around him" (Mk 3:32). When he is told his mother and brothers have arrived to take him in hand, he looks at the crowd at his feet and says, "Who are my mother and my brothers? . . . Here are my mother and my brothers! Whoever does the will of God is my brother and sister and mother" (Mk 3:33-35). In a society where kinship relations were key to personal identity, this was a startling assertion.

Jesus seems to be saying that these old kinship relationships are no longer sufficient to provide identity in the coming kingdom. This is perhaps the background of his striking assertion: "Whoever loves father or mother more than me is not worthy of me; and whoever loves son or daughter more than me is not worthy of me" (Mt 10:37). The new community, the community of the coming kingdom, turned kinship relationships on their heads. Family alone, mother and father alone, son and daughter alone, did not provide identity. One's identity was found in the new community that sat at the feet of Jesus. And this kinship would go beyond the borders of Israel to include Gentiles, sinners, women and children—the least, the lost and the losers. Jesus would transgress old boundaries of law and propriety to include prostitutes and sinners in this new community.

In Mark 7 Jesus enters into a controversy with some "Pharisees and some of the scribes." They complain that his disciples have failed to observe adequately the rituals around eating. By failing to properly wash their hands, they have made themselves unclean. Jesus argues that actually the Pharisees and the scribes are the ones who have misunderstood what is clean and unclean. "There is nothing outside a person that by going in can defile, but the things that come out are what defile" (Mk 7:15). When his disciples question him about this he tells them, "Do you not see that whatever goes into a person from outside cannot defile? . . . For it is from within, from the human heart, that evil intentions come: fornication, theft, murder, adultery, avarice, wickedness, deceit, licentiousness, envy, slander, pride, folly. All these evil things come from within, and they defile a person" (Mk 7:18-23).

This is not a critique of Jewish legalism. Neither Jesus nor Paul had a problem with the law per se. Their issue was not that Jews were seeking to be saved by keeping the law. Rather, I would argue, both Jesus and Paul were concerned to say that in the coming community of the kingdom a new set of boundaries was being set. No longer were law keeping and circumcision the exclusive marks of the people of God: now the uncircumcised were being admitted to the community of the kingdom; now the law of Christ was to guide communal relationships and personal behavior. With the coming of Israel's messiah and the announcement of the kingdom of God, everything had changed. A new community was being formed with a new community rule and a new set of kinship relationships. The difference between Jews and Christians is not that Christians believe we are saved by faith and Jews believe we are saved by keeping the law. Rather, Christians believe Jesus is Israel's messiah who announced the kingdom of God and formed a new community, and Jews do not.

In the community of Israel, relationships were determined by the so-called Holiness Code. This code prescribed the relationships between persons, places, things and times (see Lev 19–26). Certain things could be eaten. Certain things must not be eaten. Certain things could be touched. Others things should not be touched. This was done not simply because God was fastidious, but to provide Israel with an identity in a diverse and threatening world. It had, and has, served the Jews well throughout their painful and difficult history. It is perhaps no exaggeration to say the Holiness Code enabled the Jews to survive. But Jesus in Mark both teaches and demonstrates that something new is going on in his ministry. The old rules regarding clean and unclean are being radically altered, and not because the old regulations were wrong or misguided. They were from God, after all. Rather, they were being changed so that Gentiles might be included in the coming kingdom of God and because in the death and resurrection of Jesus the kingdom of God had been inaugurated. With the arrival of the kingdom, everything was changed.

Jesus demonstrates this removal of the boundaries throughout Mark's Gospel by breaching the Holiness Code. Perhaps this is seen most clearly in Mark 5. Here he deals with what could be called three impossible cases. The first case is an evidently Gentile man who is not only possessed by a whole army of demons but living with pigs in the middle of a cemetery. So far as the Holiness Code was concerned, the man was a holiness loser. In the following story, Jesus is touched by a woman with a bleeding problem and then takes a dead girl by the hand. In both cases, according to the Holiness Code, Jesus would have been ritually defiled. But rather than defiling Jesus, the demoniac, the bleeding woman and the dead girl are healed by Jesus. The old barriers are eliminated by the healing power of the Messiah. At the very end of this Gospel, when Jesus dies, the veil of the temple is torn from top to bottom (Mk 15:38). The veil shielded the holy of holies from view. It was there, on the lid of the ark of the covenant, that atonement was made. Only the high priest had access to the holy of holies and then only once a year. But at the death of Jesus the veil was torn and access was made possible for everyone.[6]

Jesus also provides a new community rule for his followers through his teaching—perhaps most provocatively in Matthew's Sermon on the Mount. In the new community, Jesus says, the law is not thrust aside but intensified. Anger, not simply murder, and lust, not simply adultery, are condemned (Mt 5:21-32). Instead of seeking vengeance, the followers of Jesus are to love their enemies (Mt 5:38-48). Jesus rejects the idea that in the kingdom there will be us and them. "Your Father in heaven . . . makes his sun rise on the evil and on the good, and sends rain on the righteous and on the unrighteous" (Mt 5:45). Jesus' disciples are to love not just their own people, but those beyond the pale—just as God loves both righteous and unrighteous. As if these expectations were not challenging enough, Jesus concludes by declaring, "Be perfect, therefore, as your heavenly Father is perfect" (Mt 5:48).

This means that, among other things, Jesus' followers are not to create scapegoats. According to René Girard, as noted above, the whole of human culture is founded upon what he calls the "scapegoat mechanism."[7] From the beginning of creation we have sought someone to blame: Adam blamed

---

[6]See Marcus J. Borg, *Conflict, Holiness, and Politics in the Teachings of Jesus* (Harrisburg, PA: Trinity Press International, 1998).

[7]See René Girard, *The Scapegoat*, trans. Yvonne Freccero (Baltimore: Johns Hopkins University Press, 1989), p. 212; René Girard with Jean-Michel Oughourlian and Guy Lefort, *Things Hidden Since the Foundation of the World,* trans. Stephen Bann and Michael Matteer (Stanford, CA: Stanford University Press, 1987); and René Girard, *I See Satan Fall Like Lightning,* trans. James G. Williams (Maryknoll, NY: Orbis, 2001). For a popular exposition of Girard's ideas, see Gil Bailie, *Violence Unveiled: Humanity at the Crossroads* (New York: Crossroad, 1995).

Eve; Eve blamed the snake. Girard argues that this is a very common human strategy. When resources are scarce, people tend to fight over them. At times this rivalry can become so fierce it threatens the very existence of the community. When the survival of the community is at stake, unity is restored by identifying a scapegoat, an enemy. It could be an alien, an other. It could be a member of the community who has violated a community rule. It could be someone chosen at random. But the anxiety and rage of the community are loaded on this scapegoat, and it is either killed or driven away. As a result, equilibrium is at least temporarily restored.

Throughout human history, Girard argues, we have used this strategy. Rulers have identified enemies, either within or without the community, in order to unify a fractious society. The enemy is sacrificed or imprisoned in order to placate the community. When the force of that unification begins to wear off, a new scapegoat must be identified and the process repeated. Virtually all people and nations throughout all human history have used this tried and true method. But Jesus, both in his teachings and in his death, undercut the scapegoat mechanism. In his teachings he insisted that, for his disciples, there was no enemy, no other. There were only "children of your Father in heaven" (Mt 5:45). Jesus died as the scapegoat to end all scapegoats. He showed that the scapegoats chosen to bring unity were actually innocent victims of communal violence and not worthy of suffering and death. Ever since, particularly in Western society, Girard argues, the effectiveness of the mechanism has been waning.

What does this all have to do with the kingdom of God? It suggests first of all that the community of Jesus is something entirely different from every other human community. It is a community that sustains itself by refusing to scapegoat. It is a community, in other words, that refuses to have enemies. There are no *others* in the community of Jesus. The kingdom of God does not scapegoat. By living out of this commitment, the Jesus community demonstrates the purity of the love of God. Followers of Jesus do not identify tax collectors and sinners to despise. The community of Jesus does not have enemies. The community of Jesus does not recognize national boundaries, racial identities or even gender differences (see Gal 3:28). As Jesus said, in this new community the old pattern of relationships, be they familial, national or religious, is shattered. As Paul would put it, "If anyone is in Christ, there is a new creation: everything old has passed away; see, everything has become new!" (2 Cor 5:17). This is what it means to be a part of the kingdom of God.

As previously noted, according to Rodney Stark in his book *The Rise of Christianity*, this is exactly what appealed to the Greco-Roman cities where Paul and others proclaimed the good news. These cities were cramped, filthy, disease ridden and appallingly violent. Stark argues that Christianity had such an impact because it simply offered a better way to live:

> Christianity revitalized life in Greco-Roman cities by providing new norms and new kinds of social relationships able to cope with many urgent urban problems. To cities filled with homeless and impoverished, Christianity offered charity as well as hope. To cities filled with newcomers and strangers, Christianity offered an immediate basis for attachments. To cities filled with orphans and widows, Christianity provided a new and expanded sense of family. To cities torn by violent ethnic strife, Christianity offered a new basis for social solidarity. . . . And to cities faced with epidemics, fires and earthquakes, Christianity offered effective nursing services.[8]

Christianity was able to do all this because of Jesus' teaching on the kingdom of God and his formation of a new community living out of a new community rule. This new community realized that the kingdom had not arrived in its fullness, but it believed that with the resurrection of Jesus from the dead it had been inaugurated. This new community was to live as if the kingdom was already here. That meant living without enemies and without borders. It meant living without the old notions of us and them and the old strategy of scapegoating. It meant living without the old love of violence:

> Perhaps above all else, Christianity brought a new conception of humanity to a world saturated with capricious cruelty and the vicarious love of death. . . . For the throngs in the stadia, watching people torn and devoured by beasts or killed in armed combat was the ultimate spectator sport, worthy of a boy's birthday treat. It is difficult to comprehend the emotional life of such people. . . . Christianity condemned both the cruelties and the spectators. . . . What Christianity gave to its converts was nothing less than their humanity.[9]

---

[8]Rodney Stark, *The Rise of Christianity: How the Obscure, Marginal Jesus Movement Became the Dominant Religious Force in the Western World in a Few Centuries* (San Francisco: HarperSanFrancisco, 1997), p. 161.
[9]Ibid., pp. 214-15.

In Isaiah 11 the prophet predicts that the Spirit of the Lord will rest on "a shoot . . . from the stump of Jesse" (Is 11:1). This shoot will set the world right by coming to the defense of the needy and the poor. "Righteousness shall be the belt around his waist, and faithfulness the belt around his loins" (Is 11:5). As a result of the activity of the Shoot, the entire order of the world will be changed:

> The wolf shall live with the lamb,
>   the leopard shall lie down with the kid,
> the calf and the lion and the fatling together,
>   and a little child shall lead them.
> The cow and the bear shall graze,
>   their young shall lie down together;
>   and the lion will eat straw like the ox. . . .
> They will not hurt or destroy
>   on all my holy mountain. (Is 11:6-7, 9)

The old violence and bloodshed so characteristic of our battered world—even, or perhaps especially, in the natural world—will be ended. The era of predator and prey will come to an end.

Clearly that era is not here yet. There are still plenty of predators around, of both the four-footed and the two-footed variety. But this vision of the kingdom of God is the vision undergirding the kingdom preaching of Jesus. It was the vision that motivated the early Christians and provided the ancient world with a saner, less violent vision of human life. It was a vision that identified with the weak rather than despising them. It cared for the poor rather than blaming them for their own poverty. It loved the marginal and despised rather than pushing them even further away. It was a vision quickly forgotten when Christianity came into power. Eventually the kingdom of God was identified with the empire. The coercive power of the empire was sanctified, and its violence against the other was justified by leaders of the church. The enemies of the empire were the enemies of the church. It became easy once again to scapegoat the other. Conquering armies were blessed. Heretics were burned at the stake. Jews were persecuted. The world returned to its old violent ways.

There were, and always have been, critics of the subservience of the church to secular powers. There have always been those who have seen this accommodation to power as a violation of the very nature of the kingdom of God. There have always been those who called the church away from its love affair with imperial power and violence back to Jesus' teaching on the kingdom of God. But they have been too few and too far between. In his famous book *Discipleship,* the modern martyr Dietrich Bonhoeffer argued that the German church of his day had been seduced by "cheap grace."[10] This was "grace without discipleship." He saw this in the too-easy accommodation of the German church to the goals of the German government. Christianity for many Germans was simply a religious veneer over their German culture and nationalistic aspirations. Such a flaccid faith was incapable of resisting the scapegoating violence of the Nazis. Their Christianity was in service of the national goals of the German people and nation rather than of the kingdom of God preached by Jesus.

I reiterate that eschatology is a profoundly practical discipline. It is not just speculation about the second coming of Jesus or the nature of the tribulation. It is about how Jesus' followers are to live out the values of the kingdom now. If the kingdom has already in some profound sense been inaugurated in the life, death and resurrection of Jesus, the new community he formed has a new way to live. Followers of Jesus become his witnesses, not just in what they say but in how they live. The community of Jesus' followers, the church, is to be the sacrament of the kingdom. In who we are and how we live we are to demonstrate a life without scapegoating violence, without the marginalization of the other—a life without enemies. This is not to say we will not have differences with others. This is not to say there is no longer right or wrong. It is rather to say that, however deeply and purely our convictions are held, they are held with love, with humility and with grace.

In 2 Corinthians 5, Paul tells his fractious church that "all this is from God, who reconciled us to himself through Christ, and has given us the ministry of reconciliation; that is, in Christ God was reconciling the world to himself, not counting their trespasses against them, *and entrusting the message of reconciliation to us. So we are ambassadors for Christ, since God is making his appeal through us*" (2 Cor 5:18-20). God has no enemies, he

---

[10]See Dietrich Bonhoeffer, *Discipleship,* vol. 4 of *Dietrich Bonhoeffer Works* (Louisville, KY: Fortress, 2003).

tells them, and neither should you. God sent Christ to bring about the reconciliation of his estranged creation, and now you, Corinthian church, are agents of that reconciliation. But it is going to be hard for you to effect reconciliation in the world if you can't get along with each other. And how can you claim to be reconciled to God if you aren't reconciled to each other? "We entreat you on behalf of Christ," he concludes, "be reconciled to God" (2 Cor 5:20).

One of the great questions of Christian history has been the so-called delay of the parousia, that is, the delay of Christ's return to set things right. Various explanations have been offered over the years. Perhaps, some say, in a sense Jesus has already returned. Perhaps, others say, God is following a timetable, and we are simply not there yet. But I have wondered if, humanly speaking, God in his exasperation has decided he is not going to return to set up the new heaven and the new earth until his people actually begin to live out of the kingdom life proclaimed by Jesus. Is God waiting until we live without enemies, without scapegoats, without sidling up to the powers and without violence against the other? I cannot say, of course. But I do know that Jesus' followers have too often been agents of division rather than agents of reconciliation. During the twentieth century, Christians in Europe slaughtered each other in the millions in the two world wars. Christian churches throughout the world still live under the pall of mutual condemnation. Our denominational divisions and theological squabbles have been a perpetual embarrassment to the gospel. We Christians have given the enemies of God good reason to scoff.

Nevertheless, it is never too late to return to our first love. It is never too late to begin living out of the presence of the kingdom. It is never too late to put aside violence and scapegoating and show the world a better way to live. It is never too late to take up the ministry of reconciliation. I have a good friend who is an Orthodox rabbi. We have been studying the book of Romans together. I explained to him that so far as Paul was concerned the kingdom had been inaugurated in the death and resurrection of Jesus. I also said that Paul thought Christians had been transformed by the Spirit of God and were already in a sense living in the age to come. He smiled at me sadly and said, "Well, we Jews haven't seen that yet." My friend and his fellow Jews have good reason to question the spiritual transformation of Christians.

And he is right to expect something more from us than he has so far experienced. It is not too late for Jesus' followers to live out the peaceable kingdom so as to demonstrate to my friend and to the wider world that the good news of Jesus can transform both individuals and society.

- God is rescuing his people - 1st Century Time of Crisis has arrived (Mk 1:15)

- Kingdom of God is fulfilment of Scriptures
  Is.
    - Kingdom has been Inaugurated
    - barriers would be broken

- Community would be redefined
    - no longer family but in Christ

- Holiness Code
    - Jesus broke it

- No more Scapegoats

- Quote pg. 95

- weak w/ strong; Poor w/ rich; marginalized w/ insiders

- Disagreements are held w/ love, ~~care~~ humility, + grace

6

Hope for Jesus' Return

THE EARLIEST CHRISTIANS CLEARLY EXPECTED JESUS to return and set the world right. After the ascension of Jesus, the gawking disciples are asked by "two men in white robes," "Men of Galilee, why do you stand looking up toward heaven? This Jesus, who has been taken up from you into heaven, will come in the same way as you saw him go into heaven" (Acts 1:10-11). A bit later Peter, preaching after healing a crippled beggar, declares "Jesus . . . must remain in heaven until the time of universal restoration that God announced long ago through his holy prophets" (Acts 3:20-21). Peter makes it clear that for the early Christians Jesus was the Messiah appointed by God to bring about this transformation. He explicitly connects Jesus' ministry and future coming with the expectations of the prophets of Israel.

The early expectation of the return of Jesus has been the source of no little embarrassment to Christians. When Jesus did not return within the first few generations of Christians, doubt set in. This doubt is expressed within the New Testament canon itself. In 2 Peter 3:3-4 "scoffers" ask, "Where is the promise of his coming? For ever since our ancestors died, all things continue as they were from the beginning of creation!" The delay, the writer declares, is not because God is indifferent or absent, "but is patient with you, not wanting any to perish, but all to come to repentance" (2 Pet 3:9). The judgment of God *is* coming. The world *will* be purified and renewed: "In accordance with his promise, we wait for new heavens and a new earth, where righteousness is at home" (2 Pet 3:13). In spite of the apparent delay, God is coming as he promised.

Traditional Jews and Christians still wait for the coming of God. But both church and synagogue have struggled to integrate this "primitive" hope into the modern and now postmodern world of attenuated expectations. In the 1990s neoliberal thinkers declared we had arrived at the "end of history."[1] The liberal-democratic state and capitalism, they argued, had brought humanity to its desired end. It was "the best of all possible worlds." Over the last decade terrorism, war, and political and economic strife have called this overconfident expectation into question. Enlightenment philosophies, neoliberal political policies, communist and capitalist economies, and imperial military powers have all failed to produce a secular kingdom of God. Humanity, having thrown off the traces of traditional religion, is now left to its own devices and finds itself at the brink of several disasters. Perhaps it is time to reconsider the ancient expectation of God's judgment and the restoration of his creation.

REINTERPRETING ESCHATOLOGY

Over the centuries Christians sought by various means to preserve the Christian faith while denying, ignoring or reinterpreting the eschatological expectations of Jesus and the early church. Two major options for the reinterpretation of eschatology emerged. One focused on the individual; the second focused on the state or the culture or both. These attempts at reinterpretation of the Christian hope entered the secular vocabulary stripped of their biblical and theological settings.

Option one: There is no second coming, only a spiritual renewal of the individual. As suggested above, biblical eschatology never did sit well with some folks. Perhaps the Corinthian believers uncomfortable with the "resurrection of the dead" (see 1 Cor 15:12) thought some sort of spiritual resurrection had already occurred. As suggested above, many Greeks would have found the notion of the resurrection of the body distasteful. Perhaps these Corinthians preferred no eschaton, no resurrection of the body, and no new heavens and new earth. Perhaps they thought Jesus was already present, had

---

[1]See Francis Fukuyama, *The End of History and the Last Man* (New York: Free Press, 1992).

already come, spiritually. Perhaps they imagined the world was already spiritually transformed to those who had eyes to see. They were evidently looking not for a new heaven and a new earth but for a more spiritual and certainly less physical existence. Perhaps among this crowd were Hymenaeus and Philetus "who have swerved from the truth by claiming that the resurrection has already taken place" (2 Tim 2:18). Since the resurrection was essential to the restoration and judgment of the last days, this amounted to a denial of the coming of Jesus and the final restoration of the earth.[2]

Although many modern Christians would not put it as those ancient Corinthians did, there are plenty who think this is the only world there is or will be. Jesus is not coming back. There is no new heaven and new earth coming. There is only the spiritual renewal of the individual and perhaps, for some, the expectation of "going to heaven when you die."[3] Others may hope to be absorbed into divinity in some way and transcend this grubby earthly existence. It could be argued that all secular attempts at self-realization and psychological healing reflect this hope of personal spiritual renewal or self-transcendence.

Option two: There is no second coming; the eschaton is fulfilled within history by human instrumentality by means of the state, the culture or various means of social improvement. Once the Roman Empire had accepted the church and the emperor himself was a Christian, it was difficult to speak of the judgment and destruction of powers and authorities or of the empire as the whore of Babylon. Not only would the church's imperial masters frown on this, but the bishops were now part of the powers and authorities themselves. Eschatological expectations needed to be tempered by political realities. The kingdom of God would not come via the coming of God and the judgment of the powers and authorities but, in fact, would be accomplished through those powers. The expected fulfillment would be accomplished through the cooperation of the church with its imperial partner. Eschatology was replaced by ecclesiology, the kingdom by the church. Theologian Jürgen Moltmann calls this "culture Christianity." It is Christianity "cut

---

[2]Jürgen Moltmann, *The Coming of God: Christian Eschatology*, trans. Margaret Kohl (Minneapolis: Fortress, 1996), pp. 20-21.

[3]N. T. Wright, *Surprised by Hope: Rethinking Heaven, the Resurrection, and the Mission of the Church* (New York: HarperOne, 2008), pp. 17-20.

adrift from early Christianity."[4] This is the logic of any church that has linked itself to the fate of a particular nation, culture or power.

This adaptation produced a kind of secular eschatology. God's kingdom would be brought to the world by the civilizing impulses of Western society, by the spread of democracy, by the enhancements of technology, by universal education or by capitalism or communism. Or the kingdom would be produced by improving social conditions, by ensuring that the hungry were fed, the poor employed and the oppressed set free. Nation-states took up the mantle of God—a God whose existence, in the case of communism, they denied. It was not the coming of God that would set things right, but the maturity of humanity. For the late nineteenth-century progressives this was an inevitable process, as unstoppable as the motion of the planets and the process of evolution. Though long discredited, this secular eschatology is still with us. Every four years in the United States our political parties nominate a new candidate for a messiah who will lead us to the new age of prosperity and power. The language and vision are frequently explicitly religious and founded on a long-forgotten expectation of God's intent to finally set the world right.

These options exist in a variety of forms and are all sub-Christian. "Christian eschatology," Moltmann writes, "teaches hope not only for the soul—the word used for existence in earlier times—but also for the body; not only for the individual but also for the community; not only for the church but also for Israel; not only for human beings but also for the cosmos."[5] Christian hope cannot be individualized or politicized. It cannot be reduced to social or personal improvement. Christian hope is not for some sort of merely spiritual presence of God or a merely spiritual personal renewal. Christian hope is for the coming of God to raise the dead, to judge and restore the earth. Anything else, as Moltmann insists, disconnects the church from early Christianity and from Jesus himself.

THE COMING OF GOD IN THE OLD TESTAMENT

The burden of the prophets was to warn and encourage Israel via the promise of the coming of God. As we saw above, Israel—battered and forlorn, her

---

[4]Moltmann, *Coming of God,* p. 10.
[5]Ibid., p. 21.

land desolate, her cities pillaged—would be, the prophets insisted, renewed and restored. Her Gentile enemies, once so powerful, would be humiliated. Her God, no longer the tribal deity of a minor people, would be seen as the Lord of all the earth. Once-proud kings would bow before him, once-powerful armies would lay down their weapons, the implements of war would be retooled for farming, and the gleaming city of Jerusalem would become the center of the world.

"When I restore the fortunes of Judah and Jerusalem," Joel records, "I will gather all the nations and bring them down to the valley of Jehoshaphat, and I will enter into judgment with them there, on account of my people and my heritage Israel" (Joel 3:1-2). This is "the day of the LORD," a time of judgment when "the sun and the moon are darkened, and the stars withdraw their shining" (Joel 3:14-15). It is the time of the coming of God:

> The LORD roars from Zion,
>> and utters his voice from Jerusalem,
>> and the heavens and the earth shake.
> But the LORD is a refuge for his people,
>> a stronghold for the people of Israel. (Joel 3:16)

The God of Israel makes his home "in Zion, my holy mountain" (Joel 3:17). "Judah shall be inhabited forever," God promises, "and Jerusalem to all generations" (Joel 3:20). Israel's enemies will be subjected and its future in the land made secure:

> The mountains shall drip sweet wine,
>> and the hills shall flow with milk,
> and all the stream beds of Judah
>> shall flow with water;
> a fountain shall come forth from the house of the Lord
>> and water the Wadi Shittim. (Joel 3:18)

The postexilic prophet Zechariah foresaw "a day . . . coming for the LORD" when Israel's God "will go forth and fight against those nations as when he fights on a day of battle" (Zech 14:1, 3). The people of Israel will not do the fighting. The LORD and his holy ones will route their enemies. "On that day," the vision continues, "living waters shall flow out of Jerusalem, half of them to the eastern sea and half of them to the western sea; it shall continue in summer as in winter" (Zech 14:8). In such an arid land this "living water" assures Israel of a constant fruitful harvest and a secure food supply. In that day, "the LORD will become king over all the earth; on that day the LORD will be one and his name one" (Zech 14:9). Israel's former Gentile oppressors "shall go up year after year to worship the King, the LORD of hosts, and to keep the festival of booths" (Zech 14:16).

Many years before, Isaiah had promised,

"Here is your God.
　He will come with vengeance,
with terrible recompense.
　He will come and save you."

Then the eyes of the blind shall be opened,
　and the ears of the deaf unstopped;
then the lame shall leap like a deer,
　and the tongue of the speechless sing for joy.
For waters shall break forth in the wilderness,
　and streams in the desert;
the burning sand shall become a pool,
　and the thirsty ground springs of water. (Is 35:4-7)

Earlier in the prophecy (though perhaps later chronologically), the prophet had declared that God would make a great feast for "all peoples," "wipe away the tears from all faces" and "swallow up death forever" (Is 25:6-8). Seeing all this, Israel's people will say,

This is our God; we have waited for him, so that he might save us.
This is the LORD for whom we have waited;
　let us be glad and rejoice in his salvation. (Is 25:9)

Such passages could be multiplied. Israel was waiting for God. When God came, Israel's enemies would be subdued. Israel's land would flourish. Israel's people would be safe, and all people would worship Israel's God. Some passages suggest God will use a scion of David's house to effect his victory and secure his rule: "I will set up over them one shepherd, my servant David, and he shall feed them: he shall feed them and be their shepherd" (Ezek 34:23). In Ezekiel, as in the other prophecies, God will cause the land to flourish and be fruitful: "I will send down the showers in their season;

they shall be showers of blessing. The trees of the field shall yield their fruit, and the earth shall yield its increase" (Ezek 34:26-27).

Ezekiel adds an important codicil to these predictions. Not only will the land be renewed, but the people themselves will be transformed: "I will sprinkle clean water upon you, and you shall be clean from all your unclean-nesses, and from all your idols I will cleanse you. A new heart I will give you, and a new spirit I will put within you; and I will remove from your body the heart of stone and give you a heart of flesh" (Ezek 36:25-26). Not only will God's people be renewed and cleansed, but "I will put my spirit within you, and make you follow my statutes and be careful to observe my ordinances" (Ezek 36:27). Ezekiel 37 is the great vision of the valley of dry bones. The prophet sees Israel's bleached-white bones restored to life by the very breath of God. The land will flourish, and the people as a whole will be renewed and restored to life by the very spirit of God.

When a young Galilean carpenter began his work of teaching, healing and making disciples, the people of Israel had suffered under a string of imperial masters: Babylon, Persia, Greece and then Rome. The people were still waiting for God. They were looking to Jerusalem, to Mount Zion, to Herod's gleaming temple with hope. Some anticipated a Davidic messiah who would rally Israel against its enemies. Jews as far west as Spain and as far east as Babylon were looking forward to gathering on Mount Zion to worship their God. Some were waiting patiently. Some were trying to force the hand of God. And then one sabbath this young carpenter made his way home to worship at his hometown synagogue.

JESUS AND THE EXPECTATIONS OF ISRAEL

Jesus took the scroll of Isaiah and unrolled it. He read:

> The Spirit of the Lord is upon me,
> > because he has anointed me
> > > to bring good news to the poor.
> He has sent me to proclaim release to the captives
> > and recovery of sight to the blind,
> > > to let the oppressed go free,
> to proclaim the year of the Lord's favor. (Lk 4:18-19)

Surely, as he read several passages from Isaiah's great prophecy, there echoed in the minds of many in the assembly the promises of the coming of God, the setting right of the world and the blessing of God's people. Jesus handed the scroll back to the attendant and sat down to teach: "Today," he declared, "this scripture has been fulfilled in your hearing" (Lk 4:21). He did not say, "soon this scripture will be fulfilled" or "someday this scripture will be fulfilled," but *today*. It seems clear that he was claiming the role of anointed messenger of God. It could be argued that he was telling them that in him God had already arrived. When he healed the sick, restored the sight of the blind, cleansed lepers and preached good news, he was doing the very work of God.

N. T. Wright has argued cogently that Jesus' life and ministry were the fulfillment of the story of Israel. In *How God Became King* he writes, "The point the gospel writers are eager to get across—that the life, death and resurrection of Jesus is in fact the climax of the story of Israel, even though nobody was expecting such a thing and many didn't like the look of it when it was presented to them—is something that like the risen Jesus himself, is visible to the eye of faith."[6] The coming of Jesus, in other words, is the promised coming of God. "The radically new thing God did was nevertheless the thing he'd always promised, the thing for which they'd always most deeply hoped and prayed."[7] God's people were being gathered, healed, cleansed and made new. God's kingdom was at hand. God would be in the midst of his people as he promised. But "what the gospels offer us . . . is a God who is in the midst *in and as Jesus the Messiah,* and a God who is then committed to remaining in the midst, through Jesus, in the person of the Spirit. Jesus himself is the new Temple at the heart of the new creation, against the day when the whole earth shall be filled with the glory of God as the waters cover the sea."[8]

Jesus died and rose. His disciples formed a new community. "This temple," Wright writes, "like the wilderness tabernacle, is a temple on the move as Jesus's people go out in the energy of the Spirit to be the dwelling of God in each place, to anticipate the eventual promise by the common and cross-

---

[6]N. T. Wright, *How God Became King: The Forgotten Story of the Gospels* (New York: HarperOne, 2012), p. 77.
[7]Ibid., p. 80.
[8]Ibid., p. 239 (emphasis original).

shaped life and work."[9] Nevertheless, the Romans were still in place in Jerusalem. The emperor was still on the throne in Rome. The Jews rebelled in the late 60s A.D. and were crushed by the legions under Titus. Jerusalem was razed, and the great temple of Herod, so recently completed, destroyed. Visitors to Jerusalem today can still see piles of rubble from the Temple Mount thrown to the streets below by the Romans. In the second century a second rebellion under a messianic pretender was quelled by Emperor Hadrian, and the city of Jerusalem was once again leveled.

How is this to be understood? If Jesus was the fulfillment of Israel's story, if Israel's God had arrived with Jesus and God's Spirit was present in his healing and exorcising, why was Jerusalem a ruin and why were God's people scattered and defeated once again? John the Baptist had evidently wondered about this. Jesus seemed to be doing the work of the Messiah, but there was John, rotting in Herod's prison. "Are you the one who is to come, or are we to wait for another?" John asked (Mt 11:3). Jesus responded by paraphrasing Isaiah 35: "the blind receive their sight, the lame walk, the lepers are cleansed, the deaf hear, the dead are raised, and the poor have good news brought to them" (Mt 11:5). Yes, Jesus seems to be saying, I am the one. I am doing the work of God, the work God promised to do when he came to renew and restore. But John could be excused if he wondered why, this being true, he was still in prison and facing death! Jesus' ministry was—and was not—what he expected. The kingdom had been inaugurated. When would the coronation of God as king finally occur?

THE COMING OF THE SON OF MAN: THE OLIVET DISCOURSE

Mark 13 and its parallels in Matthew and Luke have occasioned enormous debate among biblical scholars over the last 150 years or so. Some have seen this passage as the key to unlocking Jesus' understanding of his mission and God's plan for the future. Others have insisted Jesus never said these words at all. Certainly the Evangelists saw Jesus' warnings and predictions as enormously important. In what follows, I will argue that Jesus spoke these words for the benefit of his contemporaries but that they continue to speak a word of challenge and hope to disciples of Jesus today. They also speak

---

[9]Ibid.

to how the coming of God coincides with the coming of Jesus.

To understand Mark 13 and parallels, an even more difficult and controversial prophecy must be explored. Jesus alludes at least twice to the book of Daniel in the discourse. In Mark 13:14 he alludes to the "desolating sacrilege" (NRSV) or the "abomination that causes desolation" (NIV). This is a citation of Daniel 9:27 in the prophecy of the seventy weeks. In Daniel's context, this is likely a reference to the desecration of the temple by the Greek king Antiochus IV in the second century B.C. Luke takes Jesus' allusion to be a reference to the destruction of Jerusalem in A.D. 70. He changes the "desolating sacrilege" in Mark to "Jerusalem surrounded by armies" (Lk 21:20). Jesus warns that a fierce time of suffering will break out in connection with this event. He tells "those in Judea" to "flee to the mountains" (Lk 21:21). During the Jewish revolt, this is exactly what the early Christians did. They clearly understood Jesus' prophetic warning to refer to the crisis of the Jewish rebellion and its suppression by the Romans.

After his warning about the great time of suffering, Jesus declares: "In those days, after that suffering,

> the sun will be darkened,
>> and the moon will not give its light,
> and the stars will be falling from heaven,
>> and the powers in the heavens will be shaken.

Then they will see 'the Son of Man coming in clouds' with great power and glory. Then he will send out the angels, and gather his elect from the four winds, from the ends of the earth to the ends of heaven" (Mk 13:24-27). Jesus first quotes from Isaiah 13, from a prophecy against Babylon. The references to wonders in the sky seem to be a dramatic way of speaking about the coming judgment of God. As N. T. Wright has cogently argued, this is not a reference to the end of the world but a dramatic way of referring to the coming of God to set the world right.[10] In this case it is the Son of Man who is coming. This is Jesus' second allusion to Daniel, this time to Daniel 7.

Daniel 7 describes a dream of Daniel's in which four great beasts rise out of the sea. "The first was like a lion and had eagles' wings"; "another beast

---

[10]N. T. Wright, *Jesus and the Victory of God*, vol. 2 of *Christian Origins and the Question of God* (Minneapolis: Fortress, 1996), pp. 354-60.

appeared, a second one, that looked like a bear"; and "another appeared, like a leopard" with four wings and four heads. Finally, a fourth beast appeared "terrifying and dreadful and exceedingly strong. It had great iron teeth and was devouring, breaking in pieces, and stamping what was left with its feet" (Dan 7:4-7). This passage is parallel to the great vision of Nebuchadnezzar in Daniel 2. In that dream there are not four beasts but four segments of a great statue: gold, silver, bronze and iron. These visions have been variously interpreted, but it seems from a comparison of Daniel 2, 7 and 8 that the prophet is referring to the imperial might of Babylon, Media, Persia and Greece. In Daniel 8 the final kingdom is clearly Greece, depicted as a male goat.

Jesus quotes from the climax of the vision (see Mk 13:24-27). "Thrones were set in place, and an Ancient One took his throne, his clothing was white as snow" (Dan 7:9). Obviously, this is God taking the place of judgment. The "beast was put to death," and the other beasts had their dominion removed (Dan 7:11-12). And then,

> I saw one like a human being [literally "son of man"]
> 	coming with the clouds of heaven.
> And he came to the Ancient One
> 	and was presented before him.
> To him was given dominion
> 	and glory and kingship,
> that all peoples, nations, and languages
> 	should serve him.
> His dominion is an everlasting dominion
> 	that shall not pass away,
> and his kingship is one
> 	that shall never be destroyed. (Dan 7:13-14)

A great deal of scholarly ink has been spilled and continues to be spilled over this passage. Some have seen the Son of Man as a reference to the people of Israel, depicted as a human figure rather than a beast. Others have argued the Son of Man is an angelic figure or Israel's Messiah. Lately it has been argued that the Son of Man is a second divine figure alongside the God of Israel![11]

---

[11]See Daniel Boyarin, *The Jewish Gospels: The Story of the Jewish Christ* (New York: New Press, 2012); and Peter Schäfer, *The Jewish Jesus: How Judaism and Christianity Shaped Each Other* (Princeton, NJ: Princeton University Press, 2012).

An equal amount of ink has been spilled over Jesus' use of the phrase Son of Man as a reference to himself. Is this simply a way of speaking of himself as a fellow human being and not an allusion to Daniel at all? After all, God refers to Ezekiel as "son of man" and means nothing more than "human." Or perhaps Jesus is speaking of someone else when he promises the coming of the Son of Man. Some have argued that Jesus said some of the Son of Man sayings, but not others. When he spoke of the suffering of the Son of Man, perhaps he was speaking of himself. But it was the church, it is argued, that created the statements regarding the coming Son of Man. This thicket is too dense to untangle here, but I am convinced that Jesus did speak of himself as Son of Man, did use the phrase as a title and did allude to the book of Daniel. This is not a title likely to be created by the church. It is not found in the Epistles as a title of Jesus and not widely used by early Christians to refer to him. It was Jesus' way of referring to himself and connecting his story with the story of God and his coming with the coming of God.

This being so, what is Jesus referring to in Mark 13:24-27? Is this his so-called second coming? If so, what are we to make of the prediction that "this generation will not pass away until all these things have taken place" (Mk 13:30)? If the reference is to the destruction of the temple in A.D. 70, Jesus is certainly correct. If Jesus is speaking of the coming of God or his second coming as it is conventionally understood, he was clearly in error. Scholars like Albert Schweitzer argued this was exactly the case. Schweitzer thought Jesus expected the end of the world, the resurrection and the judgment of God, to occur in connection with his ministry. In fact, Schweitzer argues, Jesus boldly made his way to Jerusalem and a fatal confrontation with the authorities to force God to act.[12] Faced with the death of his beloved Son, God would surely act to rescue him, punish his enemies and begin the kingdom.

N. T. Wright has argued vigorously against this interpretation of Mark. He insists that Jesus is not predicting his second coming, if by that one means the end of the world. The language Jesus uses is typical apocalyptic imagery. The stars are not really going to fall from the sky (Mk 13:25). In this discourse Jesus is referring, Wright argues, to the "final judgment on the city that has now come," "the great deliverance promised in the prophets"

---

[12]See Albert Schweitzer, *The Quest of the Historical Jesus: A Critical Study of Its Progress from Reimarus to Wrede,* 3rd ed. (London: A. & C. Black, 1954).

and "the vindication of the prophet who had predicted its downfall."[13] When Jesus came to the city of Jerusalem, to the temple itself, God himself had come as the prophets predicted. In Jesus' death and resurrection, his victory over evil and death was secured. The early Christians, Wright argues, understood this: "They announced and celebrated the victory of Jesus over evil as something that had already happened, something that related pretty directly to the real world, their world. There was still a mopping-up battle to be fought, but the real victory had been accomplished."[14]

Wright does not mean that the church itself is responsible for finally bringing in the kingdom. "We do not 'build the kingdom' all by ourselves," he writes, "but we do build *for* the kingdom."[15] Nor does he imply that Jesus will not finally be present to set the world right.[16] He is rather arguing against a view of the return of Jesus that amounts to a world-denying escapism. He is insistent that Jesus is not predicting the end of the world and the escape of his people to heaven. Wright's concern is that such an escapist eschatology undermines the ministry and mission of the church. There is little incentive to work for justice, peace, truth and love since "the present world is doomed to destruction while the chosen few are snatched up to heaven."[17] It also suggests that Jesus' victory over evil was ephemeral or had very few practical implications. This was certainly not the view of the early church.

I have immense respect for Wright and his work. I am in substantial agreement with his interpretation of the life and ministry of Jesus. I must admit, however, that I am not entirely convinced by his interpretation of Mark 13 and passages like 1 Thessalonians 4—a passage I will examine shortly. I do not think it is necessary to argue that Mark 13:24-27 does not refer to the second coming of Jesus in order to oppose the notion of the rapture. Nor do I think it is necessary to deny that Jesus is here referring to his second coming in order to keep him from being wrong about the time of his coming. Jesus actually says two apparently contradictory things in

---

[13]Wright, *Jesus and the Victory of God*, p. 514.
[14]Ibid., p. 659.
[15]Wright, *Surprised by Hope*, p. 143 (emphasis original).
[16]Ibid., pp. 137-45.
[17]Ibid., p. 120.

these verses: "this generation will not pass away until all these things have taken place" (Mk 13:30), and "about that day or hour no one knows, neither the angels in heaven, nor the Son, but only the Father" (Mk 13:32). Jesus seems to affirm in the first statement what he denies in the second: "all these things" will happen in a generation. But, only God knows. So what is Jesus saying? "These things will happen in a generation—but maybe not"? This hardly seems plausible.

In Daniel 3, King Nebuchadnezzar orders everyone in his kingdom to worship a great golden statue on pain of death. In this well-known story, Daniel's three friends, Shadrach, Meshach and Abednego, refuse. Threatened with the "fiery furnace," they tell the king, "If our God whom we serve is able to deliver us from the furnace of blazing fire and out of your hand, O king, let him deliver us. But if not, be it known to you, O king, that we will not serve your gods and we will not worship the golden statue that you have set up" (Dan 3:17-18). The New International Version puts it this way: "the God we serve is able to save us from it [the furnace]. . . . *But even if he does not . . .* we will not serve your gods or worship the image of gold you have set up." I believe this is the baseline for all apocalyptic writers. Every one of them faces the violence of a powerful, hostile force. They face the destruction of their way of life, their way of worshiping and serving God. The apocalyptic writers promise God's deliverance and judgment. God is able to deliver Israel, the early church and the church today out of the hands of enemies and oppressors. That is God's final and ultimate intention. Such deliverance may appear in the current crisis. But in the meantime, even if he doesn't bring about their deliverance, God's people are commanded to be faithful to the point of death.

I would suggest that Jesus is saying something very like this to his disciples: the God you serve is able to deliver you out of the hands of the oppressors. But even if he doesn't—even if the time of final judgment and resurrection does not arrive within your lifetime—you are still to be faithful and confident in God's final purposes. This does not undermine anything Wright says about Jesus' victory over evil in cross and resurrection. It does not mean he is wrong about Jesus' ministry as the fulfillment of Israel's story—Jesus' coming *was* the coming of God. He is certainly correct that in Jesus' death and resurrection the early Christians believed the powers and authorities were defeated and God's kingdom inaugurated. The church's mission is to proclaim that victory and work for that kingdom. Christians are not to wait passively for Jesus to come and snatch them away, but they are to be active in love, grace and hope. But the church still awaits the consummation of that kingdom. This is clear in the letters of the apostle Paul.

PAUL AND THE SECOND COMING

One of the earliest pieces of Christian literature is 1 Thessalonians. It was written long before the Gospels came into their final forms. It reflects Paul's pastoral concerns for his fledgling churches in Greece. Apparently the Thessalonians were thoroughly versed in the expectation that Jesus would come to set things right. Paul, like many if not most Jews of his day, expected a great final resurrection of the dead and had taught the Thessalonians to expect it. Some Thessalonian Christians had died. Evidently, "the Thessalonian Christians were anxious that those who had died before Christ's return would miss out on any final triumphant event."[18] Paul assures them this is not true: "The dead in Christ will rise first. Then we who are alive, who are left, will be caught up in the clouds together with them to meet the Lord in the air" (1 Thess 4:16-17). Upon the *appearance* of Jesus, for that is what the word *parousia* means, he will begin the task of setting the world right. In 1 Thessalonians 5, Paul goes on to encourage the Thessalonian Christians to watchfulness and sobriety in words very similar to Jesus in the Gospels: "But you, brothers and sisters, are not in darkness so that this day should surprise you like a thief" (1 Thess 5:4 NIV).

The image of Jesus meeting the believers "in the clouds" calls to mind the promise of the angel in Acts 1 and the words of Daniel 7, Mark 13 and Jesus' assertion at his trial before the Jewish council that "'you will see the Son of Man seated at the right hand of the Power,' and 'coming with the clouds of heaven'" (Mk 14:62). This is the language of epiphany. Recall that when Jesus is transfigured and has his conversation with Moses and Elijah "a cloud overshadowed them, and from the cloud there came a voice" (Mk 9:7), the voice of God. Wright and others are quite right to argue that these are conventional ways of talking about a dramatic appearance of God and should not be taken with wooden literalness. This reunion in the sky is described

---

[18]Anthony C. Thiselton, *Life After Death: A New Approach to the Last Things* (Grand Rapids: Eerdmans, 2012), p. 98.

in terms of the visit of a dignitary to a city. The populace, including its leaders, would go outside of the city to meet the visiting dignitary and accompany him back to the city.

First Thessalonians 4 has frequently been read as describing a "secret rapture" of the church. According to this view, still very popular among dispensationalists, Christians are removed from earth to heaven just preceding a time of fierce tribulation. In fact, this appearing, this coming, as described in 1 Thessalonians 4, is anything but secret. The Lord will descend "with a cry of command, with the archangel's call and with the sound of God's trumpet" (1 Thess 4:16). This is reminiscent of Jesus' words in Matthew 24:31: "he will send out his angels with a loud trumpet call." Here too there is nothing secret about the coming of Jesus: "the sign of the Son of Man will appear in heaven, and then all the tribes of the earth will mourn, and they will see 'the Son of Man coming on the clouds of heaven' with power and great glory" (Mt 24:30). I have quoted extensively from Matthew 24 to show that these two passages clearly describe the same event. Matthew 24 with its very public "coming" cannot be separated from 1 Thessalonians 4. The latter passage simply does not describe a separate secret rapture of the church—in fact *no* passage in the New Testament does. It describes the very public appearance of Jesus to set the world right—the coming of God in the coming of Jesus.

What occurs in the wake of this appearance, so far as Paul is concerned? In Romans 8 Paul speaks of the "creation itself" being "set free from its bondage to decay." We "who have the first fruits of the Spirit" await our "adoption, the redemption of our bodies" (Rom 8:21, 23). In 1 Corinthians 15 he argues that "flesh and blood cannot inherit the kingdom of God." At the "last trumpet," Paul declares, "the dead will be raised imperishable, and we will be changed. For this perishable body must put on imperishability, and this mortal body must put on immortality" (1 Cor 15:50-53). The kingdom of God that Paul awaits, in other words, is not merely spiritual. It is not eternal life in heaven. It is a fully embodied reality. However our bodies are changed, Paul insists, they are still bodies. Earlier Paul had written that Jesus in "the end" would hand over the kingdom to God the Father, "after he has destroyed every ruler and every authority and power. For he must reign," Paul insists, "until he has put all his enemies under his feet. The last enemy to be destroyed is death" (1 Cor 15:24-26). All of this is reminiscent of the passages from Israel's prophets discussed earlier in this chapter. Paul was looking forward to the reign of God in a new heaven and a new earth when God would be all in all. Paul was anticipating what Joel, Isaiah, Zechariah and Jesus himself anticipated—the new creation.

JOHN'S REVELATION, A NEW HEAVEN AND A NEW EARTH

I will devote all of chapter seven to the book of Revelation, but here I will cite two passages near the end of Revelation that speak to the expectations of the coming of God in Jesus to set things right. In Revelation 19 the prophet sees a rider on a white horse coming with the armies of heaven: "He is clothed in a robe dipped in blood, and his name is called The Word of God" (Rev 19:13). The robe dipped in blood recalls the "Lamb that was slaughtered" of Revelation 5:12. This is clearly a reference to the risen and exalted Jesus. He defeats his enemies with a sharp sword out of his mouth (see Rev 1:16). In other words, the rider defeats the enemies of God with his message—with the *word* of God. He takes up rule as "King of kings and Lord of lords" (Rev 19:16), and as in Zechariah 14 exercises rule over the nations. That the nations are judged but not entirely destroyed is demonstrated by the fact that the "tree of life" in Revelation 22 provides leaves that "are for the healing of the nations" (Rev 22:2). As previously argued, judgment does not mean merely punishment and destruction; it means setting right.

After the great judgment John "saw a new heaven and a new earth; for the first heaven and the first earth had passed away, and the sea was no more. And I saw the holy city, the new Jerusalem, coming down out of heaven from God, prepared as a bride adorned for her husband. And I heard a loud voice from the throne saying,

> See, the home of God is among mortals.
> He will dwell with them;
> they will be his peoples,
> and God himself will be with them;
> he will wipe every tear from their eyes.
> Death will be no more;
> mourning and crying and pain will be no more,
> for the first things have passed away. (Rev 21:1-4)

John here suggests not that we go to heaven but that heaven comes to us. Our destiny is an entirely earthly destiny. We are waiting not to go to heaven when we die but to live in the new heaven and the new earth. This is what occurs at the coming of God, at the second coming of Jesus.

CONCLUSION

God's coming, God's appearing, is about the setting right of God's creation. It is about the unity of all God's people, Jews and Gentiles alike. It will involve all people and the whole creation. It will be a "universal restoration," as Peter put it (Acts 3:21). It must involve time, not simply eternity; earth, not simply heaven. With Moltmann, there is no redemption of human beings without the redemption of nature. There is no new creature without a new creation. But, also with Moltmann, God is at work in history now—and not simply in some distant future. With Wright, the church does not bring in the kingdom but works *for* the kingdom. The church is not the kingdom, but it is the sacrament of the kingdom. Moltmann cites the stunning words of Ernst Bloch: "'For only the wicked exist through their God, but the righteous—God exists through them, and in their hands is laid the sanctification of the Name, the naming of God himself, the God who moves and ferments within us.'" Moltmann concludes, "The fellowship between Christ and God in the process of mutual glorification is so wide open that the community of Christ's people can find a place in it: '. . . that they also may be in us.'"[19] In fellowship with the Trinity, God's people both bear witness to and represent the presence and purposes of God.

The church even now joins God in his work of redeeming and restoring the whole creation with full knowledge that the completion of that great work is his alone at the appearance of our great God and Savior Jesus Christ (Tit 2:13). Without the expectation of the coming of God and the new heaven and the new earth, the church is like the aforementioned luxury car without an engine—impressive perhaps, even beautiful, but powerless and ultimately useless. So what are the church and the world to expect of the coming of God? Speculation is fruitless. The second coming of Jesus may be as sur-

---

[19]Moltmann, *Coming of God*, pp. 333-35.

prising as the first! The church is called to be alert, sober and faithful. Individual Christians are called to be good stewards of the Lord's resources and to keep their lamps trimmed. "The good news must first be proclaimed to all nations" (Mk 13:10).

7

Hope in the Midst of Empire

THE BOOK OF REVELATION IS A CONVENIENT SYMBOL for the ambiguity of Christian hope. There is probably no book so beloved and so despised, so carefully studied and so terribly abused, so routinely obsessed over and so generally ignored. G. K. Chesterton famously observed, "Though St. John the Evangelist saw many strange monsters in his vision, he saw no creature so wild as one of his own commentators."[1] Revelation had detractors from the very beginning. It was a late entry into the canon and, according to early church historian Eusebius, was still disputed by some.[2] The reformers Martin Luther and John Calvin also had their doubts. Luther wrote, "I miss more than one thing in this book, and this makes me hold it to be neither apostolic nor prophetic." So far as Luther was concerned, "Christ is not taught or known in it."[3] Recent critics have been even less restrained in their opinions. D. H. Lawrence called John "a shameless power-worshipping pagan Jew, gnashing his teeth over the postponement of his grand destiny."[4] George Bernard Shaw dismissed the book as "a curious record of the visions of a drug addict which was absurdly admitted to the canon under the title of Revelation."[5]

---

[1]G. K. Chesterton, *Orthodoxy* (New York: Dodd, Mead, 1908), p. 13.

[2]Eusebius, *Ecclesiastical History* 3.23, 25.

[3]For this and more examples, see John E. Phelan Jr., "Revelation, Empire, and the Violence of God," *Ex Auditu* 20 (2004): 66.

[4]Quoted in Harry O. Maier, *Apocalypse Recalled* (Minneapolis: Augsburg Fortress, 2002), p. 47.

[5]Quoted in Leonard L. Thompson, *The Book of Revelation* (Oxford: Oxford University Press, 1990), p. 4.

As I noted in my article "Revelation, Empire, and the Violence of God," Revelation has had detractors from the beginning.

> Revelation *has* been misused terribly. It has been used to foster a dark and paranoid vision of the world. "We" are the people of God oppressed by "them," and "they" deserve anything and everything God can bring upon them. How many violent, secretive groups have seized on John's vision as a warrant for their hatred and fear? Perhaps an even more disturbing aspect of the misuse of Revelation is its appropriation by comfortable middle and upper class western Christians who long ago compromised with the "empire." There is something obscene about such materially comfortable and relatively secure people gleeful over the judgment of others.[6]

In fact, Revelation offers no comfort to the comfortable and complacent. Quite the contrary. It is, if nothing else, a view from below. In Revelation we hear the voices of the martyrs, the oppressed, the fearful and the marginalized. It is easy to be squeamish over the cries for judgment if you reside in a place of power and comfort. But if your home has been burned down, your daughter raped and your son murdered, you may look at things a bit differently. If the rich and powerful keep you from opportunities for work, learning and worship, you may find yourself calling on God to bring them down. As we have seen, the call for God's judgment in the Bible is not simply a call for revenge. It is a call for the world to be set right. It is a call for a world free of oppressors who burn, murder and rape. Revelation is about the victory of God over those very forces of violence, fear and destruction that ravage his people and his world. But, as I will argue, it is not the victory of a violent and bloodthirsty God eager to destroy his enemies. It is the victory of the slaughtered Lamb who delivers his entire world through his word, his love and his cross.

CHARACTERISTICS OF THE BOOK

If you pick up a novel to read, you immediately have certain expectations. First, a novel is a piece of fiction. It may be based on a historical situation and may even include historical figures, but its story is a figment of the author's imagination. Certain kinds of fiction follow certain sets of

---

[6]Phelan, "Revelation, Empire, and the Violence of God," pp. 66-67 (emphasis original).

rules: a mystery normally has a murder at the center of the story and a detective who solves it; a romance has a pair of lovers, initially thwarted, who eventually find their way into each others' arms. These expectations are what we mean when we speak of genre. Different pieces of literature operate on the basis of different sets of rules and different sets of expectations in the reader. So what did the readers of the book of Revelation expect when they picked it up?

Most scholars argue that the genre of Revelation is apocalyptic. The most important scholarly definition of apocalyptic is recorded by John J. Collins:

> a genre of revelatory literature with a narrative framework, in which a revelation is mediated by an otherworldly being to a human recipient, disclosing a transcendent reality which is both temporal, insofar as it envisages eschatological salvation, and spatial insofar as it involves another, supernatural world.[7]

The two clear examples of apocalyptic literature in the Bible are the books of Daniel and Revelation. Daniel is set in the Babylonian and Persian Empires after the fall of Jerusalem (narrative framework). Daniel has dreams and visions and is visited by angels who explain what he has seen in them (revelatory literature and mediation by otherworldly figures). The visions reveal God's intent for his suffering people: victory and defeat of their enemies (supernatural world, eschatological salvation). Similarly, in Revelation John is on the island of Patmos during the time of the Roman Empire when he receives a vision of the risen and exalted Jesus. He is taken to the very throne room of heaven, where he has visions of the slaughtered Lamb and the heavenly worship. He is instructed and led by an angel and shown God's intentions for his suffering and battered people: the judgment of the world and the establishment of a new heaven and a new earth.

Outside of the canons of the Old and New Testaments are many other apocalyptic works. A collection of works under the name of Enoch is perhaps the most famous and important of these works. Both Jews and Christians recorded and explained visions of judgment and salvation in books like *4 Ezra,*

---

[7]John J. Collins, *The Apocalyptic Imagination: An Introduction to Jewish Apocalyptic Literature,* 2nd ed. (Grand Rapids: Eerdmans, 1998), p. 5.

2 *Baruch* and the *Apocalypse of Abraham*.[8] Although they were very different
in their particulars, they shared the characteristics of apocalyptic mentioned
above. They also shared something else: they were composed during a time of
imperial power. According to Anathea E. Portier-Young,

> the first Jewish apocalypses emerged as literature of resistance to empire.
> Empire claimed the power to order the world. It exercised this power through
> force, but also through propaganda and ideology. . . . Resisting imperial dom-
> ination required challenging not only the physical means of coercion, but also
> empire's claims about knowledge and the world. The first apocalypses did
> precisely this.[9]

Although set in the Babylonian and Persian periods, the book of Daniel
is addressed to Jews suffering under the power of the Seleucid kingdom. The
Seleucids were the successors of Alexander the Great and gained power over
Jerusalem and its environs in the second century B.C. In order to consolidate
his empire and put down possible rebellions, Antiochus IV attacked the
religious practices of the Jews and desecrated their temple. These events are
described in 1 Maccabees, a so-called apocryphal book. The outcome of
Antiochus's assault of Judaism was a famous revolt headed by Judas Mac-
cabeus. But Daniel's visions recommend courageous resistance and patient
waiting for a God who will deliver. So far as Daniel is concerned, human
agency is of little value in the face of imperial power. Only God can bring
down the imperial beasts and establish his rule over the earth. I will have
more to say about the historical setting of Revelation shortly, but suffice it
to say here that Revelation similarly addresses a marginal group of people
helpless before a powerful empire—this time Rome. It similarly looks to
God, not human agency, for deliverance. As in Daniel, the imperial powers
are depicted as strange, even grotesque beasts threatening God's people with
compromise and even death.

The initial readers of Daniel and Revelation would not have found the
books strange or bizarre. They were used to the odd (to us) symbolism of
the books. In some ways the beastly symbols functioned for the apocalyp-
tists as political cartoons do for us. They told a story vividly and quickly.

---

[8]For a scholarly treatment of these, see ibid., chap. 7.
[9]Anathea E. Portier-Young, *Apocalypse Against Empire: Theologies of Resistance in Early Judaism*
(Grand Rapids: Eerdmans, 2011), p. xxii.

Daniel used and manipulated imperial symbols of the Near East. Revelation used and manipulated the symbols from Daniel as well as Roman imperial symbolism. The first readers and hearers of these apocalypses would understand that the heavenly trips and angel visitations were ways of asserting God's control over a world that seemed to be under the control of pagan kings and emperors. From the perspective of God, these arrogant powers could be easily swept aside. The earliest readers of apocalypses expected warning, encouragement and hope and found them in these books.

Revelation, however, is not simply an apocalypse. It begins with a series of "letters" to seven churches of Asia Minor—present-day Turkey. These letters are addressed to churches trying to be faithful to God in the midst of enormous cultural pressures to conform. In his wonderful book *Reversed Thunder*, Eugene Peterson argues that John is not a wild-eyed prophet salivating over the destruction of his enemies but a pastor.

> The pastor is the person who specializes in accompanying persons of faith "in the middle," facing the ugly details, the meaningless routines, the mocking wickedness, and all the time doggedly insisting that this unaccountably unlovely middle is connected to a splendid beginning and a glorious end.[10]

Revelation, then, is perhaps surprisingly a book of pastoral care. Just as Daniel addresses Jews under pagan rule and commends faithfulness, not compromise, so John, the wise pastor, begins with warnings and encouragement to seven small churches and their leadership. He commends and rebukes; he warns and instructs. Like Daniel, he calls, as we will see, for faithfulness, not compromise.

Finally, John not only has characteristics of apocalyptic literature and functions as a book of pastoral care; it is a prophecy. It is important to remember, however, that prophecy is not simply about what God is going to do in the future. The prophet warns about what will happen if people do not change their ways. A prophet is also an evangelist. Like Jonah, the prophet cries out warnings, not so that people can tremble in fear at the inevitable but so they can repent and seek the mercy of God. As suggested above, judgment is not simply something God does to people; it is something

---

[10]Eugene H. Peterson, *Reversed Thunder: The Revelation of John and the Praying Imagination* (San Francisco: Harper & Row, 1988), p. 8.

people bring on themselves. This will be richly illustrated in the book of Revelation. Suffice it to say that John wears the mantle of Jeremiah and Isaiah, of Ezekiel and Zechariah. He is a prophet of warning and hope using the tools of apocalyptic to get his message across to both his threatened people and their oppressors.

HISTORICAL SETTING

It seems likely that the book of Revelation was composed during the reign of Emperor Domitian at the end of the first century A.D.[11] The church father Irenaeus (ca. A.D. 180) and other early Christian writers made this claim. Domitian was the son of Vespasian, who had led the armies that crushed the Jewish revolt in A.D. 70 (although it was his elder son, Titus, who completed the destruction of the city of Jerusalem and Herod's temple). Upon the death of Titus, Domitian became emperor and ruled for some fifteen years. According to J. Nelson Kraybill, "coins of the era call Domitian the father of the gods, and Roman contemporaries report he wanted to be addressed as *Dominus et Deus noster* (our lord and god)."[12] Although most scholars doubt Domitian pursued a policy of systematic persecution of Christians, "it is likely that some Christians were caught in the bloodbath that attended Domitian's reign."[13]

Persecution of Christians at this time was likely sporadic and localized. During the reign of Domitian's successor, Trajan, an imperial bureaucrat named Pliny wrote the emperor requesting instructions on how to deal with Christians. This suggests that Pliny was not able to consult a set imperial policy regarding the treatment of Christians. Pliny saw in Christianity little more than an absurd superstition. He was unsure in his letter whether Christians recanting their faith should be spared or whether merely being a Christian was punishable by death:

> I have asked them in person if they were Christians, and if they admit it, I
> repeat the question a second and third time with a warning of the punishment

---

[11]For an imaginative and very helpful re-creation of the social and political world at the time of Domitian, see Bruce W. Longenecker, *The Lost Letters of Pergamum* (Grand Rapids: Baker Academic, 2003).

[12]J. Nelson Kraybill, *Apocalypse and Allegiance: Worship, Politics, and Devotion in the Book of Revelation* (Grand Rapids: Brazos, 2010), p. 131.

[13]Ibid.

awaiting them. If they persist I order them to be led away to execution; for whatever the nature of their admission, I am convinced that their stubbornness and unshakeable obstinacy ought not to go unpunished.[14]

This well illustrates the bland, casual brutality of the imperial powers.

Pliny's strategy for discovering the true Christians was to require them to make an offering to the image of the emperor. This was something a true Christian, he had been told, would never do. A follower of the Lord Jesus could not at the same time claim the emperor as lord and god. Those who did were released.[15] This was exactly the sort of compromise John feared the Christians of Asia Minor were about to make. According to Michael Gorman,

> these believers were faced with hard questions and decisions. Should they continue to participate in social activities that have a pagan . . . religious character? This would include most activities: watching or participating in athletic and rhetorical contexts; buying and eating meat in the precincts of pagan temples; and frequenting trade guilds, clubs and events in private homes.[16]

Perhaps their most serious question was, "Should we acknowledge the sovereignty of the emperor when asked to do so at a public event in the precincts of his temple, or at another of the many events in his honor?"[17] Some early Christians evidently saw these as meaningless patriotic gestures or civic duties that did not compromise their Christian faith. John clearly thought otherwise.

John saw such participation in the imperial cult as idolatry. He called on the churches of Asia Minor to reject such compromises even if it led to persecution and death. Cried a voice from heaven,

> Come out of her, my people,
> so that you do not take part in her sins,
> and so that you do not share in her plagues. (Rev 18:4)

This would not be easy. The "beast" would require "all, both small and great, both rich and poor, both free and slave, to be marked on the right hand or

---

[14]Cited in Kraybill, *Apocalypse and Allegiance*, p. 76.
[15]Ibid., p. 77.
[16]Michael Gorman, *Reading Revelation Responsibly: Uncivil Worship and Witness: Following the Lamb into the New Creation* (Eugene, OR: Cascade, 2011), pp. 31-32.
[17]Ibid., p. 32.

the forehead, so that no one can buy or sell who does not have the mark"
(Rev 13:16-17). Some scholars think this is an allusion to the documents
provided to those who freely participated in the imperial cult. Without
proof they had made an offering to the emperor, Christians could be cut out
of the economy and marginalized within the society. And if they fell into the
hands of an officious imperial servant like Pliny, they could lose their lives.

It is easy to see why believers in Asia Minor would try to find ways to
work around the requirements of both empire and church. It is difficult not
to sympathize with their plight. A refusal to sacrifice to the emperor could
result in a loss of business, trade, home and place in society. John was asking
them to do something extremely difficult. It seemed to guarantee suffering
one way or another. Poverty, homelessness and alienation seemed to await
them. Like John himself, they could end up banished or even killed.

This remains an enduring challenge for the Christian church. "The apparent power brokers in every generation—whether in government, social
circles, religious institutions, or professional guilds—sometimes ostracize
or slander followers of the Lamb."[18] Our nations, our employers and our
professions frequently demand loyalty that belongs to God alone. At the
beginning of the Third Reich in Germany a group of courageous Christians
gathered to declare in writing their commitment to Jesus alone. The so-
called German Christians had been thoroughly compromised by the Nazi
government. But the Confessing Church refused to buckle under government pressure. In the Barmen Declaration they insisted, "We repudiate
the false teaching that there are areas of our life in which we belong not to
Jesus Christ but another lord, areas in which we do not need justification
and sanctification through him."[19] Many of them lost jobs, homes and
freedom. Some lost their lives. John would have approved.

INTERPRETIVE APPROACHES

It is not unusual for a devoted fan of a novel to visit the places where things
"happened" in his or her favorite story. Fans of Sherlock Holmes want to track
down 221B Baker Street. Swedish entrepreneurs will take you on a tour of the
places associated with Lisbeth Salander and Mikael Blomkvist of *The Girl*

---

[18]Kraybill, *Apocalypse and Allegiance*, p. 79.
[19]*The Covenant Hymnal: A Worshipbook* (Chicago: Covenant Publications, 1996), selection 885.

with the Dragon Tattoo fame. Most fans obviously know the stories are fiction and are seeking out the locations for fun. But occasionally a preteen will be convinced that a letter from Hogwarts is coming for him or that vampires are threatening her. To imagine that a fictional tale is real is to misread the text—to read fiction as fact. Similarly, comedians like Garrison Keillor or David Sedaris tell stories that are perhaps based on actual events but are significantly exaggerated for effect. Neither would want you to press the details too closely. To imagine that their stories occurred exactly as they told them is to seriously misunderstand the genre of comedy. We expect accuracy from a reporter or a witness in court, but not from a comedian.

A work of historical scholarship operates by a different set of rules from those of a historical novel. A geography textbook serves a different purpose from a travel guide even though both cover the same territory. As stated before, different genres operate under different rules. This is true in the Bible. For example, the wise reader of the Bible differentiates the purposes of different sorts of texts. Legal texts and wisdom texts, for example, are very different. When the Ten Commandments assert, "You shall not murder," the meaning is straightforward and unambiguous. That is the nature of law. The book of Proverbs, however, contains wisdom, not law. It offers good advice and is clearly situational. This is well illustrated in Proverbs 26. Proverbs 26:4 declares, "Do not answer fools according to their folly, or you will be a fool yourself." But Proverbs 26:5 continues, "Answer fools according to their folly, or they will be wise in their own eyes." Well, which is it? The answer, of course, is it depends. The wise woman or man will know in a given situation how to address a fool. To try to make law out of wisdom is to misinterpret and misapply it.

How, then, does one interpret apocalyptic? How is one to read and understand John's great revelatory text? I have already suggested that in addition to elements of apocalyptic it has characteristics of pastoral letters and prophecy. This makes interpreting and applying the text a complex and challenging task. Nevertheless, one thing is clear. *Revelation should be read as a first-century document within a first-century historical and literary context.* It should be interpreted according to the "rules" of the genre apocalyptic and in keeping with the purposes of the author and the nature of his intended audience. If these observations had been followed from the beginning, John's great vision would not have suffered so cruelly at the hands of its many interpreters.

According to Michael Gorman in his highly recommended book *Reading Revelation Responsibly,* there have been "five interpretive strategies" for reading Revelation.[20]

The predictive approach. Over the centuries the predictive approach has been the most common. Revelation is deemed to refer to events still future to the contemporary readers of the book. As Gorman observes, "Throughout the centuries, many Christian interpreters have seen the fulfillment of the tribulations, the millennium and/or the figures in Revelation in their own time or the very near future."[21] Hardly a century has passed without someone suggesting that this or that crisis is the final crisis or that this or that political or military figure is the beast predicted by Revelation. There is something quite wrong and something quite right about this. It is quite right to look on our days as possibly the last days. It is quite right to say that in the midst of our current crisis we should, as John recommends, remain faithful, trust God and anticipate his deliverance—just as the Hebrew children did before the fiery furnace. But expectations of God's deliverance in the current crisis should always be tentative and humble. Remember that Shadrach, Meshach and Abednego said they would not bow down to the king's idol even if God did not deliver them (Dan 3:16-18). They were delivered—but they were prepared to die. Miroslav Volf has argued that apocalyptic is about the future of "yesterday, today, and tomorrow."[22] It speaks *to* every age but not exclusively *of* any age. The book of Revelation is addressed to its own time and people. It is not predicting detailed events in the distant future. And yet, its prophetic message and warnings are profound and enduring. And at least in one regard it clearly is speaking of future events: the coming judgment and restoration of the world. But if Revelation only spoke of specific events coming in the twenty-first (or twenty-fifth, for that matter) century it had little significance to its original readers. It must be to and for its contemporaries to have significance for us as well.

---

[20]Gorman, *Reading Revelation Responsibly,* pp. 64-68.
[21]Ibid., p. 65.
[22]Miroslav Volf, "After Moltmann," in *God Will Be All in All: The Eschatology of Jürgen Moltmann,* ed. Richard Bauckham (Edinburgh: T & T Clark, 1999), p. 253.

The preterist approach. This leads to the second interpretive approach, what Gorman calls the "preterist" approach, or perhaps more helpfully can be described as the "contemporary historical" approach. In this approach John is not predicting the Islamic threat to early modern Europe or a coming worldwide government controlled by the United Nations in the twenty-first century. He is rather referring to the very contemporary power of imperial Rome, one of the most successful, brutal and seductive empires of all time. According to this view, John was anticipating not thousands of years of church history and fulfillment in some distant millennium but the immediate intervention of God in the midst of Roman imperial oppression. Scholars who read Revelation as an interesting historical document providing insight into early Christianity and nothing else follow this approach. Having said this, there are scholars who read and interpret Revelation in its first-century Roman imperial setting but insist the book has enduring theological and even predictive significance. John was writing for his contemporaries as Isaiah, Jeremiah, Daniel and Jesus were writing for or speaking to theirs. But their messages of warning and hope obviously have enduring authority and significance. Nearly every modern interpreter uses the historical/contemporary approach as a base. But from this common base their approaches are frequently very different.

The poetic or theopoetic approach. The third approach Gorman calls poetic or theopoetic. He notes that it goes by many other names: idealist, spiritual, non-historical, timeless or transtemporal.[23] According to these views, the book describes the ageless struggle between the kingdom of light and the kingdom of darkness. No particular events are described or anticipated. Rather, these are struggles and judgments of Christians in every era. The church continuously meets and defeats demonic forces. Revelation offers encouragement and hope in the midst of the battle. Some interpreters anticipate a final consummation. Others do not. There is something profoundly true about this approach, but unless it is connected with the preterist approach, it can turn the book into a collection of meaningless and easily manipulated symbols. John clearly believed his symbols were connected to concrete reality. They cannot be made to mean whatever the

---

[23]Gorman, *Reading Revelation Responsibly,* p. 67.

modern interpreter wants them to mean. But they can be fruitfully used according to the principle of analogy. Since Revelation was first read, there have been many imperial beasts oppressing and seducing God's people. The warnings and encouragement of John can be fruitfully used to endure the more contemporary beasts. This is made clear in the fourth approach.

The political or theopolitical approach. Gorman's fourth approach is called political or theopolitical. This school of interpreters sees the book "as a document of comfort and (especially) protest."[24] Oppressed people in South Africa, Latin America and the United States have used Revelation to criticize imperial abuses, attack injustice and anticipate transformation. This obviously fits with the origins and purposes of ancient apocalyptic. Daniel anticipated the fall of Seleucid imperial power. John looked for the collapse of "Babylon"—his term for imperial Rome. Political approaches make analogies between the situation of ancient Jews and Christians under the abusive power of Rome and contemporary Christians confronted by military juntas in Latin America or dictatorial governments wherever they are found.

The pastoral-prophetic approach. Gorman calls the final approach pastoral-prophetic. Obviously this approach may be used with nearly all of the interpretive approaches already discussed. Drawing from the seven letters and other prophetic warnings in the book, interpreters committed to the pastoral-prophetic approach see the book "as a document of Christian formation designed to call the church to faithfulness in the face of inevitable conflicts with hostile powers."[25] Eugene Peterson's *Reversed Thunder* is a wonderful example of this approach.

Each of these interpretive approaches contributes to our understanding of the book. The book must be read and interpreted within its first-century context (preterist). Christian interpreters must allow for a future consummation (predictive or futurist). Christian interpreters must also allow for and cultivate interpretations that speak to the current social, moral and political crises (poetic, political, pastoral). The skillful interpreter of the book of Revelation steeps himself or herself in the first-century literary, historical and political setting of John and his contemporaries. Trusting in the Scriptures' authority and power, such interpreters will reflect on the analo-

---

[24]Ibid.
[25]Ibid., p. 68.

gies and connections between their time and John's, between the past and the present, believing that the God speaking at the end of the first century is speaking now as well. The secular or imperial state and its servants in the wider culture will always seek to compromise believers. They must always resist the mark of the beast in any and every century. In the modern era, the state or the economy has frequently been deified. Our loyalties continue to be subverted by the promise of material comfort and physical protection. Revelation powerfully reminds us of the dangers of such compromise and calls us to faithfulness.

THEOLOGY OF THE BOOK OF REVELATION

There is not space in a brief chapter to offer a detailed commentary on this complex book. While there are many fine scholarly commentaries, for readers looking for a succinct overview of the book I recommend Gorman's *Reading Revelation Responsibly.* Rather than offering an overview of the book here, I will explore some major theological themes. Over the years, when I have been asked for a helpful book on Revelation, I have recommended Richard Bauckham's excellent volume, *The Theology of the Book of Revelation.*[26] Much of the discussion that follows will be drawn from this valuable book.

In his volume *Apocalypse Recalled,* Harry O. Maier calls on North American churches to read the book of Revelation "as Laodiceans." John had denounced the comfortable and complacent church of Laodicea as "neither hot nor cold." "You say," John continues, "'I am rich, I have prospered, and I need nothing.' You do not realize that you are wretched, pitiable, poor, blind, and naked" (Rev 3:16-17). Maier contends, "At the end of Christendom the Christian church exists to insist on the troubling story of the cross and to form this-worldly believers who contribute to and enrich pluralistic society through lives of spirited public witness to the God incarnate in Jesus of Nazareth, who reveals a way of being human on terms other than the insatiable desire for more, military domination and national security."[27] This

---

[26]Richard Bauckham, *The Theology of the Book of Revelation,* New Testament Theology (Cambridge: Cambridge University Press, 1993).

[27]Harry O. Maier, *Apocalypse Recalled: The Book of Revelation After Christendom* (Minneapolis: Fortress, 2002), p. 28.

is necessary because North American Christians, Maier argues, have compromised with the empire. To use John's terms they have "committed fornication" with the "great whore" (Rev 17:1-2). The whore is a symbol for the Roman imperial system that offers wealth, security and comfort— but at a cost. Maier and many others suggest that early twenty-first-century Western Christians have allowed themselves to be seduced by the wealth and brutality of empire and have lost their bearings as followers of the Lamb.

According to Bauckham, "Revelation portrays the Roman Empire as a system of violent oppression, founded on conquest, maintained by violence and oppression. It is a system both of political tyranny and of economic exploitation."[28] The major symbols of Rome are the great prostitute (Rev 17–18) and the beast (Rev 13; 17). "The beast," Bauckham writes, "represents the military and political power of the Roman Emperors. . . .The beast and the harlot are intimately related. The harlot rides the beast ([Rev] 17:3) because the prosperity of the city of Rome at the Empire's expense and her corrupting influence over the Empire rest on the power achieved and maintained by the imperial armies."[29] The empire is characterized by extremes of wealth and poverty, power and weakness, perverse sexuality, and compromised piety. Political and military power was "absolutized" in the "worship of Rome and the Roman emperors."[30]

Before such absolute power and in the face of such wealth and perversity, what can the tiny, vulnerable groups of churches in Asia Minor do? John recognizes that both compromise and despair are possible. Like the Laodiceans, the churches could ape the power, wealth and perversity of the empire. Or they could faithfully endure oppression and even martyrdom that threatened if they did not conform. John's preferences are clear. But what will enable individual Christians and their communities to endure in the face of such fearful violence? Perhaps the key passage in the book is Revelation 5. In Revelation 4 John has been ushered into the divine throne room that is, according to David Aune, a parody of the Roman imperial

---

[28]Bauckham, *Theology of the Book of Revelation*, p. 35.
[29]Ibid., p. 36.
[30]Ibid., p. 37.

court.[31] But instead of seeing an emperor gloriously robed as a god or armored for battle, John "saw between the throne and the four living creatures . . . a Lamb standing as if it had been slaughtered" (Rev 5:6).

The Lamb is a messianic figure, according to Bauckham, "who is to establish God's kingdom on earth by defeating the pagan powers who contest God's rule." But, "John carefully reinterprets the tradition. His Messiah Jesus does not win his victory by military conquest, and those who share his victory and his rule are not national Israel, but the international people of God."[32] The followers of the Lamb participate in the victory not by acts of violence and bloodshed but by witness. "Just as [Rev] 5:5-6 depicts Jesus Christ as the Messiah who has won a victory, but has done so by his sacrificial death, not by military power, so [Rev] 7:4-14 depicts his followers as the people of the Messiah who share in his victory, but do so similarly by sacrificial death rather than by military conquest."[33] The Lamb wins the victory through death and witness. His final victory over the forces of evil will be won by a "sharp sword" coming out of his mouth (Rev 19:15). The Messiah here wins his victory through his word. As Bauckham puts it in his book *The Climax of Prophecy,* "The martyrs conquer not only by their suffering and death as such, but by their faithful *witness* to the point of death (cf. [Rev] 12:11). Their witness to the truth prevails over the lies and deceit of the devil and the beast. For those who reject this witness, it becomes a legal testimony *against* them securing their condemnation. But it also entails a positive possibility: that people may be won from illusion to truth."[34]

Even the dreadful plagues described in Revelation 8 and 9, for example, are not meant to be mere punishment. Rather, Revelation 8 describes the result of environmental degradation and Revelation 9 of war and violence. These are the outcomes of human ignorance and violence and not simply the acts of a vindictive God. In the end, in spite of all this, the people "did not repent of the works of their hands or give up worshiping demons and idols of gold and silver and bronze and stone and wood, which cannot see

[31]David E. Aune, "The Influence of Roman Imperial Court Ceremonial on the Apocalypse of John," *Biblical Research* 28 (1983): 5-26.

[32]Bauckham, *Theology of the Book of Revelation,* p. 68.

[33]Ibid., p. 77.

[34]Richard Bauckham, *The Climax of Prophecy: Studies on the Book of Revelation* (Edinburgh: T & T Clark, 1993), p. 237 (emphasis original).

or hear or walk. And they did not repent of their murders or their sorceries or their fornication or their thefts" (Rev 9:20-21). This suggests the intent of these plagues was to produce repentance and turning back to God. But human beings were so committed to their violent and destructive ways that even brutal suffering brought on by their ways would not turn them to God.

Christians will not win the battle over evil by trying to beat the beast at his own game. The battle is not won by automatic weapons and heavy artillery. In fact, according to Bauckham, "the continuing and ultimate victory of God over evil which the rest of Revelation describes is no more than the working-out of the decisive victory of the Lamb on the cross."[35] John's message is "'Resist!—but by witness and martyrdom, not by violence.' On the streets of the cities of Asia, John's readers are not to compromise but to resist the idolatry of the pagan state and pagan society. In so doing they will be playing an indispensible part in the working-out of the Lamb's victory."[36] Maier warns that violence will always threaten our modern world: "The sheer boredom of consumerism and hence the advent of Nietzsche's 'last man'—the modern citizen consumed with triviality, a slave to the mediocrity of creature comforts—threatens the new world order. So there will always be the temptation to return to 'the first men' of bloody history, if for no other reason than to interrupt our lives of interminable consumerist boredom."[37] It does not take too much imagination to see in our jaded culture the commitment to triviality, shallowness and violence that Maier foresees.

Unfortunately, the church, as John warned, has also been seduced by the consumerist mentality. Obsessed with trivialities, we worship our worship rather than worshiping the slaughtered Lamb. Christians, as fearful of losing our creature comforts as anyone else, put our trust in the Democrats or Republicans, the military or the stock market rather than the God of Abraham, Isaac and Jacob. We put our faith in a variety of experts to solve our medical issues and to deal with environmental threats and economic challenges. If none of these work out, we stuff our ears and refuse to listen to the warnings about our consumptive lives or we vote for the other party in

---

[35]Bauckham, *Theology of the Book of Revelation*, p. 75.
[36]Ibid., p. 92.
[37]Maier, *Apocalypse Recalled*, p. 28.

hopes that we can return to the standard of living we have come to expect. Christians who do this, John would insist, have committed adultery with the great prostitute and already bear the mark of the beast.

CONCLUSION

In the next chapter I will take a closer look at the so-called millennium, the final judgment, and the new heaven and new earth. But suffice it to say, except for this future consummation, Revelation is not a book that describes in detail events still future to us. You should not read Revelation in order to identify the antichrist (a term not used in the book). John did not predict the use of helicopters or nuclear weapons. Rather, he warned Christians in the first century and by extension Christians in every century that the beastly powers of this world will do their best to seduce and destroy God's people. He also warned Christians in the first century and in every century that their power is not found in matching imperial violence with violence— something quickly forgotten when Christians came into power themselves. Rather, their power was and is found in the power of the slaughtered Lamb. They were called, as we are, to suffer, love and bear witness as the Lamb suffered, loved and bore witness. The swords of the first-century Christians were not the murderous short swords of the Roman legions but the word of God and the message of the gospel. For Christians in the Western world I can think of no more challenging and difficult book than Revelation. Perhaps we have been so fascinated with decoding the book because taking it seriously would require us to examine too closely our own compromises and adulteries with the empire.

8

Hope for the Millennium

REVELATION 20:1-10 IS THE ONLY PLACE IN THE BIBLE where a thousand-year reign of Christ over the earth is mentioned. Nevertheless, these few verses have created enduring difficulty and challenge. Their influence is still powerfully experienced in both our religious and our secular cultures. Revelation, it is true, was not the only late-first-century or early-second-century document that anticipated a temporary messianic kingdom. As Richard Bauckham notes, a temporary messianic reign before the last judgment is also found in Jewish apocalyptic writers of the late first century and early second century (2 *Baruch* 40:3; 4 *Ezra* 7:28-29).[1] The passage in 4 *Ezra* declares, "Messiah shall be revealed with those who are with him, and those who remain shall rejoice four hundred years. And after those years my son the Messiah shall die and all who draw human breath." The resurrection and the judgment will follow seven days of "primeval silence." The statement in 2 *Baruch* is much less specific. Messiah's rule will last "until the world of corruption has ended and until the times which have been mentioned before have been fulfilled." John's expectations, however, are more elaborate and their impact much more profound.

John has the martyrs "coming to life" and reigning with Christ for a thousand years. The rest of the dead are not resurrected until *after* the

---

[1]Richard Bauckham, *The Theology of the Book of Revelation*, New Testament Theology (Cambridge: Cambridge University Press, 1993), p. 108. For 2 *Baruch* and 4 *Ezra* see James H. Charlesworth, ed., *The Old Testament Pseudepigrapha*, vol. 1 (New York: Doubleday, 1983).

thousand years. While the devil has been "bound" during these years of the Messiah's rule, at the end of the period he will be released and there will be a final rebellion and judgment followed by the new heaven and the new earth. All this seems clear enough but it is difficult to see how the scenario fits with the eschatological expectations of Jesus and Paul. For John it seems the resurrection is split into two parts—the "martyrs" at the beginning of the millennium and everyone else at the end. This does not seem to be what Jesus expected in Mark 13 and parallels or what Paul expected in 1 Thessalonians 4 and 5. There everyone appears to be resurrected at the same time. Nor does it seem to fit with Jewish expectations of a grand resurrection of the dead followed by the final judgment.

This problem caused many to see the rule of Christ depicted here as the *current* age of the church. The martyrs in this case are ruling with Christ in heaven. Christ in his resurrection and ascension has bound the devil and is ruling through his saints in heaven and on earth. This is often called *amillennialism*—the belief that there is no millennium. The name is not apt. Perhaps this view should be called *realized millennialism* in that by this interpretation the millennium is occurring now. The rebellion, the judgment, and the new heaven and new earth are still to come. There are several difficulties with this view. First, in what sense are the martyrs resurrected? If they are ruling with Christ in heaven, do they already have their resurrection bodies? Has the first resurrection already occurred in some sense in heaven? Elsewhere it seems that resurrection is a phenomenon of earth at the last day. This is complicated by the fact that the word for "resurrect" is not used here but rather the verb meaning "live." The word could be translated "lived" or "came to life." This need not refer to a resurrection at all.

One might also ask about the so-called binding of Satan under this view. That Satan is indeed bound, and evil thereby limited, seems counterintuitive, to say the least. Evil has flourished throughout the history of the church. The twentieth century was the bloodiest, cruelest century of the Christian era and the twenty-first is not starting out any better. If Satan has been bound, the bonds are pretty loose! If this millennium is the fulfillment of the expectations of the prophets, it can only be said to be a severe disappointment. Amillennialists have a variety of explanations for this—each one, in my opinion, more implausible than the last.[2] Finally, it is perhaps not unfair to note that it has been nearly two thousand years since John wrote these words. Having said this, I admit to finding the other millennial views equally troubling.

According to premillennialism, Jesus returns *before* the thousand years. He will indeed rule with his saints over the earth and fulfill the prophecies of the Hebrew prophets. This solves some problems and creates others. By this view the dual resurrection of the dead is still problematic. Will only the martyrs be raised at first? Will the rest of the saints and sinners have to wait until after the thousand years? Again, how does this comport with Mark 13 and 1 Thessalonians 4 and 5? Furthermore, in this view the return of and reign of Christ seem to lack finality. Earlier in Revelation, when Christ returns he defeats his enemies and sets up his kingdom (Rev 19:11-21). Are his enemies really to be reborn after his rule and will there be a second great time of vindication and judgment?

So-called postmillennialism shares some of the same difficulties as the other views. According to this reading, the millennium is brought on by the faithfulness of God's people. The rule of Christ is realized in history as the church proclaims the gospel and lives faithfully. A golden age is experienced as Christ rules through his church. This view motivated many Protestant missionaries in the nineteenth and early twentieth centuries. They saw preaching the gospel and, more problematically, spreading Western civilization as a means to bring in the kingdom. Nevertheless, as in the case of amillennialism, how are we to explain the resurrection of the saints? When did this resurrection occur, and what did it entail? And as in the case of premillennialism, how are we to explain the rebellion *after* the rule of Christ? Postmillennialism raises additional problems and questions I will address later on.

None of the millennial views seems to make sense of the text of Revelation 20 or comport with the eschatological texts in the Gospels and Paul. Throughout history, many have considered Revelation 20 a troublesome outlier. It has seemed to many easier simply to ignore the passage entirely or lamely joke about being a "panmillennialist" believing it will all "pan out in

---

[2]See Stanley J. Grenz, *The Millennial Maze: Sorting Out Evangelical Options* (Downers Grove, IL: InterVarsity Press, 1992), pp. 149-72.

the end." But this would be an error of the first order. In spite of its difficulty, the notion of the millennium has shaped our Christian understanding of the church, the state and the culture in profound ways. We neglect this passage to our peril. Furthermore, as Moltmann has brilliantly argued, without the expectation of an earthly reign of Christ Christianity detaches itself from hope. "Christian theology," he writes, "is not a theology of universal history. It is a historical theology of struggle and hope. It therefore does not teach the secular millenarianism of the present, as does the naïve modern faith in progress. . . . Nor does it teach that in the future everything will get worse and worse, like equally naïve modern apocalypticism."[3] No, Christian eschatology is hope for the reign of Christ over the whole earth and to that extent it is millenarian. Moltmann concludes: "Christian eschatology—eschatology, that is, which is messianic, healing and saving—is millenarian eschatology."[4] But before I explore the hopeful aspects of millenarian eschatology, I will examine, with Moltmann, the misuse of Christian millenarianism.[5]

MILLENNIAL POLITICS

The recovery of a millenarian eschatology that is "healing and saving," to use Moltmann's phrase, comes after a long and disastrous detour. On this detour both church and state co-opted the messianic rule and abused millenarian eschatology for their own purposes. Moltmann argues that "as a consequence of the turn of events under Constantine, the old apocalyptic martyr eschatology was transformed into a millenaristic imperial theology."[6] With first the tolerance of and then the acceptance of the Christian church, the Roman state identified itself with the messianic hopes and millennial expectations of the church. The book of Revelation had seen the Roman state as a beast and a whore doomed for destruction. Now the state was the promoter and protector of the cause of the church. The church went from being the persecuted to being the persecutor.

---

[3]Jürgen Moltmann, *The Coming of God: Christian Eschatology,* trans. Margaret Kohl (Minneapolis: Fortress, 1996), p. 200.
[4]Ibid., p. 202.
[5]For more on the millennial views, see Craig A. Blaising, Kenneth L. Gentry Jr. and Robert B. Strimple, *Three Views on the Millennium and Beyond,* Counterpoints (Grand Rapids: Zondervan, 1999).
[6]Moltmann, *Coming of God,* p. 159.

The early Christian historian and bishop Eusebius of Caesarea even linked Emperor Augustus and Christ: "when the Lord and Savior appeared, and when at the time of his coming Augustus, as the First among the Romans, became Lord over the nationalities, the pluralistic rule by many was dissolved and peace embraced the whole."[7] This would have surprised Christians at the end of the first and beginning of the second century! The universal peace begun under Augustus, Eusebius argued, was finished when Constantine arrived on the scene. Augustus and Christ, empire and church, came together to form the kingdom of God. When the emperor took the cross as his symbol, he completed God's plan of salvation. "Constantine," according to Moltmann, "brings this time of salvation to the peoples of the earth, and himself has messianic significance."[8] Eusebius even sees the coming of Constantine as the fulfillment of Daniel 7:18. "The Roman empire which has now become Christian was itself nothing less than the universal kingdom of Christ."[9] The implications of this move for the future of both church and state were—and are—enormous.

The result, of course, was Christendom—the melding of church and state under the rule of Christ through the ecclesiastical hierarchy on the one hand and the Christian ruler on the other. To resist one was to resist the other and to resist either was to resist God. Ironically, the Christian rulers of Rome and its successor states in Europe became the new caesars, who threatened and oppressed all who refused to conform as the Roman imperial powers had once threatened and oppressed the early Christians. Both Jews and heretics found their freedom circumscribed and their lives at risk. Religious opposition under Christendom was not merely a difference of opinion but a threat to the stability of the empire and akin to treason. With the supposed realization of the millennium in the Roman Empire, and then in the Christian empires and kingdoms of Europe, the need for eschatology came to an end. In fact, eschatology became a threat to the powerful and a tool in the hands of the weak.

During the era of Christendom, eschatology and millennial hopes went

---

[7]Eusebius, *Ecclesiastical History* 3.22.
[8]Moltmann, *Coming of God,* p. 161.
[9]Ibid., summarizing Eusebius.

underground, according to Timothy Gorringe.[10] At times, millennial theology was the purview of "the lunatic fringe of utopian politics."[11] At the same time, eschatological hopes constituted one tool with which the weak could challenge power. The powerful do not look forward to the consummation. They have already arrived. They have already succeeded. They cannot imagine God scattering those who are "proud in the thoughts of their hearts" or bringing "down the powerful from their thrones" (Lk 1:51-52). It is to their advantage to ignore or minimize eschatological hopes and expectations. Gorringe quotes theologian Karl Barth, who denounces such excising of eschatological hope from Christianity:

> A Christianity which is not wholly and completely and without reserve (*restlos*) eschatology has wholly, completely and without reserve nothing to do with Christ. . . . [W]hatever is not hope is wooden, half-baked, shackled, leaden and awkward. . . . It does not liberate but takes prisoner. It is not grace, but judgement and corruption. It is not divine leadership but fate. It is not God but an image of unredeemed human beings.[12]

Christendom dammed up eschatological hope. From a river of life it made a stagnant pool. But the critiques by Mary, Jesus and fierce old John raging against the beast continued (and continue) to burst through to offer hope and new life. Millennial eschatology, both for good and ill, informed and enflamed generations of critics of the powerful and continues to do so to this day.

"It is not 'the Christian world,'" Moltmann writes, "that mediates between church and world; it is the kingdom of God, which the church awaits for itself and the world both. As epiphany of the kingdom of God in history, the church frames the vision of the world's future, and takes it seriously in its dynamic, which is the dynamic of the provisional."[13] The church in its worship and work keeps the vision of the kingdom of God before a battered world. But what happens when the church abdicates this

---

[10]Timothy Gorringe, "Eschatology and Political Radicalism," in *God Will Be All in All: The Eschatology of Jürgen Moltmann,* ed. Richard Bauckham (Edinburgh: T & T Clark, 1999), pp. 87-114.

[11]Ibid., p. 90.

[12]Ibid., p. 96. This is Gorringe's own translation from *Der Romerbrief,* 2nd ed. (Zurich: Theologische Verlag, 1948), p. 413.

[13]Moltmann, *Coming of God,* p. 165.

responsibility? What happens when the church becomes convinced of its own imperial power? What happens to Christianity when, in the words of Moltmann, the power of "the kingdom of God on earth and the Christian empire were represented before God no longer by the holy emperor but by the 'Holy Father'"?[14]

THE IMPERIAL CHURCH

The church had found a secure place in the world when it was recognized by the emperor. But what happens when Roman imperial power begins to disintegrate? How is the millennial rule of a unified empire and church to be understood when Rome, the "eternal city," is sacked and ruled by "barbarians"? While a variety of rulers held on to the pretensions of imperial power (notably the so-called Holy Roman emperor), "the idea of the Christian empire was transferred from the Christian emperor to the pope. From Gelasius I onwards, both the kingdom of God on earth and the Christian empire were represented before God no longer by the holy emperor but by 'the Holy Father,' as *pontifex maximus.* The pope became the successor of both Peter and the Roman caesars."[15] Rome is no longer the great whore and home of the murderous beast but the holy city, and the pope is a benevolent ruler of both church and world. Later popes, with limited success, would claim the right to crown and depose secular rulers and would even lead their own troops in battle.[16]

The implications of this were enormous. The church "ceases to see itself as the struggling, resisting, and suffering church; it is now the church victorious and dominant. It no longer participates in the struggle and sufferings of Christ, but already judges and reigns with him in his kingdom."[17] This Moltmann calls "a millenarian concept of the church."[18] Although the Reformation challenged the papacy and many aspects of Roman Catholic theology and practice, it inculcated in the state churches of northern

---

[14]Ibid., p. 198.
[15]Ibid.
[16]See Paul Johnson, *A History of Christianity* (New York: Touchstone, 1976), pp. 125-26, 274; Diarmaid MacCulloch, *Christianity: The First Three Thousand Years* (New York: Viking, 2010), pp. 363-95.
[17]Moltmann, *Coming of God*, p. 179.
[18]Ibid.

Europe the same notions of the imperial church and retained the links between the church and the state. This is not to say such links remained unchallenged. The imperial church was challenged in the Roman Catholic setting by the monastic orders and in the Protestant setting by the Anabaptists and the Pietists.[19]

Monasticism and Pietism both represented a protest against the structure and vision of the imperial church. The church had morphed from a community to a hierarchy. One could argue that this change began early. The early-second-century bishop Ignatius of Antioch, in letters written on his way to Rome and martyrdom, repeatedly called for obedience and submission of the church to the bishop.[20] As Rome's power grew and its authoritarian structures solidified, Moltmann observes,

> Christian fellowship *in* the church is replaced by communion *with* the church and its head, who represents Christ. . . . The dissolution of the church in the religion of the Christian world, and this elevation of the church to the spiritual rule over the nations are both millenarian dreams. They demand of politics and church more than they can give, and destroy the world.[21]

I repeat that this was not simply a characteristic of the Roman church. Rome was not the only communion with millenarian pretensions. The state churches of Germany, Scandinavia and Great Britain made similar claims to temporal as well as spiritual power. According to Rodney Stark, the result for Protestantism was a flaccid church and an under-evangelized populace.[22] The consequences of such millennial assumptions were disastrous. The church in Germany, linked with the German state and national identity, found itself, with honorable exceptions, incapable of resisting the blandishments of Hitler. And all the state churches of Europe were no match for Enlightenment skepticism on the one hand and material prosperity on the other. Christian faith slipped away in northern Europe as easily and quickly as it was acquired.

The humble, embattled Christian community has always existed

---

[19]MacCulloch, *Christianity,* pp. 312-18, 622-25, 738-47.

[20]Ignatius, *Letter to the Smyrnaeans* 8.1-2.

[21]Moltmann, *Coming of God,* p. 182 (emphasis original).

[22]Rodney Stark, *The Triumph of Christianity: How the Jesus Movement Became the World's Largest Religion* (San Francisco: HarperOne, 2011), pp. 331-32.

alongside and within the imperial church. From the rule and communities of Saint Benedict to the Irish monks in their hide-covered coracles to Saint Francis and his elected poverty to the martyred Anabaptists, slaughtered by Catholics and Protestants alike, the church at the margins has endured. Today it is clear to nearly everyone that the Constantinian era is over. Christendom has come to an end. As Stanley Hauerwas and William Willimon put it, the church has lost its home-field advantage.[23] We are *all* at the margins. This, in my opinion, is a good thing.

The church, in fact, can no longer afford the illusion of millennial rule—an illusion that has compromised its message and sapped its strength. Moltmann argues,

> Before the millennium, there is no rule of the saints. Only in the millennium will the martyrs rule with Christ and judge the nations. Before the millennium, the church is the brotherly and sisterly, charismatic, non-violent fellowship of those who wait for the coming of the Lord and in the power of the Spirit, who is the giver of life, enter into Christ's struggle and bear their cross and his discipleship.[24]

The church in the West must confront its imperial past and its Laodicean present. But the church must also confront dangerous secular millennial illusions spawned by the very collapse of its hegemony. To this secular millenarianism I now turn.

THE SECULAR MILLENNIUM

Postmillennialism, as suggested above, saw a golden age on the horizon. Through the efforts of the church to evangelize, civilize and moralize, the world would turn to God, and the rule of Christ would be realized. Such a view obviously appealed to Christian activists, reformers and missionaries who were convinced, especially in the late nineteenth century, that a world transformation could be effected through their efforts. The twentieth century put a dent in such optimism, to say the least. But postmillennialism was more than a religious phenomenon. As suggested in chapter two, the entire modern project was itself religious, even millennial, in character. For

[23]Stanley Hauerwas and William H. Willimon, *Resident Aliens: Life in the Christian Colony* (Nashville: Abingdon, 1989).
[24]Moltmann, *Coming of God*, p. 184.

many intellectuals, activists, politicians and preachers, advances in technology, economics and politics rooted in human reason and directed toward human good would produce a golden age, indeed, the end of history. Both liberal democratic capitalism and communism could be seen as millennial projects intended to produce human flourishing.

Communism clearly had millennial characteristics. Marx and his heirs believed its coming, like that of Christ, was inevitable. It was part of an unstoppable historical process that would produce a just and prosperous social order. Communists like Lenin thought their violence was simply a way of helping the process along. The eschatological omelet unfortunately required the breaking of a few historical eggs. It would become clear to many devotees of communism that this was, as a famous volume puts it, "the God that failed."[25] The vicious purges of Stalin, the crowded gulags of Siberia, and the poverty and starvation in places like the Ukraine did not point to a golden age. Within less than a century the entire creaky structure of communism collapsed and virtually disappeared.

Communism succeeded early on, according to Tony Judt and Timothy Snyder, exactly because it took on the characteristics of Christian millennial and missionary thinking: "The ultimate purposes of history—attained and understood in the light of the Revolution—became homologous with the immortal soul: to be saved at any price. . . . For decades, it ascribed to 'revolution' a mystery and a meaning that could and did justify all the sacrifices—especially those of others and the bloodier the better."[26] Intellectuals, having abandoned their Christian or Jewish faith, found in communism a vision of the future and a missionary zeal that were entirely familiar. Communism, like the church, was an international community formed around a common purpose and cause. This purpose and cause entailed more than a political party; it was an inevitable process of history. When this god failed, the loss of this meaning and community was most painful.[27]

Liberal democracy and capitalism have never had the religious force of communism. But this is a god also in the process of failure. It is becoming

---

[25]Richard H. Crossman, ed., *The God That Failed*, with 2001 foreword by David C. Engerman (1950; repr., New York: Columbia University Press, 2001).
[26]Tony Judt and Timothy Snyder, *Thinking the Twentieth Century* (New York: Penguin, 2012), p. 96.
[27]Ibid., p. 97.

clearer to many of us that the European and American civilization of expansion is not sustainable. In fact, Moltmann concludes, "the expansion and spread of this culture of domination is accelerating, and in proportion to this acceleration ecological catastrophes in all countries are increasing."[28] In the United States boosters of the American way of life have resolutely refused to acknowledge the dangers of our consumptive lifestyle. "Foolishness on this scale," writes Wendell Berry, "looks disturbingly like a sort of national insanity. We seem to have come to a collective delusion of grandeur, insisting that all of us are 'free' to be as conspicuously greedy and wasteful as the most corrupt of kings and queens."[29] Berry goes on to argue that our "industrial fundamentalism" insists on an economy and lifestyle characterized by "limitlessness." This, Berry points out, is a characteristic of God. "The idea of a limitless economy implies and requires a doctrine of general human limitlessness: *all* are entitled to pursue without limit whatever they conceive as desirable—a license that classifies the most exalted Christian capitalist with the lowliest pornographer."[30]

The inevitable outcome of our greed and wastefulness—its environmental destructiveness and the inevitable hunger, poverty and death that follow—is perhaps reflected in the judgment of the seven trumpets in Revelation 8: a third of the earth is burned up, a third of the sea creatures are destroyed, the waters are poisoned, the earth is darkened and the suffering of humanity is immense. Our faith in our abilities to solve through technology the problems of declining fuel reserves, poisoned groundwater, infertile topsoil and the disappearing ozone layer would be touchingly naive if it were not so disastrous. Communism put its faith in revolution as an inevitable historical process. Liberal democracy and capitalism have put their faith in the imaginary "invisible hand"[31] of the marketplace and the unfettered desires of human beings. Both looked for a golden age. Both sowed to the wind and reaped, or are in the process of reaping, the whirlwind. While the church staunchly opposed the former, it has done little to challenge the latter.

The Bible, however, is not the account of human limitlessness. Quite the

---

[28]Jürgen Moltmann, *Ethics of Hope,* trans. Margaret Kohl (Minneapolis: Fortress, 2012), p. 134.
[29]Wendell Berry, "Faustian Economics," in *What Matters? Economics for a Renewed Commonwealth* (Berkeley, CA: Counterpoint, 2010), pp. 41-42.
[30]Ibid., p. 43 (emphasis original).
[31]This term was coined by eighteenth-century Scottish philosopher Adam Smith.

contrary. The snake appeals to the woman in Genesis and brings about her fall with the allure of limitlessness. It has always been very appealing to human beings to be like God—omniscient and all-powerful. The story of the Bible, however, is the story of proper human limitation. The Torah of Israel provides an account of human limits and divine expectations. The teachings of Jesus, of Paul and, indeed, of the entire New Testament put the lie to the heresy of human limitlessness. A human life, a good life, is a life lived within the parameters given by God. "Our human and earthly limits, properly understood," Berry writes, "are not confinements but rather inducements to formal elaboration and elegance, to *fullness* of relationship and meaning."[32] The gospel is at least in part about accepting our place within creation, within the divine order, and perhaps ironically finding freedom within those boundaries and limitations.

I think this is a particularly difficult message for American Christians. Capitalism and the American way of life have been intertwined with our Christian faith from the very beginning. It seems to some of us that to criticize the one is to attack the other. Even before there was a United States of America there was a sense that this new land (new at least to the European immigrants) was a promised land. Away from the oppressions and limitations of Europe, immigrants could live as they pleased, worship as they pleased and expand as they pleased. The newly formed United States increasingly understood itself as a redeemer nation. It would show the oppressive European monarchies with their corrupt aristocracies the way to liberty and equality. This political message was taken up enthusiastically by religious leaders: "Famous preachers founded seminaries and schools in the newly won West. In his famous address 'A Place for the West,' Lyman Beecher declared that the United States was destined 'to lead the way in the moral and political emancipation of the world' and that the necessary resources could be found in the west of the continent."[33]

Clearly, nineteenth-century America set itself a millennial task. Through the promotion of moral and political emancipation and the celebration of entrepreneurship and individualism a new world order would be produced. It is no diminishment of the genuine accomplishments of American de-

---

[32]Berry, "Faustian Economics," p. 50 (emphasis original).
[33]Moltmann, *Coming of God,* p. 173.

mocracy to suggest that such unquestioning and naive optimism had and has a shadow side. For people on both the left and the right of American politics, freedom has become a kind of shibboleth. In general, conservatives want to be free to do whatever they want with their property. Liberals want to be free to do whatever they want with their bodies. Libertarians, of course, want to be free to do whatever they want with both. Liberals and conservatives believe in some limits—but generally for other people, not for themselves. And no one, it seems, wants to explore too deeply the implications of their freedoms for future generations.

Paul's letter to the Galatians is, in part, an exploration of the tensions between law and freedom. "For freedom Christ has set us free," he wrote. "Stand firm, therefore, and do not submit again to a yoke of slavery" (Gal 5:1). But for Paul freedom did not mean autonomy, and he was certainly not antinomian. He would go on to warn the Galatians, "Do not use your freedom as an opportunity for self-indulgence, but through love become slaves to one another" (Gal 5:13). There were "works of the flesh" to be avoided and "fruit of the Spirit" to be cultivated (Gal 5:19-26). And all of this was to be directed to the common good: "The whole law is summed up in a single commandment, 'You shall love your neighbor as yourself'" (Gal 5:14). Christian freedom is clearly not limitless. We are responsible to and for our neighbors. We are responsible to God and for the proclamation of his will and purpose. Whether we are communist or capitalist, American or German, Western or Eastern, we are not the instruments of millennial accomplishment. Our economic structures, political systems and national boundaries are contingent. The kingdom is God's accomplishment, not ours.

THE COMING OF JESUS AND THE MILLENNIUM

A clear tension exists within the Bible and its interpreters between two understandings of the end. In Matthew 24–25 Jesus speaks of the "'Son of Man coming on the clouds of heaven' with power and great glory." This is followed by a trumpet call and the gathering of the elect (Mt 24:30-31). Subsequently, Jesus illustrates through a number of memorable parables the judgment of the nations and the inheritance of the kingdom by the righteous (Mt 25:31-46). This same scenario appears in 1 Thessalonians 4:13–5:11—the coming of the Lord, the sound of God's trumpet, the gathering of the saints and the judgment of the unrighteous. Although 2 Thessalonians warns of a "lawless one" coming before the consummation, it seems clear that it too anticipates judgment and deliverance to arrive along with Jesus (2 Thess 1:5–2:12). None of these passages seems to anticipate one thousand years of rule by the Messiah followed by yet another rebellion. Nor indeed is there any anticipated rapture of the church.

On the other hand, it is also clear, as discussed above, that neither Jesus nor Paul nor any other New Testament writer anticipated spending eternity in heaven rather than ruling with the Messiah in the new creation. Christians do not believe the immortal soul abandons the body for ethereal existence in the realm of God. Christians, rather, believe in the resurrection of the dead and a new heaven and a new earth. Christians anticipate "the holy city, the new Jerusalem, coming down out of heaven from God, prepared as a bride adorned for her husband" (Rev 21:2). In the end, Christians don't go to heaven; rather heaven comes to them: "See, the home of God is among mortals. He will dwell with them; . . . and God himself will be with them" (Rev 21:3). Jesus and Paul, just like John, believed in the kingdom of God, the rule of God over all the earth through his King and Messiah. All of them believed in a God who makes all things new—even this battered old world. While neither Jesus nor Paul taught anything like the millennial reign of Messiah described in Revelation 20, they certainly believed in such a reign. There is no evidence they thought this reign temporary as John did. But that there would be such a reign, a reign of justice, healing and peace, they had no doubt.

Why is a millennial reign of the Messiah, whether it lasts a thousand years or not, so important to the church even today? First, according to N. T. Wright:

> The classic Christian doctrine . . . is actually far more powerful and revolutionary than the Platonic one. It was people who believed robustly in the resurrection, not people who compromised and went in for a mere spiritualized survival, who stood up against Caesar in the first centuries of the Christian era. A piety that sees death as the moment of "going home at last," the time when we are "called to God's eternal peace," has no quarrel with the power-mongers who want to carve up the world to suit their own ends. Resurrection, by contrast, has always gone with a strong view of God's justice and

of God as the good creator. These twin beliefs give rise not to a meek acquiescence to injustice in the world but to a robust determination to oppose it.[34]

That God will reign and God will judge on this earth makes what happens here all the more important. This was certainly the burden of Jesus' warnings in the famous parables of Matthew 25. It matters whether you clothe the naked, feed the hungry and visit the prisoners. What happens in this world will be accounted for in this world. If you pray "your kingdom come on earth" and live as if it will not actually come on earth and does not matter, you are the living embodiment of hypocrisy.

Second, the reign of Messiah on the earth is critical because it is an affirmation of the creation itself. The fledgling Christian church faced its greatest challenge not from the Roman emperors or pagan or Jewish opponents but from within. According to an ostensible group of Jesus followers who came to be called Gnostics, the creation was an evil place and the body a prison. Their goal was not a new creation and a resurrection body but an ascent to the divine. The actual world, its rivers and trees, its mountains and seas, did not matter and would eventually disappear. But for Paul the creation is not inherently evil but rather "was subjected to futility." He anticipated that one day "the creation itself will be set free from its bondage to decay and will obtain the freedom of the glory of the children of God" (Rom 8:20-21). The Jewish prophets would have agreed.

How we treat other people matters. How we live on the earth matters. To violate another human being is to court God's judgment. To violate God's creation is also to court God's judgment. These two are intimately connected. More than one of the Jewish prophets linked the violation of God's laws with the infertility of the land (see Is 5:8-10; Hag 1:1-11; Mal 3:8-12). If we live in anticipation of the kingdom of God, the rule of the Messiah, and a new heaven and a new earth, we are to live on this earth with justice, love and hope. We are to treat both the land and the people with respect and love. In the last chapter I will explore how the church is to live on the earth in anticipation of the kingdom of God. I will argue that we do not simply passively wait for the kingdom; we actualize the kingdom in our communal life

---

[34]N. T. Wright, *Surprised by Hope: Rethinking Heaven, the Resurrection, and the Mission of the Church* (New York: HarperOne, 2008), p. 33.

and mission. Although postmillennialism was flawed in many respects, it was correct in insisting that the church had the task of living toward the coming rule of God and anticipating that rule in its life on the earth.

Third, the rule of Messiah on the earth is important for its vindication of the prophets of Israel and of the Jews. I dedicate an entire chapter to the biblical importance and eschatological hope of Israel and the Jews, but suffice it to say here that I agree with Moltmann that "the millenarian hope of Christians has maintained a future for Israel *as* Israel."[35] Clearly Jesus, Paul and Revelation's John anticipated the fulfillment of Israel's prophets. They shared the expectations of Isaiah, Jeremiah, Ezekiel and Daniel for the salvation and restoration of Israel and the Jewish people. In the next chapter I will argue that the notion that the church has superseded the Jews as the people of God is a misunderstanding of the New Testament. Something new had clearly occurred in Jesus of Nazareth, but as Paul would insist, "the gifts and the calling of God are irrevocable" and, startlingly, "all Israel will be saved" (Rom 11:26, 29). Without the rule of the Messiah over a renewed earth, we lose the heart of Israel's prophets and potentially the people of Israel themselves.

Fourth, however we work to actualize the kingdom of God in our communities and our lives, the history of the church's cozy and disastrous relationship with the powers, whether political, religious or economic, is a sober warning about compromising the Christian gospel for the sake of ideology. From Constantine to the great state churches of Europe to the postmillennial naiveté of nineteenth-century American Christianity to the contemporary identification of evangelicalism with the Republican Party, the powers have easily seduced us to their purposes. Capitalism, communism and liberal democracy have all made millennial claims and sought to co-opt the church's message. We work toward the kingdom, we actualize the kingdom, but we are justifiably wary of those who would call us to join them in building a secular kingdom of God.

EXPECTATIONS

It is easy to understand why many Christians are more comfortable with going to heaven when they die than with the reign of the Messiah over a new

---

[35]Moltmann, *Coming of God,* p. 197 (emphasis original).

heaven and a new earth. The first is clearly acceptable to our culture. It is vague enough and comforting enough to be accepted by people who have no particular religious convictions. You don't need to believe in Jesus or anyone in particular to believe you go to heaven when you die. Such a notion does not threaten life on this earth or human ambitions. It can even ignore human misdeeds since far fewer people believe in hell than believe in heaven. The resurrection of the dead and the direct rule of God's Messiah over the earth may sound rather primitive in comparison.

It is one of the burdens of this book that something significant to Christian faith and practice is lost when the concreteness of God's promised future is lost. There is nothing human beings anticipate more than the end of the death, suffering and violence that characterize life on this earth. There is nothing we desire more than the drying of our tears, the healing of our diseases and the restoration of our dead. Christians worship a God who sets all things right. If the church spiritualizes such expectations or projects them into the heavenly realm, life on this earth is robbed of hope. The Bible warns us not to try to figure out when all this will occur or how it will appear. We are called to be alert, awake, aware and alive in our anticipation of God's coming kingdom but to leave the fulfillment to God in God's good time. But the promise of a millennial reign, whether or not it lasts a literal one thousand years, remains the fulfillment of human hopes and divine promises: "See, I am making all things new. . . . It is done! I am the Alpha and the Omega, the beginning and the end. To the thirsty I will give water as a gift from the spring of the water of life. Those who conquer will inherit these things, and I will be their God and they will be my children" (Rev 21:5-7).

9

Hope for Israel

THE ORIGINAL THEOLOGICAL PROBLEM of the early church, I would suggest, was the failure of significant numbers of Jews to respond to the good news regarding Jesus of Nazareth. Certainly many Jews did respond to the gospel early on, and a distinct form of Jewish Christianity survived for centuries. But it is quite clear that the great majority of Jews were either indifferent or hostile to the message of Messiah Jesus. As early as Paul's letter to the Romans, it seems clear that the Jewish mission had for the most part been a failure. Paul speaks movingly of his "great sorrow and unceasing anguish" over the failure of "my own people, my kindred according to the flesh . . . Israelites," to respond to his message (Rom 9:2-4). Paul's missionary efforts had seen success among the Gentiles, but the book of Romans reveals a rising conflict between the growing Gentile faction and the Jewish followers of Jesus in the church in Rome. The tide of Gentile converts would eventually overwhelm the early Jewish core of the church in Rome and elsewhere. Paul had his own explanation for the failure of the Jewish mission, which I will explore later in this chapter.

As the Jesus movement became increasingly Gentile, however, the lack of response from Jews became less of a problem. It became common to argue that the church of Jesus Christ had simply replaced the people of Israel as the covenant people of God. The failure of the Jews to respond to Jesus was not a disappointment, but demonstrated their unworthiness to be the bearers of the covenant promises. Jesus' parable of the tenants was read, wrongly in my opinion, to mean that the owner of the vineyard, God, had taken the vineyard, Israel, away from the unworthy tenant farmers, the Jews, and given it to others, the church (see Mk 12:1-12 and parallels). Some Christians saw the destruction of the temple in A.D. 70 and the final rebellion and obliteration of the city of Jerusalem in A.D. 135 as a judgment on the Jews and a vindication of the Christian movement. For years Christian pilgrims visited the ruins of Jerusalem not to visit holy sites but to gaze in satisfaction at the judgment of Israel.

The view that Christianity had replaced Israel is frequently called supersessionism. According to George Lindbeck, "the understanding of the church as the replacement of Israel is the major ecclesiological source of Christian anti-Judaism."[1] Some church fathers argued for the preservation of the Jews not because they were followers of the same God worshiped by Christians but in order to demonstrate through their humiliation the triumph of the church. The early church did fend off an attempt to make the break with Israel complete. The church rejected Marcion's attempt in the second century to demonize both the Hebrew Scriptures and the God they revealed. Marcion had rejected the Hebrew Scriptures and argued for a truncated version of the New Testament devoid of all Jewish elements.[2] Marcion's critics insisted that the Hebrew Scriptures were Christian Scriptures and the Jewish God, the Christian God. In spite of Marcion's condemnation, the echoes of his heresy are still heard every time someone speaks of the "Old Testament God of wrath" and the "New Testament God of love."

Tragically, by the fourth century the lines between Jews and Christians had hardened. Views that could be ignored or laughed off by Jews when the Christian movement was small and weak became deadly when Christians acquired imperial support. The Jews were increasingly written out of their own story and eliminated from their own hopes. In Europe they were forbidden many roles in society and severely criticized for the ones they were permitted. They were relegated to ghettos and viewed with suspicion by their often superstitious neighbors. Even if they rose to positions of wealth

---

[1]George Lindbeck, "What of the Future?: A Christian Response," in *Christianity in Jewish Terms*, ed. Tikva Frymer-Kensky et al. (Boulder, CO: Westview, 2000), p. 358.
[2]On Marcion, see Diarmaid MacCulloch, *Christianity: The First Three Thousand Years* (New York: Viking, 2010), pp. 125-27.

and power, they were always vulnerable to the avarice and envy of both kings and commoners. In spite of this, the Jews created and sustained their own rich and vital world of piety and scholarship and contributed mightily to the intellectual, spiritual and commercial prosperity of Europe.[3]

Supersessionism remained the most common Christian view of Judaism well into the twentieth century. Among many Christians, of course, it is still the typical understanding of the relationship between Judaism and Christianity. This was exacerbated by the fact that many Christians had little or no contact with Jews. It was easy to countenance their replacement since, for some Christians, especially in the United States, Jews were not contemporaries, neighbors who lived on the same block, but ancient people living in dusty Palestine. Their understanding of Judaism was frequently based on misunderstanding and polemic. Judaism, they were taught, was a religion of grim legalism, and Jewish life was characterized by an endless process of ethical nitpicking. The exemplar of the Jew was a caricature of the Pharisee in the New Testament—harsh, condemning, narrow minded and perverse. It didn't seem to occur to its critics that if Judaism was truly as Christians imagined, it was amazing it had survived at all. But in the middle of the twentieth century everything began to change.

THE ZENITH OF ANTI-SEMITISM

Anti-Semitism had long been characteristic of European Christianity, but in the mid to late nineteenth century it grew in sophistication and virulence. European biblical scholarship took a page out of Marcion's book and worked to purge Christianity of Jewish practices. This did not mean wholesale rejection of the Hebrew Scriptures as with Marcion, but a selective purging of what were considered distasteful elements. The prophets were used to criticize the rest of the Hebrew Scriptures. Legalism was rejected, cultic practices repudiated and the apparent violence of God critiqued, with the result that God ultimately appeared to be a perfectly respectable Victorian gentleman. Scholars, particularly in Germany, argued that a more appropriate background for understanding the New Testament writings was the Greco-Roman, rather than the Jewish, world. Some went so far as to argue that

---

[3]On the sad and bitter history of relations between Christians and Jews, see MacCulloch, *Christianity,* index s.v. "Jews," and follow the trail of references.

Jesus was not actually a Jew at all since he was born in Galilee, where, they argued quite wrongly, there were more Gentiles than Jews.[4] Although the evidence for this entire movement to Hellenize Jesus and the early church was scant, it heavily impacted New Testament scholarship until nearly the end of the twentieth century and still has many adherents to this day.

Anti-Semitism, however, was not only religious. All over Europe there were nationalistic anti-Semites who saw Jews as alien elements in French or German or Italian society. For their countries to grow strong and endure, such elements needed to be eliminated. Many Jews in northern Europe were by this time secular and, so they thought, fully integrated into Christian society. They thought of themselves as good, patriotic citizens of Germany or France or Great Britain. Some of them despised "peasant" Jews every bit as much as their Gentile fellow citizens did. But to the convinced nationalistic anti-Semite, this made no difference. Some of these critics of the Jews were secular despisers of Christianity. They hated Judaism because it gave the world Christianity, particularly Roman Catholic Christianity. These have been dubbed the anti-Christian anti-Semites. Were it not for the Jews, they argued, we would not have to contend with the church in Rome. Jews became, as they had frequently been in the past, a convenient scapegoat for the perceived ills of society.

Jews were faced with religious opposition, right-wing nationalistic opposition and left-wing secular opprobrium by the end of the nineteenth and beginning of the twentieth century. All this abetted the rise of fascism in Germany in the wake of the devastation of the First World War. For Hitler and his fanatical followers, the Jews were convenient scapegoats for the misery and humiliation of the Germans. The Jews were accused of being the capitalist bankers sucking the life out of Germany and the communist agitators eager to plunge it into chaos and bloodshed. Fantasies about an international Jewish conspiracy fueled the paranoia of the Nazis and their followers. The bitter outcome of this is well known. Throughout Europe millions of Jews went to their deaths for no other crime than being Jewish. They were shot, hanged, gassed, starved and worked to death—men, women and children, peasants, scholars and artists.

---

[4]On European biblical scholarship and the Jews, see Susannah Heschel, *The Aryan Jesus: Christian Theologians and the Bible in Nazi Germany,* paperback ed. (Princeton, NJ: Princeton University Press, 2010).

In the wake of the war the full horror of this became apparent to Jews, Christians and secularists alike. However secular and even pagan Hitler and his minions were, Christians had to face the grim fact that years of Christian mistreatment of Jews had contributed to the murders of six million. Many Christians had participated in these murders, and many others had ignored the signs that they were occurring. Christians were clearly complicit in the slaughter of a people with whom they shared a text, a tradition and a God. A reassessment of the relationship between Jews and Christians was demanded. Deep sorrow and sincere repentance were necessary. Thus began a series of painful and fruitful dialogues between Jews and Christians. Some Jews, with good reason, wanted nothing to do with such conversations. Others courageously confronted the very people who considered their tradition passé and contributed to a new understanding and respect between Jews and Christians from the Roman Catholic, Protestant and more recently the evangelical tradition. These conversations are ongoing.

THE STATE OF ISRAEL

Subsequent to the Second World War something else occurred that radically altered the nature of the conversation: the state of Israel was established. For the first time in thousands of years the Jews were in possession of their ancestral land and eventually the holy city of Jerusalem. While Israel clearly aspired to be a secular state and a place for all Jews, religious or otherwise, to find a homeland, this raised significant theological, ethical and political questions for Christians. Some Christians saw the establishment of the state of Israel as a sign of the end times. They supported the Jews' return to the land as a fulfillment of prophecy and a necessary precursor to the return of Jesus. Others saw the creation of the state as a just recompense for the Holocaust and rejoiced that the Jews finally had a homeland. Others were troubled by the expulsion of the Palestinians from their lands and villages and worked to limit or turn back Jewish expansionism. Christian interest and interference in Israel and the holy land continue unabated to this day. I will have more to say about this later in the chapter.

THEOLOGICAL IMPLICATIONS

In the wake of these horrific and startling events, it became clear to many

Christian thinkers that supersessionism needed to be rethought. Contacts between Christians and Jews demonstrated not only significant and enduring differences but surprising and important similarities between the two traditions. Many Christians discovered to their shame that their caricature of Jews as narrow-minded, nitpicking legalists was a perverse misunderstanding at best and gross insult at worst. At the same time, Christian biblical scholarship was beginning to reassess the Jewishness of Jesus, Paul and the early church. In spite of ongoing and fruitless attempts to find a background for Jesus in the Greco-Roman world, scholars like E. P. Sanders, James Dunn and N. T. Wright insisted Jesus, Paul and the early church could only be understood in their Jewish context.[5] Jewish New Testament scholarship contributed significantly to this reassessment beginning with Samuel Sandmel, who was ably followed by Mark Nanos, A. J. Levine and many others.[6]

Jewish and Christian scholars from many disciplines have met in recent years to share papers and hear responses for the sake of greater mutual understanding. Several publications have resulted from these conferences. Notable examples include *Christianity in Jewish Terms,* edited by Tikva Frymer-Kensky and others, and, recently, *Covenant and Hope,* edited by Robert W. Jenson and Eugene Korn.[7] Christian theology and practices have been clearly shown to be consistent with Jewish origins even where Christians took their theology and practices in entirely different and, so far as Jews were concerned, inappropriate directions. We are more alike than we think. All this work should lead to a more hopeful future for Jewish-Christian relations.

Having said this, Christians need to hear David Blumenthal's warning:

> The bloody history of Christian-Jewish relations over two millennia does not allow the traditional Jew to identify with a doctrine that is specifically Christian, even if it were otherwise true. Christianity has simply been too

---

[5]See E. P. Sanders, *Jesus and Judaism* (Philadelphia: Fortress, 1985); N. T. Wright, *The New Testament and the People of God,* vol. 1 of *Christian Origins and the Question of God* (Minneapolis: Fortress, 1992); James D. G. Dunn, *The Theology of Paul the Apostle* (Grand Rapids: Eerdmans, 1998).

[6]See Amy-Jill Levine and Mark Zvi Brettler, eds., *The Jewish Annotated New Testament: New Revised Standard Bible Translation* (New York: Oxford University Press, 2011).

[7]See Tikva Frymer-Kensky et al., eds., *Christianity in Jewish Terms* (Boulder, CO: Westview, 2000); and Robert Jenson and Eugene Korn, eds., *Covenant and Hope: Christian and Jewish Reflections: Essays in Constructive Theology from the Institute for Theological Inquiry* (Grand Rapids: Eerdmans, 2012).

> cruel to Jews and Judaism, even if, in very recent times, some Christians have
> taken a different attitude toward us. "How can one sing the songs of the Lord
> on alien soil?" It would be a betrayal of all our ancestors to do so. It would
> render the death of thousands of martyrs an act of futility.[8]

Christians must hear the truth of this hard word with deep sorrow and humility. Commonality does not mean unanimity. Understanding does not mean full acceptance. Given the ugly history of misunderstanding and abuse of Jews, Christians would be wise in these ongoing dialogues to listen more than they speak. Unfortunately, Christians must acknowledge they have given Jews good reasons to reject their gospel. I will have more to say about this later in the chapter.

This important work, in addition to forging more positive relationships between Jews and Christians, has forced a reassessment of supersessionism. It also raises a crucial eschatological question for Christians: What is now the hope for Israel as Israel? If supersessionism is at best simplistic and at worst simply wrong, do the Christian Scriptures, let alone the Hebrew Scriptures, anticipate a future for Israel as Israel? If Israel, as traditionally thought by Christians, has simply been swept aside as the people of God and replaced by the church, any future for Israel is simply subsumed within the Christian church. In this case, the only future Jews have is if they convert before the end.

However, does Christian eschatology, the hope of Christians for a new heaven and a new earth, really require supersessionism? Does it not make a place for Israel as Israel? Increasingly, Christian theologians are insisting that it does. Jürgen Moltmann famously argued that what he calls millenarianism does entail a hope for Israel as Israel. The term *millenarianism* refers to belief in the thousand-year earthly rule of God referred to in Revelation 20:1-6. For Moltmann, millenarianism anticipates a very earthly hope for both the people of Israel and the followers of Messiah Jesus. Millenarianism is the hope of an earthly kingdom—God's direct rule over a new heaven and a new earth as promised by Israel's prophets.

For most of its history, the church rejected the notion of an earthly kingdom as a Jewish dream. As discussed in an earlier chapter, the prevailing view was

---

[8]David Blumenthal, "*Tselem:* Toward an Anthropathic Theology of Image," in *Christianity in Jewish Terms*, ed. Tikva Frymer-Kensky et al. (Boulder, CO: Westview, 2000), p. 347.

amillennialism—the belief that there was no thousand-year rule of God. Rather, God was already ruling with his saints through the church and Christian empire. Moltmann argues that this Christian empire was the chief reason for the historical rejection of millenarianism, the future rule of Messiah on the earth, in spite of the clear expectations of Jesus, Paul and the early church. "We shrug our shoulders over the people of the election, and hence over chiliasm [the belief in the thousand-year earthly kingdom] too," declared one Christian thinker.[9] When the messianic kingdom was identified with the rule of a Christian king or emperor alongside bishops and clergy, the expectation of an earthly kingdom ruled by a Jewish messiah became less attractive— especially for the emperors and bishops. Moltmann, as seen in a previous chapter, intends to reclaim millenarian eschatology for both Israel and the church. He insists that there is a Christian hope for Israel as Israel.[10]

According to Moltmann:

> The presuppositions for a Christian hope for Israel are these: (a) Israel has an enduring "salvific calling," parallel to the church of the Gentiles, for God remains true to his election and his promise (Rom. 11:1f). (b) The promises given to Israel are as yet only fulfilled in principle in the coming of the Messiah Jesus, and in him without conditions, and hence universally *endorsed* (2 Cor. 1:20); and in the outpouring of the Spirit "on all flesh" are as yet realized only partially. . . . Through the gospel and the Holy Spirit, the divine promises given to Israel are extended to all nations, for whom therefore dawned what Paul calls the time of the gospel—in the language of Maimonides, the *praeparatio messianica*. (c) Christianity is God's "other community of hope" parallel to Israel and over against Israel. Parallel to the people of God, it is the missionary and messianic church of the nations. It can therefore only remain true to its own hope if it recognizes Israel as the older community of hope alongside itself. In its hope for the nations the church also preserves the "surplus of hope" in Israel's prophets, and therefore waits for the fulfillment of Israel's hopes too. In the very fact of turning wholly to the Gentile nations with the gospel, it confirms and strengthens Israel's hopes: all Israel will be saved when the fullness of the Gentile arrives at salvation (Rom. 11:25f).[11]

---

[9]Jürgen Moltmann, *The Coming of God: Christian Eschatology,* trans. Margaret Kohl (Minneapolis: Fortress, 1996), p. 197.
[10]Ibid., pp. 196-99.
[11]Ibid., pp. 197-98 (emphasis original).

Moltmann clearly argues here against any notion of supercession or theory of replacement. Israel, he insists, has not lost its standing before God or forfeited its covenant. He makes his argument from the apostle Paul and principally from the book of Romans.

Before turning to Romans, however, I want to make two important points. First, a relativistic approach to God's saving intent for the world is an insult to both Judaism and Christianity. To say in effect that it doesn't matter whether you are a Jew or Christian ignores or minimizes genuine differences between the two traditions and trivializes the sufferings of the aforementioned martyrs. So, second, I read Paul and interpret his hope for a future for Israel as Israel *as a Christian* reader. I cannot and do not expect all or any Jews (or Christians, for that matter) to agree with me in my reading. Like Paul, I am a follower of Jesus who sees a future for Israel and my Jewish friends. With him, I affirm that "all Israel will be saved" (Rom 11:26). And with him I expect that salvation to come through Messiah Jesus. Jews clearly disagree with this, for reasons already mentioned. Nevertheless, I would insist that Jews have not been replaced by Christians, have not lost their covenant and are still included in God's intentions to make a new heaven and a new earth. I don't expect to inherit the new world without them.

PAUL'S ANGUISH: ROMANS 9–11

Some have argued that the entire book of Romans was written to address the question of why Israel had rejected the gospel. Earlier I mentioned Paul's anguish and perplexity at this rejection. He would go so far as to say, "I could wish that I myself were cursed and cut off from Christ for the sake of my own people" (Rom 9:3). But Paul does not argue that because of this rejection Israel is cut off from God, their covenant and their hope. Quite the contrary. In what follows, note the present tense: "To them belong the adoption, the glory, the covenants, the giving of the law, the worship, and the promises; to them belong the patriarchs, and from them, according to the flesh, comes the Messiah" (Rom 9:4-5). So far as Paul was concerned, all these things continued as possessions of the Jewish people. Rather, he argued, their rejection was part of a divine strategy.

At the beginning of Romans 11 Paul reiterates that God had not rejected his people. Some had, of course, responded, and yet most had not. To Paul, they seemed to be in a kind of stupor or suffering from a form of blindness. They had stumbled, but, Paul insists, they had not fallen beyond recovery (Rom 11:11). "But," he continues, "through their stumbling salvation has come to the Gentiles, so as to make Israel jealous. Now if their stumbling means riches for the world, and if their defeat means riches for Gentiles, how much more will their full inclusion mean!" (Rom 11:11-12). So far as Paul was concerned, their rejection was a temporary matter. He famously compares the current situation to an ancient olive tree. The Gentiles are wild olive branches grafted into the cultivated tree of Israel. Some branches have been removed in order for them to be grafted. But Paul fully expects that the old branches will be grafted in once more (Rom 11:17-24).

The next few verses are even more startling. "A hardening has come upon part of Israel," Paul argues, "until the full number of the Gentiles has come in. *And so all Israel will be saved*" (Rom 11:25-26). Paul still expects God to fulfill his covenant with Israel:

"Out of Zion will come the Deliverer;
    he will banish ungodliness from Jacob."
"And this is my covenant with them,
    when I take away their sins."

As regards the gospel they are enemies of God for your sake; but as regards election they are beloved, for the sake of their ancestors; *for the gifts and the calling of God are irrevocable.* (Rom 11:26-29)

Whatever new thing God was doing with the Gentiles through Messiah Jesus, he had not and would not reject his covenant with Israel. The promises made through the great prophets Isaiah and Jeremiah were as secure after Jesus as before. God was at work among the Gentiles, but the promises of salvation to Israel had not and would not be abrogated.

What does this mean? Is Paul saying that every single Jew will be saved? Is he implying that the Jews have a parallel way of salvation that does not entail faith in Jesus? Does he mean to suggest that at some point in the future God will forcibly convert every Jew alive to Messiah Jesus? The mechanics of this salvation do not seem to interest Paul as much as the certainty of it. "God has imprisoned all in disobedience," he writes, "so that he may be merciful to all" (Rom 11:32). Paul looked forward, in keeping with the prophets of Israel and Jesus himself, to the resurrection of the dead, the rule of Messiah and the restoration of the whole earth.

In 1 Corinthians Paul writes,

> Then comes the end, when he [Christ] hands over the kingdom to God the Father, after he has destroyed every ruler and every authority and power. For he must reign until he has put all his enemies under his feet. The last enemy to be destroyed is death. . . . When all things are subjected to him, then the Son himself will also be subjected to the one who put all things in subjection under him, so that God may be all in all. (1 Cor 15:24-28)

Paul firmly believed in the final salvation of Israel in accordance with the promises of the covenants. He believed that salvation included all Israel and all those Gentiles who had responded to Jesus. For Paul, Christians were destined not to replace Israel but to inherit God's promised kingdom alongside them. Paul would have been astonished and perplexed that some followers of Jesus ever thought otherwise.

THE LAND OF ISRAEL

Integral to the hope of Israel is the hope for the land. Following the destruction of the first temple by the Babylonians, the Jews were exiled from their land and holy place. In spite of a brief time of Jewish power under the Hasmoneans, even when they were present in the land in significant numbers, they were relatively powerless. At the time of Jesus their Roman overlords kept a tight rein on the land and punished any rebellion with extreme ruthlessness and cruelty. But the Romans were only one example of many brutal overlords before and after the birth of Jesus. The land of Israel was subject to Babylonians, Persians, Greeks, Romans, Byzantines, Muslims, European Crusaders, the Ottoman Empire and finally, following World War I, the British. The latter were persuaded to guarantee the Jews a homeland in their ancient lands over the vociferous objections of the Arab inhabitants. The story of the creation of the state of Israel in 1948 is both stirring and controversial.[12]

I mentioned earlier that some Christians have seen the establishment of the state of Israel as a precursor to the coming of Christ. Many of them have

---

[12]See Martin Gilbert, *Israel: A History* (New York: Harper Perennial, 1998).

supported the expansion of Israel's holdings to include the occupied terri-
tories and the West Bank and have opposed any efforts to swap land for
peace. Other Christians, as suggested earlier, have taken a much more jaun-
diced view of the Jewish state. Some would be happy if the state and its Jews
disappeared from the map. Many, if not most, Christians are not sure what
to make of the status of the state of Israel in relation to Bible prophecy and
may be troubled by particular actions of the state of Israel, but support a
homeland for the Jews. They want Israel to prosper, and they feel a kinship
with the Jewish people.

What are we to make of the prophetic promises of land and a future in
relation to the contemporary state of Israel? How should Christians view the
state? Has Israel been reestablished in light of the coming kingdom of God?
The importance of the land in both the Old and New Testaments is in-
escapable. The prophets of Israel promised a future for God's people in their
own land. In spite of postexilic disappointments, prophets like Haggai insisted God had a plan for the glorification of the land and the people: "Once
again, in a little while, I will shake the heavens and the earth and the sea and
the dry land; and I will shake all the nations, so that the treasure of all nations shall come, and I will fill this house with splendor, says the LORD of
hosts" (Hag 2:6-7). This house, of course, was the temple in Jerusalem, the
great symbol of God's presence among his people. God would once again,
Haggai promised Zerubbabel governor of Judah, dwell in the land, in his
house, among his people.

The prophet Zechariah promised that the LORD would eventually come
to Jerusalem to fight on behalf of his people:

> The LORD will become king over all the earth; on that day the LORD will be
> one and his name one. The whole land shall be turned into a plain from Geba
> to Rimmon south of Jerusalem. But Jerusalem shall remain aloft. . . . And it
> shall be inhabited, for never again shall it be doomed to destruction; Jeru-
> salem shall abide in security. (Zech 14:9-11)

Such passages are consistent with preexilic expectations that the returning
exiles would walk through a flowering desert in safety.

> And the ransomed of the LORD shall return,
>   and come to Zion with singing;

everlasting joy shall be upon their heads;
> they shall obtain joy and gladness,
> and sorrow and sighing shall flee away. (Is 35:10)

Jewish exiles, whether in Babylon or Brooklyn, have always longed for a return to the land. For many, if not most, this return entailed the victory of God's messiah over the forces of resistance and oppression. For many, if not most, it still does. Is not the contemporary denial of a future for Jews in the land of Israel, their ancient homeland, another form of supersessionism?

But what about the specifically Christian vision of the future of the land of Israel? Jesus clearly locates the climax of judgment and redemption in the land of Israel, although the judgment impacts the entire world (see Mk 13 and parallels). The language of his Olivet Discourse is reminiscent of Zechariah 14. Jerusalem and the land of Israel are still at the heart of things. In the Revelation of John, the final great conflict between God and his enemies is at Armageddon in the land of Israel (Rev 16:16). After the creation of the new heaven and new earth, John sees

> the holy city, the new Jerusalem, coming down out of heaven from God. . . . And
> > I heard a loud voice from the throne saying,

"See, the home of God is among mortals.
He will dwell with them;
they will be his peoples,
and God himself will be with them;
he will wipe every tear from their eyes.
Death will be no more;
mourning and crying and pain will be no more,
for the first things have passed away." (Rev 21:1-4; cf. Is 25:6-9)

Jerusalem and the land of Israel continued to inform the eschatological imagination of Christians. They still anticipate life in the new Jerusalem.

Some Christians, as we have seen, have argued that all the references to the land of Israel and the city of Jerusalem are only symbolic. There is no literal new Jerusalem. Perhaps, they say, this is a reference to heaven, the realm of God, but it has nothing to do with the actual city of Jerusalem and the actual land of Israel. The kingdom of God is not the literal rule of God over the earth but a spiritual rule within the church or within the individual.

An expectation of the rule of God within a renewed city of Jerusalem in the land of Israel is, they argue, a primitive and crudely literalistic reading of the Scriptures. Such a reading, however, requires a massive reinterpretation of both Jewish and Christian texts and a reorientation of Jewish and Christian hopes. Why is it deemed necessary? As I previously suggested, it began when the glorious future promised by God was transferred from the future rule of the Messiah to the current rule of the Christian emperor. God's rule was already being realized on earth. The Jews and their hopes had already been crushed and replaced. Why was a future judgment and redemption centered in the land of Israel even necessary? Hope for the rule of God in the land was one of the Jewish elements purged from Christian thought in the nineteenth century, and its return has been steadfastly resisted by many in the twentieth and twenty-first centuries.

Among the Jews themselves the significance of the return to the land is also debated. For secular Jews, the value of Israel has nothing to do with the fulfillment of prophecy or hope for the return of the Messiah. Israel is important because it provides the Jews with a homeland and a way to protect themselves in a hostile world. It gives the people a land and a place. Religious Jews are divided. Some religious Jews, like secular Jews, celebrate Israel as a Jewish homeland although they still anticipate the coming of Messiah. They anticipate the day when the state will be not only a Jewish homeland but the fulfillment of the hopes and expectations of the Hebrew Scriptures and the long-frustrated longings of the Jewish people. Some religious Jews, however, consider the current government of the state of Israel illegitimate. The state can only be reconstituted, they believe, when the Messiah comes.

Some Jews and Christians believe the restoration of Jews to their homeland is biblically and theologically significant. Others do not. Some Jews and Christians think the current government of Israel is religiously and theologically illegitimate. Others do not. It is undeniable, however, that both the Hebrew Scriptures and the New Testament foresee a future for the land of Israel and the city of Jerusalem. They anticipate that the land and the city will be, in God's good time, the very center of the world and the dwelling place of God. This can be minimized and spiritualized, but it cannot be entirely swept away by the indifference or hostility of interpreters. That the

Jews, after an absence of more than two thousand years, find themselves back in the land of Israel in an intentionally Jewish state is an astonishing achievement. That it is a controversial state with many critics, both religious and secular, is not surprising. But its presence and endurance should at least give all its critics pause—especially those Christian critics who think Israel has been replaced by the church and that its hopes for the land are passé.[13]

Some interpreters of biblical prophecy (called dispensationalists) believe that the presence of Israel within the family of nations once again is a sign of the restarting of the eschatological clock. I find their approach unconvincing. Nevertheless, the current state of Israel, whatever its faults and failings, not only provides a place for Jews to live in safety in their own land; it anticipates the promises of God to renew not only Jerusalem but heaven and earth and to draw all people to worship him there. The famed twentieth-century rabbi Joseph Soloveitchik wrote:

> This longing for creation and the renewal of the cosmos is embodied in all of Judaism's goals. And if at times we raise the question of the ultimate aim of Judaism, of the telos of the Halakhah in all its multiformed aspects and manifestations, we must not disregard the fact that this wondrous spectacle of the creation of worlds is the Jewish people's eschatological vision, the realization of all its hopes.[14]

Jewish obedience to Torah is in anticipation of and for the purpose of the renewal of creation promised by God—the new creation. In the final chapter I will explore the question of Christian life and obedience in anticipation of the coming kingdom of God. Suffice it to say here that Jews faithful to Torah and Christians faithful to the teachings of Jesus, whether in Israel or not, live lives of obedience in anticipation of "this wondrous spectacle of the creation of worlds." Both live *toward* the redemption of

---

[13]Perhaps it should go without saying, but the conviction that Israel as Israel has a place and future in its ancient homeland should not suggest, as some Jews and Christians seem to believe, that the current state of Israel should be supported regardless of its actions. Israel, like the United States and, for that matter, Iran, is subject to criticism when its actions betray its essential commitments. It is no more anti-Jewish or anti-Semitic to criticize Israel than it is anti-Muslim to criticize Iran. It is true, nonetheless, that some criticisms directed to both states grow from hostility to their religious traditions and ethnic identities. Israel should be criticized when appropriate but not demonized. The same is true for Iran, the US and Saudi Arabia.

[14]Joseph B. Soloveitchik, *Halakhic Man*, trans. Lawrence Kaplan (Philadelphia: Jewish Publication Society of America, 1983), p. 99.

Israel and the kingdom of God. Both anticipate the new creation in their practices of obedience and love.

EVANGELISM OF JEWS?

The most difficult part of the Jewish-Christian conversation is the question of Jewish evangelism by Christians. It is quite obvious that the early Christians preached the good news to Jews. "I am not ashamed of the gospel," Paul wrote; "it is the power of God for salvation to everyone who has faith, to the Jew first and also to the Greek" (Rom 1:16). It should be said, however, that it is unlikely that Paul was thinking that he was a Christian preaching to Jews. He was a Jewish follower of Messiah Jesus calling both Jews and Gentiles to respond to the new thing God was doing in Jesus. Be that as it may, it is undeniable that Jews formed the backbone of the early Christian community. As indicated earlier in this chapter, by the fourth century Christianity had become substantially Gentile, gained imperial support and become increasingly hostile to the Jews. It was set on a path of shameful cruelty and brutality toward a people that shared a history, a text and a hope.

Some years ago a student at North Park Theological Seminary suggested to me that in light of this horrendous history Christians should exercise a discipline of silence regarding witness to Jews. He meant by this that Christians through their abuse of the Jews over many centuries had forfeited the right to preach the gospel to them. A history of pogroms, ghettoizations, forced conversions and outright murder had given Jews good reasons to be wary of Christians' motivations for entering into conversation with them. We would do well, he argued, to listen more than speak. Perhaps at some point in the future we might earn the right to speak of what we have found in Jesus. But until then we should acknowledge with humility and grief that our tradition had failed miserably to follow the way of justice, love and peace laid out for us by Jesus of Nazareth.

Christians enter into conversations with Jews as Christians. They can do no other. As I suggested before, a flaccid relativism is an insult to both parties. We are followers of Jesus who anticipate that God through him will make all things new. At the same time, with Paul we insist that God has neither rejected his people the Jews nor abrogated his covenant with them. In some manner that we cannot now anticipate we expect to inherit the promises of his kingdom along with them. In the meantime, we live together with our very real differences with both humility and hope. We insist that the Christian hope is not only hope for the Gentiles but hope for the Jews as well. It is hope for Israel as Israel. It is, indeed, hope for the entire creation: "The creation waits," Paul wrote, "with eager longing for the revealing of the children of God. . . . The creation itself will be set free from its bondage to decay and will obtain the freedom of the glory of the children of God" (Rom 8:19, 21). That is our hope for Christians, for Jews, for the entire created order.[15]

---

[15]For a provocative and fruitful reflection on the issues raised in this chapter, see Scott Bader-Saye, *Church and Israel After Christendom: The Politics of Election* (repr.; Eugene, OR: Wipf & Stock, 2005).

10

Hope for the Church

IN *CHRISTIANITY AFTER RELIGION*, DIANA BUTLER BASS argued that the first decade of the twenty-first century was disastrous for the Christian church—especially in North America and Europe. The decade began with the attacks of September 11. In the early days following the attack, Islam was denounced as a religion of terror and violence. But "as time passed, the media, politicians, columnists, and pundits began to blame *religion* for the attacks."[1] No longer was Islam alone at fault, but religion itself was to blame. Christopher Hitchens argued that "people of faith are in their different ways planning your and my destruction, and the destruction of all the hard-won human attainments. . . . Religion poisons everything."[2] Religious folk were depicted as angry, hateful and full of rage against unbelievers. It did not help this perception that many Christians, evangelical and otherwise, were at the forefront of calls for vindictive and bloody retaliation against Muslims regardless of their political affiliations and responses to the attacks. Unfortunately, Hitchens and the other new atheists had plenty of ammunition at their disposal to use against religion in general and the Christian church in particular.

As the decade wore on, the Roman Catholic Church was wracked by a sex-abuse scandal that exposed not only the horrendous and inexcusable

---

[1] Diana Butler Bass, *Christianity After Religion: The End of Church and the Birth of a New Spiritual Awakening* (San Francisco: HarperOne, 2012), p. 77 (emphasis original).
[2] Ibid., pp. 77-78.

actions of some of its priests but the equally inexcusable cover-up and min-imization of those actions by the hierarchy. Mainline Protestants spent the decade in endless, vicious debates over homosexuality. "Newspapers, cable television, and a new cadre of bloggers," Bass writes, "reported on every threat of division, elevating ecclesiastical dirty laundry and theological meanness to a point not witnessed since the pamphlet wars of the Protestant Reformation."[3] The evangelical world was not spared. Younger evangelicals showed themselves unwilling to fight the battles of their elders. They soured on President Bush and the Iraq War. They showed a growing interest in issues of social justice and were unwilling to demonize their gay friends. The numbers are, for evangelicals, ominous: "In 1985, 26 percent of young adults under twenty-nine claimed to be evangelicals; that number now hovers around 15 percent."[4]

As a result of all this, the Christian church and its leaders are now held in scorn by an increasing number of people in North America and Europe. The moral authority of pastors, priests, bishops and popes has declined precipi-tously. Many of their own members now look at ecclesiastical hierarchies askance, whether the Roman Catholic Vatican, the Protestant denomina-tional headquarters in New York or Chicago, or their local elder boards or church councils. The voices from above always seem to come with hidden agendas. Elites, it appears, only want to hold on to power, generate income and preserve their prerogatives rather than serve the interests of the people or, for that matter, the gospel. So, increasingly, people old and young are voting with their feet and leaving those desperate elites to their own devices and dwindling resources. Mainline Protestant denominations—a prime ex-ample—are shedding jobs and churches in record numbers.

In 1990 Jürgen Moltmann wrote, "The church will have no future if it simply extrapolates into the future the path it took in the past. It will have a future only if it anticipates the Kingdom of God in Jesus' name and is pre-pared to be converted to his future, freeing itself from imprisonment in its past."[5] I would argue that it is clear that this will not be accomplished by

---

[3]Ibid., p. 79.
[4]Ibid., p. 81.
[5]Jürgen Moltmann, *The Church in the Power of the Spirit: A Contribution to Messianic Ecclesiology*, trans. Margaret Kohl (San Francisco: HarperCollins, 1991), p. xiv.

reinvigorating current ecclesial leadership and shoring up its power. It will not happen because of a clever program developed at the denominational offices or rolled out by the local megachurch. "The future of the church," says Moltmann, "is only described through the medium of a church of hope for other people and with other people."[6] It will, in other words, be an *eschatological church*, living *toward* the kingdom of God, the hope for the new heavens and new earth where righteousness dwells. Our eschatology provides our mission and our hope for the church.

In this chapter I want to call the church back to life and health by calling it back to the kingdom mission of Jesus. I will argue that, at least in part, the church's misunderstanding and misappropriation of biblical eschatology has brought it to its current unenviable state of missional collapse. Eschatology properly understood is formational for mission. Misunderstood, it distorts and hampers the mission of the church. I argued earlier that the church's millennial views often reflect the relationship between it and the powers that be. Amillennial eschatology, I have argued, was developed in the wake of the conversion of the Roman Empire and served to affirm the wedding of church and state. Through the power of the hierarchy of the church and the imperial power of the state, it was thought, the promised millennial reign of Christ would be realized. The kingdom would be pushed from the top to the bottom, from the clergy to the laity, from the aristocracy to the common people.

This view of the church endures not only in the Roman Catholic Church and the imperial pomp of the Vatican but wherever the church is the leadership—wherever the mission of the church lies with and is controlled by the hierarchy or the clergy alone. Constantinianism, in fact, lies in the background wherever the purpose (stated or unstated) of the church is the preservation of the institution, whether in its local, national or international manifestations. But imperial metaphors are not the only indicators of Constantinianism. Wherever local churches are considered franchises and pastoral leaders middle management, something has gone badly wrong with the metaphors as well as the mission of the church. Ecclesial leaders are not CEOs, and local pastors are not regional sales managers. The imposition of

---

[6]Ibid., p. xviii.

such hierarchal structures on the church has been, in my opinion, a disaster for the church and its mission.

And yet these models, often unacknowledged or unrecognized, are alive and well in episcopal palaces and megachurch corner offices around the world and emulated by desperate pastors looking for cheap and efficient ways to grow their churches. In spite of the aura of power emanating from the aforementioned palaces and offices, their metaphors have crippled the mission of the church and produced, in part, the crisis of confidence discussed earlier. The church has everywhere and always been compromised by aping cultural models of power.

The growth of premillennial eschatology in the nineteenth century did not help. While classic amillennialism argued that the partnership of church and state would produce the kingdom, classic premillennialism, especially in its dispensational form, argued that the world was going to get worse and worse while the church stood by helplessly. God's plan was for the world to descend into chaos and violence from which Jesus would rescue Christians at his return by an application of God's own brand of violence and chaos. Living toward the kingdom was at best beside the point and at worst hindering God's plan. Since the 1980s the religious right in the United States has offered a rather odd combination of both approaches. While still, for the most part, holding to the fatalism of premillennialism, the religious right has struggled to gain power in Washington so as to mandate certain policies and behaviors by means more in keeping with Constantine than with Jesus of Nazareth. Theologically they are premillennialist, while in practice they are amillennialists.

As Bass argued, in the United States and Europe the Christian church in all its manifestations is in a state of crisis. But in this crisis, I would argue, is the greatest opportunity for re-grounding the church's mission in the mission of Jesus: the proclamation and life of the kingdom. And perhaps ironically the frequently mocked and misunderstood views of the so-called postmillennialists may offer a new and hopeful direction for the church. The kingdom will not be imposed by the top-down power of church and state (whether in its Roman Catholic, mainline Protestant or evangelical religious right form). Nor is our effort as Christians to live toward the kingdom doomed to failure and frustration in that we can do nothing to precipitate or prevent the arrival of the kingdom. On the contrary, I will argue that we are called to a partnership with God for the sake of realizing his purposes in his world. God has empowered his church with the Spirit to live toward the kingdom. That power will be manifested as local congregations live in love and hope regardless of the foibles of their denominational leaders.

RETHINKING GOD

This will require not only rethinking our eschatology but rethinking our understanding of God. Whether we recognize it or not, the contemporary Western view of God was shaped powerfully by the god of the eighteenth-century rationalists. Their god was not the God of Israel, intimately involved with his people. The rationalists' god was the "unmoved mover" of Aristotle, the divine "watchmaker" who created the world and set it on its course. This view of a remote, untouchable god was frequently combined with the predestinarian views of Calvin and his followers to produce a god that set from eternity the inexorable fate of the world. Whatever happened, then, was ultimately the will of this god, whether it was the death of young mothers of cancer, toddlers succumbing to the flu or the indiscriminate slaughter of Europe's Jews in a war that consumed millions.

The new atheists justifiably wonder, what kind of god would will such things? What divine purposes are served by such brutality, such injustice? Devotees of theodicy, the defense or justification of God, spend their time, fruitlessly in my opinion, trying to defend God of the charges against him. But in the presence of the Rwandan genocide, the mass graves of Bosnia, and raped and abused women and children everywhere, their defenses ring hollow. Christians can no longer afford to follow the god of the philosophers. Christian thinkers need to give up on their efforts to defend this god, because in truth this is not the God and Father of our Lord Jesus Christ but a modern, idolatrous construct. This is a god who justifies the power of the elites and renders their actions inevitable and justifiable. This is the god whose ways cannot be challenged even when they appear to be monstrous or, at least, monstrously indifferent. The god of the elites, the unmoved mover who keeps all in place as it should be, is an idol that needs to be thrown down.

THE STRANGE GOD OF THE BIBLE

The God of the Bible is a God whose will can be thwarted. His people can and frequently do disobey his laws and ignore his will. Their disobedience and violence are the reasons for the hunger, desperation and fear in the world. Israel, so far as the prophets were concerned, had the power to obey or disobey, follow God or follow Baal. They could join God in partnership or follow their own whims and wills. In the Hebrew Scriptures, obedience and disobedience matter. Certainly God was sovereign and powerful, but not even God could force the Israelites to do his will—however much he punished them. In the Old Testament, and I dare say the New, human actions matter and have consequences. God through his prophets expresses enormous frustration with his people. Jesus expresses amazement that his disciples are so dense (see Mk 8:14-21) and weeps over the disobedience and indifference of Jerusalem (see Mt 23:37-39). What we do and do not do can frustrate the purpose of God for his world. And what we do and do not do can further the purposes of God for his world. Our actions matter!

Philosophers and theologians have long pondered how this might be so. Did God decide to limit his freedom in order to give us our own? Has God simply backed out of the world to give us the space to obey or disobey his will? Or does God genuinely need the involvement of his people to accomplish his purposes? These questions and others like them have occasioned a vigorous and worthwhile debate in recent years.[7] But it seems clear from the Bible at least that God's will can be resisted and his plans undermined. Otherwise, why do the prophets rage and Jesus weep? Otherwise, why do Paul's letters offer ethical warnings and John's Revelation excoriate the church at Laodicea? Although God's ultimate purposes are clear in the new heaven and the new earth where righteousness dwells, in our penultimate world things go badly wrong. Horrors occur that are surely not part of some grand divine plan.

The Bible is not a philosophical or theological treatise. It bristles with what appears to be, for the Western mind, blatant incongruities. How could God's creation go so wrong that he had to start over with Noah? How could God decide in frustration to destroy the people of Israel, only to have Moses

---

[7] See John Sanders, *The God Who Risks: A Theology of Divine Providence*, 2nd ed. (Downers Grove, IL: InterVarsity Press, 2007).

stop him with his prayers and pleas? How is God all powerful and yet incapable of getting his people to obey him? The Jews were not philosophers rigid in their categories. The Bible is quite willing to hold contradictory ideas in tension: God is powerful and sovereign and will work his will in the world. God is also frustrated and disappointed by the human disobedience that thwarts his plans and intentions. God on the one hand appears all-powerful and on the other hand seems weak. In Hosea 11 the anguish of God, what Abraham Joshua Heschel calls "the divine pathos," is clearly demonstrated.[8] Although God has declared through the prophet that he will destroy Israel, in the end he cries out:

> How can I give you up, Ephraim?
>> How can I hand you over, O Israel?
> How can I make you like Admah?
>> How can I treat you like Zeboiim?
> My heart recoils within me;
>> my compassion grows warm and tender.
> I will not execute my fierce anger;
>> I will not again destroy Ephraim;
> for I am God and no mortal. (Hos 11:8-9)

Because he is God, he changes his approach, he alters his direction.

This is not the god of the philosophers. This is the God who empowers and loves his people. This is the God who works alongside them, cajoles them, praises them, warns them and judges them. At the same time, this is not a predictable or safe God. Consider the story of Job. At the end of the book the beleaguered hero finally gets his way. For many chapters he has been calling on God to defend himself. In Job 38, God finally shows up, and Job eventually rather wishes he hadn't. "Who is this that darkens counsel by words without knowledge?" God asks (Job 38:2). Several chapters of rhetorical questions follow: "Where were you when I laid the foundation of the earth?" (Job 38:4). When Job is finally able to get a word in edgewise, he stammers,

> I am of small account; what shall I answer you?
>> I lay my hand on my mouth.

---

[8]Abraham Joshua Heschel, *The Prophets*, 2 vols. in 1 (1962; repr., Boston: Hendrickson, 2007).

> I have spoken once, and I will not answer;
>> twice, but will proceed no further. (Job 40:4-5)

But God plunges relentlessly on. In the end, however, something startling occurs. After all Job's complaints against God's justice, after his near-blasphemous questions and assertions, and after all God's rhetorical assaults on Job, God says something amazing. Addressing Job's erstwhile friends he says, "My wrath is kindled against you . . . for you have not spoken of me what is right, *as my servant Job has*" (Job 42:7). God actually says this twice. How is it that Job is the one who spoke "what is right" of God? After all, God had just spent several chapters excoriating Job! But consider: Job had engaged God, while his friends only spoke about God as if he were a distant power or remote unchanging principle. God evidently valued Job's engagement, questions and struggles more than the smug pronouncements of his more theologically sophisticated friends. Job was right to engage, question and dispute with God even if, in God's estimation, he didn't know what he was talking about. This strange and wonderful God of the Bible wants his people engaged with him—even when they are wrong.

RETHINKING THE CHURCH'S MISSION

What does this all mean for the mission of the church? How does it help us live toward the kingdom? It means, first of all, that we join in partnership with God to accomplish his will. In *Surprised by Hope,* N. T. Wright insists that

> to hope for a better future in this world—for the poor, the sick, the lonely and depressed, for the slaves, the refugees, the hungry and homeless, for the abused, the paranoid, the downtrodden and despairing, and in fact for the whole wide, wonderful, and wounded world—is not something *else*, something extra, something tacked on to the gospel as an afterthought. And to work for that intermediate hope, the surprising hope that comes forward from God's ultimate future into God's urgent present, is not a *distraction from* the task of mission and evangelism in the present. It is a central, essential, vital and life-giving part of it.[9]

---

[9]N. T. Wright, *Surprised by Hope: Rethinking Heaven, the Resurrection, and the Mission of the Church* (New York: HarperOne, 2008), pp. 191-92 (emphasis original).

For Wright, the gospel entails addressing the wounds of the world, wounds that clearly demonstrate the absence of the fullness of God's kingdom. Caring for these wounds in little and large ways is what living toward the kingdom entails, the kingdom when "the eyes of the blind shall be opened, and the ears of the deaf unstopped," when "the lame shall leap like a deer, and the tongue of the speechless sing for joy" (Is 35:5-6). According to Wright, this kingdom was set loose in the world by the resurrection of Jesus. Those who follow him live out of that first resurrection and toward the final great resurrection and reconciliation of the world.

Wright points out that after his long, complex and rich description of the coming resurrection in 1 Corinthians 15, Paul did not finish with "Therefore since you have such a great hope, sit back and relax because you know God's got a great future in store for you." Rather, Paul says, "Therefore, my beloved ones, be steadfast, immovable, always abounding in the work of the Lord, because you know that in the Lord your labor is not in vain" (1 Cor 15:58).[10] In 2 Corinthians 5 Paul insists that the new creation has already come. "Everything old has passed away," he writes; "see, everything has become new!" (2 Cor 5:17). We are already living in the age to come. We are already living toward the kingdom. But as in 1 Corinthians 15 we are not to simply bask in our expectations. "All this is from God," Paul continues, "who reconciled us to himself through Christ, and has *given us the ministry of reconciliation; that is, in Christ God was reconciling the world to himself, not counting their trespasses against them,* and entrusting the message of reconciliation to us. So we are ambassadors for Christ, since God is making his appeal through us; we entreat you on behalf of Christ, be reconciled to God" (2 Cor 5:18-20). We have been commissioned by God as ambassadors of reconciliation. This does not entail reconciling the world to God. God has already done the work of reconciliation "in Christ." God does not need to be reconciled—the world does. And note that it is the world, the entire created order that is to be reconciled—not just people. In Romans 8, Paul talks about the groaning of the creation in futility and its longing to "be set free from its bondage to decay" (Rom 8:21).

Our task as ambassadors, then, entails not only the estranged people of

---

[10]Ibid., p. 192.

the world but the creation itself. It involves all the systems that enslave and abuse people as well as all the systems that abuse the planet—our very source of life. Whatever we do when we live toward the kingdom, Wright insists, contributes to this process of healing and reconciliation: "What you *do* in the present—by painting, preaching, singing, sewing, praying, teaching, building hospitals, digging wells, campaigning for justice, writing poems, caring for the needy, loving your neighbor as yourself—*will last into God's future.* These activities are not simply ways of making the present life a little less beastly, a little more bearable. . . . They are part of what we may call *building for God's kingdom.*"[11] In God's economy, as we live toward the kingdom nothing is lost. Every faithful act of love builds and sustains the kingdom's fabric.

The Jews call this *tikkun olam,* the mending of the world. According to Jewish thinker Irving Greenberg, one could argue that the reason for Israel's existence as a people is to engage in this process of mending and restoration, "the cause of *tikkun olam.*"[12] God called Israel into being as "an avant-garde to serve as pacesetter for humanity, a cadre of humans to undertake the task of working toward redemption at so high a level as to inspire others to greater efforts by their example. . . . The Bible works with one small group; that family of Abraham is elected to be the pacesetters for humanity."[13] Greenberg argues that Christians, followers of Jesus, were called to "bring the message of redemption to the rest of the nations." The Christian community, according to Greenberg, was "not intended as a replacement of Abraham's family; nor were its achievements the proof of divine repudiation of Sarah's covenant." Rather, this new body, swimming "in the sea of the Gentile people and their culture," brought the faith of Abraham in the one God to the whole world.[14] Christians too may, indeed must, contribute to the *tikkun olam.*

Greenberg boldly argues that "both Jews and Christians have a revolutionary dream of total transformation and yet remain willing to accept the finitude and limitations of humans and to proceed one step at a time. Both

---

[11]Ibid., p. 193 (emphasis original).
[12]Irving Greenberg, "Judaism and Christianity: Covenants of Redemption," in *Christianity in Jewish Terms,* ed. Tikva Frymer-Kensky et al. (Boulder, CO: Westview, 2000), p. 143.
[13]Ibid., p. 144.
[14]Ibid., p. 150.

groups persist in preaching their message despite the difficulties they have encountered along the way; they press ahead in the face of their historical suffering." They continue in their God-given mission to engage in the repair of the world's torn fabric, in *tikkun olam*.[15] Now, both Christian and Jewish thinkers would raise objections to Greenberg's assertions. Many Jews would object to sharing their covenant responsibilities with Christians. Many Christians would insist the mantle of the world's mending has passed to the church. Be that as it may, Greenberg's description of the role of Israel as God's covenant people in the world is suggestive. The task of *tikkun olam*, or to use Paul's phrase, "the ministry of reconciliation," is given to a community who lives as God's avant-garde in the world. This community lives in light of the world to come and by its obedience and love repairs that shattered fabric. This community consists of Jews and Greeks, male and female, bond and free (see Gal 3:28).

The church, by its life and love in the world, acts as an agent of reconciliation in the world. All that is shattered and divided, torn and disintegrating, flawed and broken, is mended by our acts of love and faithfulness. Our actions matter—by them, we engage either in the reconciliation of the world or the dissolution of the world. As Wright insists,

> When God saves people in this life, by working through his Spirit to bring them to faith and by leading them to follow Jesus in discipleship, prayer, holiness, hope and love, such people are designed . . . to be a sign and foretaste of what God wants to do for the whole cosmos. What's more, such people are not just to be a sign and foretaste of that ultimate salvation; they are to be *part of the means by which* God makes this happen in both the present and the future.[16]

The kingdom has already been inaugurated; the ministry of reconciliation has already been assigned; the mending of the world has already started. The church is called to the task of participating in this great eschatological work of healing and reconciliation.

Wright recognizes that some will object to this. "'Doesn't that sound,' they will ask, 'as though you're trying to build God's kingdom by your own ef-

---

[15]Ibid., p. 158.
[16]Wright, *Surprised by Hope*, p. 200 (emphasis original).

forts?'" Of course, Wright agrees, God builds God's kingdom. But, he insists, "God ordered his world in such a way that his own work within that world takes place not least through one of his creatures in particular, namely, the human beings who reflect his image."[17] We are the stewards of his project of creation, he continues, and are now called to reflect his presence into his world. But I wonder if Wright gives too much away here. To say "of course God builds God's kingdom" may suggest that we are somehow only pawns in God's great game of kingdom building rather than responsible partners. But, if we are responsible partners and our part goes wrong, is not the whole project in danger?

Over and over again, the church, at least it seems to me, has dug the wrong foundation. When the church's foundation was an imperial foundation, it collapsed in ruin when the empire engaged in acts of violence rather than acts of reconciliation. When the church's foundation was set on ecclesial power, it collapsed in ruin when those powers were corrupted and despised. When the church's foundation was set on cultural accommodation, it collapsed in ruin when the society shifted its vision of the good. When the church's foundation was set on cultivated isolation from the culture, it collapsed in irrelevance. An indifferent society wondered about the reasons for its very existence. A church that craves political power, social influence, cultural relevance or safety from harm becomes an irrelevance in the face of a shattered and fearful world.

In one of the greatest books of the nineteenth or any century, Fyodor Dostoyevsky's *The Brothers Karamazov*, Ivan Karamazov tells the story of the Grand Inquisitor. As the story goes, in the midst of the brutal persecutions of the Inquisition Jesus comes to Seville. The old Inquisitor recognizes him and immediately has him arrested. "Is it you?" he wonders when he confronts the prisoner. "Why have you come to hinder us?" Although the people have praised Jesus today, the Inquisitor warns him that when he condemns him the next day they will rush to add fuel to the fire. Why would he condemn Jesus, the one he claims to follow? The church cannot abide the return of Jesus! It is too much of a risk. The problem with Jesus, the old man argues, is that he came along and offered people freedom—a terrible gift

---

[17]Ibid., p. 207.

they could not bear. In reality, the old man insists, it was the devil that had
it right. He offered Jesus what he needed to establish his kingdom—miracle,
mystery and authority. This is the way that human beings can be controlled,
he insists. You, he charges Jesus, think too much of them, expect too much
of them. They are slaves, rebellious in nature and need to be controlled. You
should have taken up Caesar's sword. If you would have grasped Caesar's
purple, you could have founded a universal kingdom and given peace to the
whole world. They want bread, they long for mystery and they require power,
he argues, but you rejected all three. But at great cost we gave it to them, he
says. We brought them under control. We reduced them to the servitude
they needed to be happy and took away that terrible gift of freedom you
offered in your foolishness. You came and threw away the chance at world
dominion, but we have spent fifteen hundred years correcting your work.
Tomorrow, he concludes, I will burn you for daring to come and hinder us.

Dostoevsky has Ivan say,

> When the Inquisitor ceased speaking he waited for some time for his Prisoner
> to answer him. His silence weighed down upon him. He saw that the Prisoner
> had listened intently all the time, looking gently in his face and evidently not
> wishing to reply. The old man longed for Him to say something however bitter
> and terrible. But He suddenly approached the old man in silence and softly
> kissed him on his bloodless aged lips. That was all his answer. The old man
> shuddered. His lips moved. He went to the door, opened it, and said to Him:
> "Go, and come no more. . . . Come not at all, never, never!" And he let Him
> out into the dark alleys of the town. The Prisoner went away.[18]

Jesus, who refused the way of power, miracle, mystery and authority (see Lk
4:1-13), could not be borne. Jesus, who preferred the way of weakness and suffering, the way of the cross, could not be followed. He could not be, as he was,
a model for the powerful. He had to be altered, ignored or sentimentalized.

Jesus expected too much of people. He expected them to live with a kind
of freedom and joy that the Inquisitor and his colleagues thought was impossible. In spite of Jesus' work, the people were weak, silly and evil creatures that needed to be taken in hand. They, in fact, had to be infantilized,

---

[18]Fyodor Dostoevsky, *The Brothers Karamazov*, trans. Constance Garnett (Garden City, NJ: International Collectors Library, [1880]), pp. 241.

kept under strict control, subject to threats and fears. If you gave them bread and a good show and threw in the occasional threat of hell, you could keep them in line. Otherwise, they were nothing but trouble. Power was the only way to the kingdom: power over people from whom little can be expected and power over a world that threatens the existence of the church as an institution.

I would suggest that this troubling story speaks powerfully to the failure of the church. To this day the Christian church, in its Roman Catholic, Protestant, Orthodox and evangelical forms, still fears Jesus' terrible gift of freedom and his model of weakness and suffering. It does not trust its own members. It is unsure of its own gospel and lacks faith in its transforming power. It has not formed disciples but has collected adherents and frequently infantilized them. It has produced substantial structures of control—ecclesiastical hierarchies, creeds and confessions, moralistic disapproval, and rigid ecclesial patterns—but it has failed to live as it should toward the kingdom. The crucified Jesus is admired but not followed, worshiped but not emulated.

The church has done amazing things. Its history is full of acts of love and justice. Saints stand before us as exemplars of faithfulness and integrity. But can we really look at the last eighteen hundred years of the church's ministry and argue that it has fulfilled its duty to the ministry of reconciliation? Earlier in the book I told the story of explaining to a Jewish friend of mine Paul's understanding of the Christians' transformation in Christ. It bears repeating here. According to Paul, I told him, we have already died and been raised with Christ. We are already in a profound sense living in the world to come. We already possess the transforming power of the resurrection. He sat quietly for a while and then said, "Well, we Jews have not seen it." It was a fair charge. Very quickly God's people the Jews found themselves attacked and marginalized by the church. For centuries they suffered in ghettos, prevented from taking up all but a few trades, threatened by pogroms and arbitrary violence. No, they haven't seen it.

Our divisions, of course, make it worse. How can we claim to be agents of reconciliation when we can't manage to get along with each other? The rest of society is right to scoff at a people who claim to be able to bring the world together as one when we cannot even worship God through Jesus as one, when we cannot even break bread together. The aforementioned squabbles within and between the various Christian bodies give the rest of the world a perfect right to say that, like the Jews, they haven't seen it either. Hierarchies will exercise power, but individual groups of Christians engaged in *tikkun olam* will change the world. This is why Moltmann insists that it is the local community of God's people that is important. It is God's ambassadors living with and among the people who are important. By individual and communal acts of love and righteousness we engage in *tikkun olam*—in the mending of the world.

RECLAIMING POSTMILLENNIALISM

Earlier in the chapter I suggested that the much-maligned postmillennial position may have something to teach us. The earlier postmillennialists were naive to imagine that the civilizing work of world mission and social reform could win the world to Christ and usher in the kingdom of God. As often noted, the optimism of the late-nineteenth-century reformers and missionaries came to grief in the brutality of the Somme and was destroyed completely by the ovens of Auschwitz. But those great missionaries and reformers did the church a great service by focusing its mission outward. The reformers and missionaries of the second half of the nineteenth century built on the work of the abolitionists in Great Britain and the United States, who fought the oppression of slavery. They built on the work of revivalists like Charles Finney, who saved souls, built schools and addressed social ills. They addressed the plight of poor women, disadvantaged children, abused workers, marginalized immigrants and abusive governments. They did this for the sake of bringing in the kingdom. Perhaps they were naive—but in my opinion we could use naiveté like that today. Many were saved. Many were healed. Much was mended.

LIVING TOWARD THE KINGDOM

So how do we proceed? In *Christianity After Religion*, Diana Butler Bass describes the post-Christian renewal of the church in terms of believing, behaving and belonging. She argues that these aspects of Christian life and practice need to be rethought in terms of our disenchanted postmodern situation. This does not mean that the traditional faith and practices of the church are to be discarded. In fact, she insists that the church needs to reclaim and reframe the tradition rather than ignore it. The church needs to read the Bible intensely and well rather than not at all. It needs to claim its historic identity and mission as ministers of reconciliation. It needs to worship with integrity and love without reservations. It needs to work toward a fourth great awakening. Bass offers a number of suggestions to prepare for this awakening the church so desperately needs.

First, she suggests, the church needs to "prepare by reading and learning the holy texts of faith in new ways." Many Christians suffer from a profound ignorance of their own sacred text. They need to reclaim the Bible as their own. Jesus' followers should read in new translations, listen to alternative voices of interpretation and listen intently with their community. They should ask, "Where is God's spirit active here?" Second, the church should encourage its members to "engage two new practices of faith." They should perhaps start with one inner practice and one outer practice, one to serve their own spiritual life and one to serve their community. They should, in other words, be formed as disciples. Third, the church should encourage people to "have fun. Play. . . . These are hard times, worrisome times, and serious times. Try to enjoy the life you have and play along the way." Life is God's good gift to be celebrated. Life in the body, life in God's creation is to be treasured. Fourth, God's people should "participate in making change. Show up for the awakening. . . . Spiritual transformation happens only as we jump in and make a difference."[19] Bear witness to Jesus' love. Heal the sick. Feed the hungry. Visit the prisoners. Mend the earth.

These are simple things—perhaps, we think, too simple. Sometimes I think we are rather like Namaan the Syrian. Remember that he went to the prophet Elisha for healing and was told to wash seven times in the Jordan River. Namaan was outraged at this and stomped off in fury exclaiming that there were better rivers in Syria than the Jordan. He had expected an elaborate rite and powerful prayer. All he got was a muddy river. His servant convinced him that if the prophet had assigned him some great task he would have taken it up with relish. Instead, Elisha asked of him something simple. Finally, Namaan obeyed and was healed and became a worshiper of the God of Israel (see 2 Kings 5).

---

[19]Bass, *Christianity After Religion*, pp. 225-26.

The church today is not being asked to do something great. Individual Christians are not being called to impossible tasks. In Western society we always look for the grand plan, the big deal, the sure-fire method of success. But we are being called away from the seductive powers of hierarchy, on the one hand, and the equally seductive appeal of infantilism and isolation, on the other. We are being called to the freedom of the gospel that binds us to one another in love. We are being called with the people, to the people. We are being called to live toward and build for the kingdom. We are being called to do this in simple acts of obedience and love. We are sustained in this by the stories of our community, the promises of the gospel and the hope for the new heavens and the new earth. We will certainly not bring in the kingdom through our own efforts. But by our healing of the world, our *tikkun olam,* we will prepare the way by lifting up valleys and bringing down hills.

Jürgen Moltmann writes, "According to Jewish insights, God puts the sanctification of his Name, the doing of his will, and hence the coming of the kingdom in the hands of men and women. He waits for his glorification through the people of his choice." But this does not mean he leaves us alone in our task. "God does not restrict himself in order to concede human beings freedom; he differentiates himself in order to be beside them in their wandering." So it is that Moltmann can say with Ernst Bloch, "only the wicked exist through their God, but the righteous—God exists through them, and in their hands is laid the sanctification of the Name."[20] In the end we are not called to great things but to the sanctification of the name of God—to obedience, love, compassion and justice—to the mending of the world. Dare we believe that our lives matter? Dare we believe that our communities matter? Dare we believe that our God lives in our world through us? Dare we believe that we can be, for this reason, ambassadors of reconciliation for the entire world? We can and we must.

If all this seems too simple, too ordinary, recall Rodney Stark's assertion that the early church moved from being a tiny sect to being the most powerful force in the Roman world without elaborate churches or grand plans. They met in obscure house churches and lived in fear of the outbreak of local

---

[20]Jürgen Moltmann, *The Coming of God: Christian Eschatology,* trans. Margaret Kohl (Minneapolis: Fortress, 1996), pp. 332-33.

persecutions. The elites despised them, considering them atheists and calling them cannibals. And yet, they lived toward the kingdom. When the plagues came, believing in the resurrection of the dead they risked death to care for the suffering and dying. They provided a home for those who had lost everything and a place of honor for the dishonored and despised. They demonstrated courage in the face of persecution and death and bore witness with their blood to the Savior who died for them and was raised from the dead for them. They transformed cities divided by hostility and fear and formed a new family that transcended the barriers of race, culture, gender and station.[21]

They were not perfect—neither are we. But they were patient—and we generally are not. We want something that will work yesterday. We want that fourth great awakening to start now. It took the primitive church hundreds of years to have an impact in its world. And it may take the Christian church hundreds of years to reclaim its identity and rethink what it means to live toward the kingdom. It may take hundreds of years for us to shed our addiction to miracle, mystery and authority. But the God who made the world and called us to a ministry of reconciliation is nothing if not patient. Perhaps now, in the wake of our failures, we have a chance to start over again in all simplicity. Perhaps now we can proclaim and live the gospel, mend the world, as ambassadors of reconciliation.

---

[21]Rodney Stark, *The Rise of Christianity* (Princeton, NJ: Princeton University Press, 1996).

Bibliography

Aune, David E. "The Influence of Roman Imperial Court Ceremonial on the Apocalypse of John." *Biblical Research* 28 (1983): 5-26.

———. *Revelation.* 3 vols. Word Biblical Commentary. Nashville: Thomas Nelson, 1997–1998.

Bader-Saye, Scott. *Church and Israel After Christendom: The Politics of Election.* Eugene, OR: Wipf & Stock, 1999.

Baker, Sharon L. *Razing Hell: Rethinking Everything You've Been Taught About God's Wrath and Judgment.* Louisville, KY: Westminster John Knox, 2010.

Balthasar, Hans Urs von. *Dare We Hope: "That All Men Be Saved"?* Translated by David Kipp and Lothar Krauth. San Francisco: Ignatius Press, 1988.

Bass, Diana Butler. *Christianity After Religion: The End of Church and the Birth of a New Spiritual Awakening.* San Francisco: HarperOne, 2012.

Bauckham, Richard. *The Climax of Prophecy: Studies on the Book of Revelation.* Edinburgh: T & T Clark, 1993.

———, ed. *God Will Be All in All: The Eschatology of Jürgen Moltmann.* Edinburgh: T & T Clark, 1999.

———. *The Theology of the Book of Revelation.* New Testament Theology. Cambridge: Cambridge University Press, 1993.

Beasley-Murray, George R. *Jesus and the Last Days: The Interpretation of the Olivet Discourse.* Repr., Vancouver, BC: Regent University Press, 2005.

Bell, Rob. *Love Wins: A Book About Heaven, Hell, and the Fate of Every Person Who Ever Lived.* New York: HarperOne, 2011.

Beker, J. Christiaan. *Paul's Apocalyptic Gospel: The Coming Triumph of God.* Minneapolis: Fortress, 1982.

Berry, Wendell. "Faustian Economics." In *What Matters?: Economics for a Renewed Commonwealth*, pp. 41-42. Berkeley, CA: Counterpoint, 2010.

———. "Manifesto: The Mad Farmer Liberation Front." In *New Collected Poems,* pp. 173-74. Berkeley, CA: Counterpoint, 2012.

Blaising, Craig A., Kenneth L. Gentry Jr. and Robert B. Strimple, eds. *Three Views on the Millennium and Beyond.* Counterpoints. Grand Rapids: Zondervan, 1999.

Blount, Brian K. *Can I Get a Witness?: Reading Revelation Through African American Culture.* Louisville, KY: Westminster John Knox, 2005.

———. *Revelation: A Commentary.* New Testament Library. Louisville, KY: Westminster John Knox, 2009.

Blumenthal, David. "*Tselem:* Toward an Anthropathic Theology of Image." In *Christianity in Jewish Terms,* ed. Tikva Frymer-Kensky et al., pp. 337-47. Boulder, CO: Westview, 2000.

Bonhoeffer, Dietrich. *Discipleship.* Vol. 4 of *Dietrich Bonhoeffer Works.* Louisville, KY: Fortress, 2003.

Borg, Marcus J. *Conflict, Holiness, and Politics in the Teachings of Jesus.* Harrisburg, PA: Trinity Press International, 1998.

Boyarin, Daniel. *The Jewish Gospels: The Story of the Jewish Christ.* New York: New Press, 2012.

Casey, John. *After Lives: A Guide to Heaven, Hell, and Purgatory.* New York: Oxford University Press, 2009.

Charlesworth, James H., ed. *The Old Testament Pseudepigrapha.* 2 vols. Garden City, NY: Doubleday, 1983–1985.

Chesterton, G. K. *Orthodoxy.* New York: Dodd, Mead, 1908.

Clouse, Robert G., Robert N. Hosack and Richard V. Pierard. *The New Millennium Manual.* Grand Rapids: Baker, 1999.

Cohn, Norman. *The Pursuit of the Millennium: Revolutionary Millenarians and Mystical Anarchists of the Middle Ages.* Rev. ed. New York: Oxford University Press, 1970.

Collins, John J. *The Apocalyptic Imagination: An Introduction to Jewish Apocalyptic Literature.* 2nd ed. Grand Rapids: Eerdmans, 1998.

———, ed. *The Origins of Apocalypticism in Judaism and Christianity.* Vol. 1 of *The Encyclopedia of Apocalypticism,* edited by John J. Collins, Bernard McGinn and Stephen J. Stein. New York: Continuum, 1998.

Collins, John J., and Daniel C. Harlow, eds. *The Eerdmans Dictionary of Early Judaism.* Grand Rapids: Eerdmans, 2010.

Crockett, William V., ed. *Four Views on Hell.* Grand Rapids: Zondervan, 1992. Citations refer to the 1996 paperback edition.

Crossman, Richard H., ed. *The God That Failed*. With 2001 foreword by David C. Engerman. 1950. Reprint, New York: Columbia University Press, 2001.

Dostoevsky, Fyodor. *The Brothers Karamazov*. Translated by Constance Garnett. Garden City, NJ: International Collectors Library, [1880].

Dunn, James D. G. *The Theology of Paul the Apostle*. Grand Rapids: Eerdmans, 1998.

Freedman, David Noel, ed. *Eerdmans Dictionary of the Bible*. Grand Rapids: Eerdmans, 2000.

Frymer-Kensky, Tikva, David Novak, Peter Ochs, David Fox Sandmel and Michael A. Signer, eds. *Christianity in Jewish Terms*. Boulder, CO: Westview, 2000.

Fukuyama, Francis. *The End of History and the Last Man*. New York: Free Press, 1992.

Gilbert, Martin. *Israel: A History*. New York: Harper Perennial, 1998.

Girard, René. *The Scapegoat*. Translated by Yvonne Freccero. Baltimore: Johns Hopkins University Press, 1989.

Gorman, Michael J. *Reading Revelation Responsibly: Uncivil Worship and Witness; Following the Lamb into the New Creation*. Eugene, OR: Cascade, 2011.

Gorringe, Timothy. "Eschatology and Political Radicalism." In *God Will Be All in All: The Eschatology of Jürgen Moltmann*, ed. Richard Bauckham, pp. 87-114. Edinburgh: T & T Clark, 1999.

Green, Joel B. *Body, Soul, and Human Life: The Nature of Humanity in the Bible*. Grand Rapids: Baker Academic, 2008.

Green, Joel B., Scot McKnight and I. Howard Marshall, eds. *Dictionary of Jesus and the Gospels*. Downers Grove, IL: InterVarsity Press, 1992.

Greenberg, Irving. "Judaism and Christianity: Covenants of Redemption." In *Christianity in Jewish Terms*, ed. Tikva Frymer-Kensky et al., pp. 141-58. Boulder, CO: Westview, 2000.

Grenz, Stanley J. *The Millennial Maze: Sorting Out Evangelical Options*. Downers Grove, IL: InterVarsity Press, 1992.

Grimsrud, Ted, and Michael Hardin, eds. *Compassionate Eschatology: The Future as Friend*. Eugene, OR: Cascade, 2011.

Hanson, Paul D., ed. *Visionaries and Their Apocalypses*. Philadelphia: Fortress, 1983.

Harris, Murray J. *Raised Immortal: Resurrection and Immortality in the New Testament*. Grand Rapids: Eerdmans, 1983.

Hauerwas, Stanley, and William H. Willimon. *Resident Aliens: Life in the Christian Colony*. Nashville: Abingdon, 1989.

Hawthorne, Gerald F., Ralph P. Martin and Daniel G. Reid, eds. *Dictionary of Paul and His Letters.* Downers Grove, IL: InterVarsity Press, 1993.

Heschel, Abraham Joshua. *The Prophets.* 2 vols. in 1. 1962. Reprint, Boston: Hendrickson, 2007.

Heschel, Susannah. *The Aryan Jesus: Christian Theologians and the Bible in Nazi Germany.* Paperback ed. Princeton, NJ: Princeton University Press, 2010.

Jenson, Robert, and Eugene Korn, eds. *Covenant and Hope: Christian and Jewish Reflections: Essays in Constructive Theology from the Institute for Theological Inquiry.* Grand Rapids: Eerdmans, 2012.

Jersak, Bradley. *Her Gates Will Never Be Shut: Hope, Hell, and the New Jerusalem.* Eugene, OR: Wipf & Stock, 2009.

Johnson, Paul. *A History of Christianity.* New York: Touchstone, 1976.

Judt, Tony, and Timothy Snyder. *Thinking the Twentieth Century.* New York: Penguin, 2012.

Kraybill, J. Nelson. *Apocalypse and Allegiance: Worship, Politics, and Devotion in the Book of Revelation.* Grand Rapids: Brazos, 2010.

Ladd, George Eldon. *The Presence of the Future: The Eschatology of Biblical Realism.* Rev. ed. Grand Rapids: Eerdmans, 1974.

Levenson, Jon D. *Resurrection and the Restoration of Israel: The Ultimate Victory of the God of Life.* New Haven, CT: Yale University Press, 2006.

Levine, Amy-Jill, and Marc Zvi Brettler, eds. *The Jewish Annotated New Testament: New Revised Standard Bible Translation.* New York: Oxford University Press, 2011.

Lewis, C. S. *The Great Divorce, a Dream.* New York: Macmillan, 1946. Reprint, San Francisco: HarperCollins, 2009.

Lindbeck, George. "What of the Future?: A Christian Response." In *Christianity in Jewish Terms,* ed. Tikva Frymer-Kensky et al., pp. 357-66. Boulder, CO: Westview, 2000.

Longenecker, Richard N., ed. *Life in the Face of Death: The Resurrection Message of the New Testament.* Grand Rapids: Eerdmans, 1998.

MacCulloch, Diarmaid. *Christianity: The First Three Thousand Years.* New York: Viking, 2010.

Madigan, Kevin J., and Jon D. Levenson. *Resurrection: The Power of God for Christians and Jews.* New Haven, CT: Yale University Press, 2008.

Maier, Harry O. *Apocalypse Recalled: The Book of Revelation After Christendom.* Minneapolis: Fortress, 2002.

Martin, Ralph P., and Peter H. Davids, eds. *Dictionary of the Later New Tes-*

tament and Its Developments. Downers Grove, IL: InterVarsity Press, 1997.

Martínez, Florentino García, ed. *The Dead Sea Scrolls Translated.* Translated by Wilfred G. E. Watson. 2nd ed. Grand Rapids: Eerdmans, 1996.

McKnight, Scot. *A New Vision for Israel: The Teachings of Jesus in National Context.* Grand Rapids: Eerdmans, 1999.

Moltmann, Jürgen. *The Church in the Power of the Spirit: A Contribution to Messianic Ecclesiology.* Translated by Margaret Kohl. San Francisco: HarperCollins, 1991.

———. *The Coming of God: Christian Eschatology.* Translated by Margaret Kohl. Minneapolis: Fortress, 1996.

———. *Ethics of Hope.* Translated by Margaret Kohl. Minneapolis: Fortress, 2012.

———. *In the End, the Beginning: The Life of Hope.* Translated by Margaret Kohl. Minneapolis: Fortress, 2004.

———. *Sun of Righteousness, Arise!: God's Future for Humanity and the Earth.* Translated by Margaret Kohl. Minneapolis: Fortress Press, 2010.

———. *Theology of Hope: On the Ground and the Implications of a Christian Eschatology.* Translated by James W. Leitch. New York: Harper & Row, 1967.

Mounce, Robert H. *The Book of Revelation.* Rev. ed. New International Commentary on the New Testament. Grand Rapids: Eerdmans, 1998.

Murphy, Frederick J. *Apocalypticism in the Bible and Its World: A Comprehensive Introduction.* Grand Rapids: Baker Academic, 2012.

Newman, Carey C., ed. *Jesus and the Restoration of Israel: A Critical Assessment of N. T. Wright's Jesus and the Victory of God.* Downers Grove, IL: InterVarsity Press, 1999.

Peterson, Eugene H. *Reversed Thunder: The Revelation of John and the Praying Imagination.* San Francisco: Harper & Row, 1988.

Phelan, John E., Jr. "God, Judgment and Non-Violence." In *Compassionate Eschatology,* edited by Ted Grimsrud and Michael Hardin, pp. 116-33. Eugene, OR: Cascade, 2011.

———. "Revelation, Empire, and the Violence of God." *Ex Auditu* 20 (2004): pp. 65-84.

Pitre, Brant J. *Jesus, the Tribulation, and the End of the Exile: Restoration Eschatology and the Origin of the Atonement.* Grand Rapids: Baker Academic, 2005.

Polkinghorne, John. *The God of Hope and the End of the World.* New Haven, CT: Yale University Press, 2002.

Portier-Young, Anathea E. *Apocalypse Against Empire: Theologies of Resistance in Early Judaism.* Grand Rapids: Eerdmans, 2011.

Ratzinger, Joseph. *Eschatology: Death and Eternal Life.* Translated by Michael Waldstein. Translation edited by Aidan Nichols. 2nd ed. Washington, DC: Catholic University in America Press, 2007.

Reddish, Mitchell G., ed. *Apocalyptic Literature: A Reader.* Peabody, MA: Hendrickson, 1995.

Reiser, Marius. *Jesus and Judgment: The Eschatological Proclamation in Its Jewish Context.* Translated by Linda M. Maloney. Minneapolis: Fortress, 1997.

Riddlebarger, Kim. *A Case for Amillennialism: Understanding the End Times.* Grand Rapids: Baker, 2003.

Rowland, Christopher. *The Open Heaven: A Study of Apocalyptic in Judaism and Early Christianity.* New York: Crossroad, 1982.

Russell, D. S. *The Method and Message of Jewish Apocalyptic: 200 B.C.–A.D. 100.* Philadelphia: Westminster, 1964.

Sanders, E. P. *Paul and Palestinian Judaism: A Comparison of Patterns of Religion.* Philadelphia: Fortress, 1977.

———. *Jesus and Judaism.* Philadelphia: Fortress, 1985.

Sanders, John. *The God Who Risks: A Theology of Divine Providence.* 2nd ed. Downers Grove, IL: InterVarsity Press, 2007.

Schäfer, Peter. *The Jewish Jesus: How Judaism and Christianity Shaped Each Other.* Princeton, NJ: Princeton University Press, 2012.

Schwarz, Hans. *Eschatology.* Grand Rapids: Eerdmans, 2000.

Schweitzer, Albert. *The Quest of the Historical Jesus: A Critical Study of Its Progress from Reimarus to Wrede.* 3rd ed. London: A. & C. Black, 1954.

Segal, Alan F. *Life After Death: A History of the Afterlife in the Religions of the West.* New York: Doubleday, 2004.

Soloveitchik, Joseph B. *Halakhic Man.* Translated by Lawrence Kaplan. Philadelphia: Jewish Publication Society of America, 1983.

Stark, Rodney. *The Rise of Christianity: How the Obscure, Marginal Jesus Movement Became the Dominant Religious Force in the Western World in a Few Centuries.* Princeton, NJ: Princeton University Press, 1996.

———. *The Triumph of Christianity: How the Jesus Movement Became the World's Largest Religion.* San Francisco: HarperOne, 2011.

Tanenbaum, Marc H., Marvin R. Wilson and A. James Rudin, eds. *Evangelicals and Jews in Conversation on Scripture, Theology, and History.* Grand Rapids: Baker, 1978.

Thiselton, Anthony C. *Life After Death: A New Approach to the Last Things.* Grand Rapids: Eerdmans, 2012.

Travis, Stephen H. *Christ and the Judgement of God: The Limits of Divine Retribution in New Testament Thought.* 2nd ed. Peabody, MA: Hendrickson, 2008.

Turkle, Sherry. *Alone Together: Why We Expect More from Technology and Less from Each Other.* New York: Basic Books, 2011.

Volf, Miroslav. "After Moltmann." In *God Will Be All in All: The Eschatology of Jürgen Moltmann,* ed. Richard Bauckham, pp. 233-58. Edinburgh: T & T Clark, 1999.

Walls, Jerry L. *Purgatory: The Logic of Total Transformation.* New York: Oxford University Press, 2012.

Witherington, Ben, III. *Jesus, Paul and the End of the World: A Comparative Study in New Testament Eschatology.* Downers Grove, IL: InterVarsity Press, 1992.

Wright, N. T. *How God Became King: The Forgotten Story of the Gospels.* New York: HarperOne, 2012.

———. *Jesus and the Victory of God.* Vol. 2 of *Christian Origins and the Question of God.* Minneapolis: Fortress, 1996.

———. *The New Testament and the People of God.* Vol. 1 of *Christian Origins and the Question of God.* Minneapolis: Fortress, 1992.

———. *The Resurrection of the Son of God.* Vol. 3 of *Christian Origins and the Question of God.* Minneapolis: Fortress, 2003.

———. *Surprised by Hope: Rethinking Heaven, the Resurrection, and the Mission of the Church.* New York: HarperOne, 2008.

Yoder, John Howard. *The Jewish-Christian Schism Revisited.* Edited by Michael G. Cartwright and Peter Ochs. Grand Rapids: Eerdmans, 2003.

Name Index

Subject Index

Scripture Index